Posthumous Love

Posthumous Love

Eros and the Afterlife in Renaissance England

Ramie Targoff

The University of Chicago Press

Chicago and London

Ramie Targoff is professor of English at Brandeis University. She is the author of *Common Prayer: The Language of Public Devotion in Early Modern England* and *John Donne, Body and Soul*, also published by the University of Chicago Press.

The University of Chicago Press, Chicago 60637
The University of Chicago Press, Ltd., London
© 2014 by The University of Chicago
All rights reserved. Published 2014.
Printed in the United States of America

23 22 21 20 19 18 17 16 15 14   1 2 3 4 5

ISBN-13: 978-0-226-78959-0   (cloth)
ISBN-13: 978-0-226-11046-2   (e-book)

DOI: 10.7208/9780226100462.001.0001

Library of Congress Cataloging-in-Publication Data
Targoff, Ramie, author.
   Posthumous love : eros and the afterlife in Renaissance England / Ramie Targoff.
      pages ; cm
   Includes bibliographical references and index.
   ISBN 978-0-226-78959-0 (cloth : alk. paper)   1. Love poetry, English—History and criticism—16th century.   2. Love poetry, English—History and criticism—17th century.   3. Renaissance—England.   4. Love in literature.   5. Immortality in literature.   I. Title.
   PR539.L7T37   2014
   821'.3093543—dc23
                                                              2013039226

For Stephen

Find the mortal world enough

—W. H. Auden, "Lullaby"

CONTENTS

ACKNOWLEDGMENTS

This book began and ended in Rome, where I had the great pleasure to spend two years on academic leave. I am immensely grateful to the American Council of Learned Societies and the John Simon Guggenheim Memorial Foundation for their generous support, and to the American Academy in Rome, where I was lucky enough to live as a scholar in residence. I want to thank the two directors of the American Academy during my time there—Carmela Vircillo Franklin and Christopher Celenza—for their wonderful hospitality and friendship. I am also greatly indebted to Brandeis University for allowing me to take time away from my teaching and administrative responsibilities in order to write.

The ideas in this book have been greatly shaped by the conversations and exchanges I have had at the universities where I have had the privilege to present my work, and I want to express my gratitude to the English departments and Renaissance colloquia at the University of Cambridge, Emory University, the Free University of Berlin, Harvard University, the Ludwig Maximilian University of Munich, Princeton University, Stanford University, the University of Pennsylvania, the University of Pittsburgh, the University of Rome, and Yale University, for their kind invitations over the past five years. The Wissenschaftskolleg in Berlin and the Free University cosponsored an international conference that I organized on the idea of posthumous love in the Latin West, and I am grateful to both of these institutions, and to my colleagues Bernhard Jussen and Joachim Köpper for their collaboration on this event.

Among the many people who have helped make this book what it is, I want to thank those who have played especially important roles. James Simpson first invited me to write a conference paper on Wyatt and Petrarch, an occasion that gave birth to my idea for the book, and I am grateful for his continued engagement with the project over the past few years. Brian Cummings and Jeffrey Knapp each read a first draft of the manuscript, and their comments and suggestions guided me through the revision and expansion of the book. Paul Alpers, Amy Appleford, Oliver Arnold, Leonard Barkan, Mary Bing, Sarah Cole, Margreta de Grazia, Meg Koerner, Joseph Koerner, Thomas Laqueur, Yoon Lee, Blyth Lord, Lisa New, John Plotz, Leah Price, Gerhard Regn, Richard Rambuss, Kellie Robertson, Catherine Robson, Luisella Simpson, Nigel Smith, Gordon Teskey, Nicholas Watson, and Michael Witmore have all been rich interlocutors at different stages in the project. I had two extraordinary readers at the University of Chicago Press, Gordon Braden and Kenneth Gross, and I am deeply indebted to their generosity in reading the manuscript with such care. I am grateful as well to my wonderful editors at the press, Alan Thomas, Randy Petilos, and Ruth Goring, for bringing this book to print. I would also like to thank my very fine research assistants, Angelo Calderone and Benjamin Woodring. Finally, my parents, Cheri Kamen Targoff and Michael Targoff, remain an abiding source of encouragement and support.

My greatest debts are to my immediate family, who give me every day the ordinary and precious gift of their companionship. To my son, Harry, who is a constant source of joy that I hope never to take for granted; and to my husband, Stephen, who has inspired me to think and to write and to love in ways I never would have done without him. Together, they have helped me to understand the true meaning of *carpe diem*.

An earlier version of chapter 2 was published as "Passion" in *Cultural Reformations: Medieval and Renaissance in Literary History*, ed. Brian

Cummings and James Simpson (Oxford: Oxford University Press, 2010), 609–34, reprinted by permission of Oxford University Press. An earlier version of sections of chapter 4 appeared in "Mortal Love: Shakespeare's *Romeo and Juliet* and the Practice of Joint Burial," *Representations* 120, no. 1 (2012): 17–38.

INTRODUCTION

Burying Love

So this one Tombe / may hold them neere / In death, as linckt in life.

—Epitaph for Elizabeth Brewster, d. 1609

In the National Etruscan Museum of Villa Giulia in Rome, secluded in a corner all to themselves, lie the most splendid of couples. Resting in a semi-reclined position, the husband drapes his arm over the right shoulder of his wife; his left arm is propped up on a pillow, with her left arm just below his. Their eyes are wide open as they gaze intensely straight ahead; their hands are caught midgesture as if pointing forward to what lies before them. The ancient sarcophagus, which dates to the second half of the sixth century BCE, startles us in its vivacity: the couple seem more likely to rise and cross the gallery than to remain frozen in time for all eternity. The tomb startles us as well in its suggestion of marital intimacy: here are a husband and wife so comfortable in their proximity, so relaxed in their posture, that they seem to exude an erotic contentedness, as if they needed no other afterlife beside the warmth of their shared terracotta bed.

The *Sarcophagus of the Bride and Bridegroom* from Cerveteri is one of the most compelling of all Etruscan sarcophagi, but it is by no means an unusual example.[1] Etruscan couples were regularly buried together and were also regularly depicted in effigies on the lids of their sarcophagus. How the Etruscans understood this joint burial, and what it tells us about their expectations for the afterlife, remains a matter of speculation.[2] Did they envision a shared fate for their souls as well as their bodies? Where did they think the afterlife would transpire—at the site of their graves in the necropolis or in a special land of the dead? Did they hope that the joint effigies on their tombs would influence their chances for a future together, or did they intend the sculptures merely as a form of commemoration? Why, in short, were couples like the *Bride and Bridegroom* of Cerveteri buried together, and what might their burial tell us about their understanding of posthumous love?

The question of what awaits earthly lovers after death lies at the heart of this book. The culture that I examine is not ancient but early modern; the works of art I explore are literary texts, not sculptures. But the issues raised by the Cerveteri tomb echo throughout representations of love in Renaissance England and help to define the ways that men and women during this period thought about the afterlife. More pointedly, what the Cerveteri tomb seems to hold tantalizingly before us is the prospect of an eternal life lived together, the dream of posthumous intimacy without either temporary or permanent rupture. This is a dream shared by lovers and spouses across the centuries, and English couples in the sixteenth and seventeenth centuries were no exception.

What is particular to Renaissance England is the emergence of a body of literature that vehemently rejected posthumous love, a body of literature that almost uniformly insisted that however much couples might hope that their love would extend from this world to the next, their love was inevitably mortal. In the poetry written in England between the 1530s and the 1660s, there are almost no representations of continuity between earthly and heavenly love. There are not even good examples of poems that attempt to cross the boundaries between the two realms: the Orpheus myth, for example, had no real traction in English culture during this period, whereas in Italy it remained central to the erotic imagination.[3] Of the scores of sonnet series written in England in the last decades of the sixteenth century, many of which were openly dependent upon Petrarchan norms and conventions, none reproduces the central division of Petrarch's *Rime sparse* between poems written to Laura *in vita*, while she is alive, and those written to Laura *in morte*.[4] Death plays, in fact, startlingly little role in the English sonnet series. However faithful or unfaithful, present or absent, the beloved remains decidedly alive.

In addition to the absence of lyric poetry that records—or attempts to transcend—the death of the beloved in the Petrarchan manner, Renaissance English literature did not produce any epic poetry that, in the spirit of Dante's *Divina Commedia*, extends love to the heavens. The period's great epic on the subject of human love, John Milton's *Paradise Lost*, turns on Adam's decision to remain with Eve even if this decision carries with it the burden of mortality. Although the archangel Raphael informs Adam, in proper Neoplatonic fashion, that earthly love is "the scale / By which to heav'nly love thou may'st ascend," Adam ultimately chooses a terminal love with Eve. When he first encounters Eve after she has eaten of the fruit, he does not consider even for a moment that he might forsake her. Instead, he recognizes with "horror chill" the fate that awaits them both: "And me with thee hath ruined," he says to himself, "for with thee / Certain my resolution is to die."[5] What it means for our "first parents" to be a couple is not to aspire to the heavens in the manner Raphael describes, whereby their intimate bond would be translated into another form (although Raphael does blush as he describes the sex life of heavenly spirits).[6] What it means for Adam and Eve to be a couple is to leave paradise together with no guarantee of a shared afterlife. Their love will bring them a "paradise within": it is self-fulfilling, not a preparation for something to come.

This book tells the story of how a body of poetry that insisted on love's mortality developed during the English Renaissance, and what that poetry ultimately gained—both aesthetically and emotionally—through this insistence. The result of denying posthumous love was not a negative void or lack where there had once been something positive and affirming. Instead, a new mode of poetry emerged that derived its power by firmly asserting love's mortal limits. To be sure, there were plenty of earlier examples of poems both in England and on the Continent that did not embrace the idea of a continuous love after death. But what this book describes is not a handful of examples from different traditions or period. It is rather the emergence of a literary norm. Mortal

poetics—a poetics that has at its core the belief that love cannot transcend the mortal world, and that derives some kind of positive gain from
the imposition of temporal boundaries—became the dominant form of
love literature in early modern England. *Posthumous Love* attempts to
explain why such a poetics developed and how we might define its central achievements.

This book begins by exploring the social and religious contexts in
which Renaissance English love poetry was written. In the remainder
of the introduction we will look at tombs erected for spouses during
the period, and in chapter 1 we will consider the attitude of the Church
of England toward the possibility that love might transcend the grave.
Each subsequent chapter focuses on a central episode in the poetic narrative I am tracing, in which poets developed increasingly rich and compelling compensations for the lack of posthumous love.

Chapter 2 begins this narrative at the earliest point of contact—and
tension—between a Petrarchan understanding of posthumous love and
that of an early modern English poet: Thomas Wyatt's translations of a
selection of Petrarch's *Rime sparse*. Wyatt systematically strove to transform Petrarch's paradigm of transcendent love, I argue, into a strictly
mortal understanding of erotic bonds. In so doing he erased *in morte*
poems from the English sonnet.

In chapter 3 I turn to some of the lesser-known Elizabethan sonnet
series, which expand Wyatt's desire to escape from love into a kind of
death-drive. The idea that death would bring an absolute end to tortur-
ous erotic affections does not lead to a consoling vision of a heavenly
afterlife with the divine. Instead this poetry is overwhelmingly secular, often suggesting a strain of materialism that seems more consonant
with classical than with Christian models for the afterlife.

The relentless secularism and materialism of English love literature
finds its most potent expression in Shakespeare's *Romeo and Juliet*. In
chapter 4 I will consider the ways in which Shakespeare transformed
the Italian story that was his source for the play, a story that in all of
its versions entails Romeo and Giulietta's affirmation that their souls
will be reunited in heaven, where they will live together for all eternity.
When Shakespeare reworked these materials, he stripped away any expectation that Romeo and Juliet's love might continue in the afterlife.

Not only did he eliminate the hope of a heavenly afterlife together, but he also rejected the comfort for the couple that might come from a private tomb. In Shakespeare's refusal to give the lovers the kind of posthumous intimacy that early modern couples so often desired for their bodies, he in effect doubles the force of the tragedy.

In chapter 5 I return to the Elizabethan sonnet, but with a focus on the more affirmative (and, not coincidentally, more celebrated) examples of the genre, which pursue literary forms of immortality. This pursuit of literary immortality differs from both its classical and Petrarchan counterparts in its explicit self-understanding as compensation for the fact that earthly love is mortal (for the Latin elegists there is very little of this sentimental strain, whereas for Petrarch immortal fame complements, rather than compensates for, a shared heavenly future). Within the English love sonnet, the afterlife of love gets displaced from eschatology onto the literary artifact itself.

If the great Elizabethan sonnets of Spenser and Drayton and Shakespeare, to name a few, imagine that love might continue through the literary artifact long after the lovers are gone, the most powerful genre of love poetry in the seventeenth century—the *carpe diem* lyric—rejects such consolation as purely sentimental. In chapter 6 I consider *carpe diem* poetry as the most extreme and uncompromising expression of mortal poetics. This classical genre was almost entirely missing from the Petrarchan canon—it was clearly incompatible with the idea that love would endure for all eternity—but it surfaced with renewed energy, and with new resonance, in Renaissance England. English *carpe diem* poetry exploits the positive consequences of the tradition that began with Wyatt's translations of Petrarch. What emerged was an embrace of the present whose intensity and poignancy were built upon the full recognition of what was being left behind.

Posthumous Love concludes with a consideration of two seventeenth-century poems that at first glance seem to be exceptions to the general argument of the book: Henry King's "An Exequy To his Matchlesse never to be forgotten Freind" and John Milton's "Methought I saw my late espoused Saint." Both rehearse the longing of a grieving husband to be reunited with his deceased wife. When we look at these poems carefully, however, we discover how deeply King and Milton were influenced by the prior hundred or so years of English poetry that denied posthumous love. In both poems the prospect of a heavenly reunion occurs early on, only to be overwhelmed by more pressing—and more corporeal—desires. In their respective struggles to locate an alternative to death as an absolute parting, King and Milton ultimately affirm the central features of the tradition that preceded them.

Each of the chapters in *Posthumous Love* examines a different response to the idea of love's mortality, and each offers a different form of consolation. But the imaginative project of English love poetry from Wyatt to Marvell is in the broadest sense a shared one: the project of exploring what happens to the experience of love if that love is limited to this world alone.

I. Spousal Tombs

Renaissance English love poetry reflects a flourishing of creativity and invention on a subject that had long preoccupied not only poets and artists but also ordinary husbands and wives confronting the deaths of their loved ones. In what follows, I want to consider the expectations of English spouses who were buried together during the sixteenth and seventeenth centuries. I have chosen to begin the book with Renaissance epitaphs in order to emphasize not simply the relevance but the absolute centrality of the topic of posthumous love for a majority of the adult population: those men and women who had spouses who left them, or whom they left, behind. The question of posthumous love was not, in other words, an abstract question belonging to the realm of theology or metaphysics. Instead, it was a pressing existential concern. What will happen to my husband if he dies before me; will I eventually be buried with him; will we meet again in the afterlife, or will death be our final parting? These or related questions must have been raised by many English wives in this period facing the deaths of their husbands (and likewise by English husbands confronting the deaths of their wives); they are the critical questions of people with any curiosity or fear about death and its aftermath. Thus when English poets wrote about the fate of posthumous love, they were dealing with materials that were of fundamental concern. And when they denied the possibility of love's continuing past the grave, they were dashing the hopes of many couples that longed for posthumous intimacy.

Because very few people specified in their wills what they hoped would await them after death, the best way to gauge these expectations is to look at the hundreds of tombs and epitaphs that either survive or were recorded from the period. (This also means we are looking only at married couples, and not lovers, whose passions were not recorded on epitaphs—with a few notable exceptions.) If we were to limit ourselves to the tombs from any single parish church, or even from a large cathedral, it would be difficult to make sense of the different types of burials we would find. As anyone who has ever stepped inside an old English church well knows, these churches typically contain tombs that span the centuries and therefore include Catholic and Protestant burials as well as monuments for individuals, couples, and entire families. What we find, in other words, is a long-term jumble of tombs that does not easily lend itself to a clear picture of how spouses from any particular period expressed their hopes for their posthumous lives.

Let us make our way, then, through an imaginary English church filled with tombs from only the sixteenth and seventeenth centuries. All of the tombs in our imaginary church are genuine: they are culled from antiquarian volumes that date back to the late sixteenth century, when John Stow first published his *Survay of London*, which was subsequently expanded to include by 1633 all of the funerary inscriptions in the parish churches of greater London and Westminster. This was an extraordinary achievement, which Stow explains as a "duty that I willingly ow to my native mother & Countrie," to show "what *London* hath beene of auncient time . . . as what it is now."[7] Stow's efforts were imitated in counties across England, and the result is an impressively vast collection of epitaphs that far exceeds what could ever be assembled from surviving tombs.

In our fictitious church we will bury only spouses—this will be a Protestant version of the pagan fields of Elysium, reserved for the ghosts of lovers—and we will stroll around and look at their tombs. Doing so will put in clear relief the central ideas that couples had about the fate of their marriages after death, and our task will be made even easier by the fact that the tombs have been conveniently arranged into three groups, each occupying its own space in the church.

The first two types of marital tombs map neatly onto the central division that Erwin Panofsky identifies in his magisterial survey of funerary sculpture from ancient Egypt to seventeenth-century Italy, *Tomb Sculpture*, in which he differentiates between the "prospective" and the "retrospective" tradition.[8] The prospective tomb is epitomized by the burials of the ancient Egyptians. These were tombs whose reliefs and sculptures focused on the future of the dead with no eye toward the past; the graves were filled with objects deemed necessary for both survival and pleasure in the next world (tools, jewelry, pottery, weapons, and, above all, containers of food).[9] Such prospective tombs not only looked forward to the posthumous future: they also attempted to shape that future, to perform, through their representations of the deceased and the deceased's possessions, what Panofsky describes as a type of "magic manipulation" (16).

Panofsky contrasts the prospective with the retrospective tradition, whose origins he locates in ancient Greece, where the tomb served as a monument, a record of the earthly fame of the deceased. The ancient Roman tombs followed in the same tradition as their Greek predecessors, whereby surviving family members offered loving care to funerary monuments in order to preserve the dead's earthly memory.[10] In the Greek and Roman traditions the emphasis fell on commemoration rather than anticipation. On expensive tombs, the deceased was often represented by a portrait-bust or effigy, which might be accompanied by friezes depicting events from his or her life. On less extravagant tombs, inscriptions commonly mentioned the deceased's social status, means of livelihood, and other biographical details.[11]

In addition to its prospective and retrospective tombs, our church contains a third type of tomb that Panofsky did not seem to have encountered, or at least did not recognize as worthy of attention. This third type focused neither on the past nor on the future, but instead on the subterranean present. Its concern was for the corpses to cohabit the grave, and nothing more. There was no intimation, that is, of a correspondence between burial together in the ground and a heavenly reunion. Instead, there was simply the hope for continued cohabitation in the earth.

II. Heaven

The first set of tombs we encounter corresponds to Panofsky's "prospective" category. The epitaphs for these tombs include some biographical details about the deceased, but their orientation is toward the heavenly future. This focus on heavenly prospects might seem at first glance to belong to a Catholic, not Protestant, tradition. Catholic epitaphs routinely ask for prayers for the dead to hasten the journey to salvation; this was the burden, in fact, of most Catholic graves. Because Protestantism prohibited prayers for the dead, scholars often assume that Protestant epitaphs stayed far away from the deceased's heavenly prospects.[12] But this was by no means universally true. In fact, on spousal tombs, inscriptions declaring the couple's desire to be reunited in heaven occur much more frequently in the post-Reformation period than before. There are multiple reasons why this may be so—including the rise of companionate marriages, a topic I will consider in chapter 1—but the most likely explanation is that Catholics generally had other priorities when contemplating what work they wanted their epitaphs to do.

In the century or so before the Reformation, epitaphs for couples usually petitioned for each spouse's passage to heaven. A typical example is this inscription for Richard and Margery Ballard, erected in a church in Romford in 1517, which beseeches onlookers to pray for the souls of both husband and wife:

> Most glorious Trinity on God and persons thre
> Have mercy on the sowlys of Richard Ballard, and his wyf Margery.
> Whos bodyes her befor yow lyn closyd in cley.
> Every man and woman of yowr cheritie do yow prey:
> That to the blis of heven sweet Iesu do their soulys bring
> Unto the plas celestial befor owr hevenly King.[13]

The two bodies are lying together, "closyd in cley," but the prayer does not aim to secure a similar proximity between them in heaven. Instead, it strives to propel the two souls upward, to assist Richard and Margery in their parallel but separate quests for salvation.

In the spousal epitaphs that we come upon through the doors of our imaginary church, by contrast, the longing to be in heaven is routinely expressed as a longing for togetherness.[14] The first tomb to catch our eye is a beautiful marble slab fastened to the west wall, which was erected by Sir Francis Knowles for his wife, Lady Katherine, who was buried in 1568 in the floor below. The lengthy Latin epitaph concludes:

> . . . Haec tecum multos
> Utinam vixisset in annos,
> Et tua nunc conjux [sic]
> Facta fuisset anus:
> Noluit at Deus, hoc voluit
> Sed sponsa maritum
> In Coelis maneas
> O Katharina, tuum.[15]

(Would that she had lived with you for many years, and now your wife would have become an old woman. But God did not want this; rather he wished that you, pledged bride, await your husband in heaven.)

The focus moves distinctly from what has been lost in this world to what the couple might expect in the next. Katherine becomes once again a betrothed woman, awaiting her husband in heaven for the renewal of their vows.

On the neighboring tomb for Sir John Windham and his wife Florence, erected in 1596, this dialogue is inscribed:

Maritus	When changelesse fate to death did change my life,
	I praied it to be gentle to my wife.
Uxor	But shee who harte & hande to thee did wedd
	Desir'd nothyng more than thys thy bedd
Fatum	Brought your soules that linckt were in each other
	To reste above, your bodyes heer togeither.[16]

The exchange between the faithful "Maritus" and "Uxor" concludes with the voice of Fate, which assures the couple of a double reunion: their bodies remain "heer togeither," their souls "that linckt were in each other" have risen to eternal rest.

Just in front of the tomb for John and Florence Windham is the monument for Sir William Stone and his wife Barbara, whose epitaph describes a similar double reunion of the spouses' bodies and souls:

> Here likewise lyes
> Inhumed in one bed,
> Dame Barbara,
> The welbeloved wife
> Of this remembred Knight:
> Whose soules are fled
> From this dimme Vale,
> To everlasting life.
> Where no more change,
> Nor no more separation
> Shall make them flye
> From their blest habitation. (307)

Since Barbara lived five years longer than William—she died in 1612 and he in 1607—and since genealogical records indicate that she remarried in 1610, it is not clear when this epitaph was composed, or by whom. But it was not uncommon, as we shall see, for a second husband to bury his wife with her first husband, especially when the first marriage had produced offspring and the second marriage had not (Barbara bore William nine children). Whether Barbara oversaw the preparation of the tomb before her death or whether it was arranged posthumously by her second husband or children, the message of its inscription is unequivocally monogamous: she and her first husband will share a matrimonial "bed" in the earth while their souls ascend to an "everlasting life" together.

It is important to recognize that the idea that the burial ground is the earthly complement to the celestial meeting of the souls is distinct from the idea that the spouses' heavenly reunion will be delayed until the general resurrection. If the latter were true, the joint burial would simply serve as a kind of holding pattern or temporary arrangement to ensure that the ultimate reunion occurs. (This is what John Donne, for example, has in mind in his poem "The Relique," in which he famously describes the corporeal remains of himself and his mistress in the grave—"A bracelet of bright haire about the bone"—as a "loving couple" who combined their remains in order "[t]o make their soules, at the last busie day / Meet at this grave, and make a little stay.")[17] The epitaphs that we are considering, by contrast, do not see these two reunions as sequential but as simultaneous. Thus on the marble tomb erected in 1612 for John Pearse and his wife Jane, who died some twenty-three years apart, we find:

> ... By nature they were two[:] by love made one
> By Death made two. Againe with mourneful mone
> O cruell death: in turning odde to even
> Yet blessed death: in bringing both to heaven
> On earth they had one bed: in earth one toombe
> And now their soules in heaven enioy one roome
> Thus Pearse. Being peirced by death doth peace obtaine
> Oh happie peirce. Since Peace is Pearses Gaine.[18]

The author of this epitaph clearly fancied himself a great wit, but behind the multiple puns on the couple's name is the underlying claim of continuity between John and Jane's love in this world and in the next. The shared bed they enjoyed on earth is transposed to its two posthumous equivalents: the "toombe" and heavenly "roome." The long period of their earthly separation—Jane died in 1589 and John in 1612—is entirely elided with the prospect of eternity before them.

A similar conceit governs the marble slab on the west floor for John Edwards and his wife, Izan:

> As love (in life)
> Conjoyn'd us once,
> And God (by death)
> Disjoyn'd us twaine:

So love (by death)
Rejoyn'd our bones,
And God (in joy)
Joyn'd us againe. (220)

In this case, Izan remarried after her husband John's death in 1591; according to the prose inscription above these verses, her second husband, Baron Clarke, erected the tomb following Izan's death in 1613. There were twenty-two years, and a second marriage, dividing Izan from John Edwards; and yet, for reasons we cannot recover, it was Izan and John, not Izan and Baron, whom Baron "[j]oyn'd . . . againe."

Before we leave the group of prospective tombs, a few final monuments deserve our attention. These are tombs that contain multiple spouses of a single husband or wife, and whose epitaphs petition for a collective heavenly reunion. It was certainly more typical to be buried with only one spouse (and the historian Barbara J. Harris has shown that wealthy widows routinely specified in their wills which husband it would be).[19] But here we find several tombs in which men were buried with multiple spouses, creating newly polygamous families.[20] The sculpted effigies that grace many of these monuments are typically arranged with the husband lying between his two wives; those husbands buried with more than two wives are either flanked by multiple wives on their left and right sides or, as is the case with the spectacular monument for Richard Covert in a private chapel in the south aisle, the three wives are lined up behind their husband in a row (the surviving fourth wife, who presumably erected the monument on behalf of her deceased husband, was eventually buried elsewhere).[21]

The inscriptions for multiple spouses that gesture toward heavenly reunion are distinctive in their attempts to secure domestic arrangements in the afterlife that had no equivalent on earth. Outside the Covert chapel along the south wall of the church is a monument to William Lambe, with this first-person inscription carved on the front of the tomb:

With wives three
I joyned wedlocke band,

Which (all alive)
True lovers were to me:
Joane, Alice and Joane,
For so they came to hand,
What needeth praise,
Regarding their degrees
In wively truth
None stedfast more could be.
Who though in earth
Death's force did once dissever,
Heaven yet (I trust)
Shall joyne us all together. (356)[22]

What exactly this reunion shall entail remains unspecified: there is no suggestion here or elsewhere of carnal relations, and the implicit understanding in all of these tombs is of a reunion—at least initially—among souls rather than bodies. What is clear is that Lambe sees nothing problematic about inscribing in stone his desire to join with Alice and the two Joanes all at once.

Sir John Hawkins, who died in 1595, lies between his two wives, Katharine and Margaret. The epitaph for the three of them reads:

Dame Margaret,
A widdow well affected,
This Monument of memory erected . . .
Kind to his Wives,
Both Gentlewomen borne,
Whose counterfeits with grace this work adorn.
Dame Katharine
The first, of rare report,
Dame Margaret
The last, of Court consort,
Attendant on the Chamber and the Bed
Of Englands Queene
Elizabeth . . .
Thus he and she,

Alike their compasse ending,
Asunder both
By death of flesh alone,
Together both in soule,
Two making one,
Among the Saints above,
From troubles free,
Where two in one shall meet,
And make up three.
The Christian Knight
And his good Ladies twaine,
Flesh, Soule and Spirit
United once againe. (140–41)

The epitaph makes clear that Margaret, the second wife, erected the tomb for her husband and his first wife, Katharine, and imagines the three of them forming a kind of mystical union: "two in one shall meet, / and make up three."

One striking feature that characterizes this group of prospective epitaphs—and differentiates them formally from the retrospective tombs we are about to consider—is their pervasive use of rhyme. This preference for verse over prose is not, I would argue, coincidental: it reflects the fact that these inscriptions are simultaneously operating as subtle acts of prayer. Although praying for the dead was not allowed in the reformed church, when Protestant spouses wanted to express their hopes for a heavenly future, they quietly conformed to the use of metrical verse that was associated with Catholic superstition: namely, the idea that rhyme itself had an intercessionary power.[23]

III. Memoria

As we move forward along the south aisle of the church, we come upon a group of tombs whose epitaphs are strictly memorial. These tombs record the names of those buried, the number of children that the couple had, the date of each spouse's death. Some make note of the professional life of the husband, some the lineage of either husband or wife.

Many of these tombs were erected by a surviving spouse, who may or may not have been buried alongside the deceased.

The first tomb we come upon is for a young woman, Jane Hansby, who is remembered in this brass inscription erected by her husband Ralfe:

Iane the wife of Ralfe Hansby Esquire, daughter to William Vavasour Esquire, Grandchild to Thomas Manners Knight, died the 22 day of Iuly, in the yeere of our Lord 1617. and of her age the 23. To whose blessed memory her deare husband hath dedicated this sad monument to signifie that with her his joy lies here interred. (473)

Next to Jane Hansby's tomb is the monument for Anne Farrar, with this epitaph engraved on a small gilt plate:

[Here] Lieth buried the body of *Anne*, the wife of *Iohn Farrar*, Gentleman, and Merchant Adventurer of this City, daughter of *William Shepheard*, of Great *Rowlright*, in the County of *Oxenford*, Esquire. She departed this life the 12. day of Iuly, *An. Dom. 1613.* being then about the age of 21. yeeres. To whose well-deserving memory, this Monument is by her said husband erected. (277)

The third grave in this initial cluster is marked by a marble slab with an inscription for Anne Andrewes, composed by her husband Nicholas:

Nicholas Andrewes to his dearest wife Anne, doth this last office of love: for she was,

Religious,	Loving,
Chaste,	Faire,
Discreet,	Obedient.

She lived but 25 yeeres, and dyed at Chigwell in Essex, the 12. day of Iune 1606. and was here-under interred (in great sorrow) the munday following: leaving behind her living, two sonnes, William and Nicholas. (132)

Each of these tombs records the life of a wife who died in her twenties, leaving her husband (and in Anne Andrewes's case, her children) behind. Each also records a marriage that was past: a union that had been but was no more. The poignancy of these inscriptions lies in their sense of irrecoverable loss, their submission to the mortality of the human bonds that had linked the couple together. The widower was filled with sadness, his joys were buried with the body of his wife, and he did not dare to imagine anything further between them.

As we walk farther up the southern aisle, we come next to a set of tombs in which husbands and wives are buried together. There is a particularly beautiful monument along the wall for David Smith, who was buried in the floor below with his wife Katharine. The inscription on the monument reads:

> *David Smith*, Embroyderer to Queene *Elizabeth*, &c. deceased the tenth day of August, 1587. aged 63. yeeres, and lyeth here-under buried: whose honest, vertuous, and compassionate care for the needy, both in soule and body, is expressed by his benevolence that way extended, like a good Steward, making others partakers of his well-imployed Talent. Who had to wife *Katharine* (by whom he had eight sonnes and eight daughters) at whose proper charges (in memory of her said loving husband) is erected this Monument, the 25 of March, in An. 1596. Who living his faithful Widdow till the fourth day of February 1607. aged 78 yeeres, lyeth also here-under buried. (406)

Katharine erected the monument following David's death in 1596; the date of her subsequent burial beside her husband eleven years later and, presumably, the description of her "faithful Widdow[hood]" were appended to the epitaph after her death.

A more modest monument along the southern wall marks the burial place below of Margery Turner, whose second husband, Humfrey, buried her with her first husband, Isaac Sutton, with whom she had twelve children:

> Here before this place, lyeth buried the body of Margery, late the Wife of Humfrey Turner, Gent. Who deceased the 10 day of December 1607, being of the age of 56 yeeres. As also the body of her first husband, Master Isaac

Sutton, late Citizen and Goldsmith of London, who deceased the 2 day of
May, 1589. (153)

Just past this tomb is a marble inscription erected by Richard Leigh for
his wife, Anne, and her first husband, Richard Brattuph, along with
three of Anne and Richard's children:

> May 22. 1618. Richard Leigh, Merchant and Citizen of London, placed
> this stone in memoriall of his deare wife Anne Leigh; Who lyeth heere
> interred by the body of Richard Brattuph her first husband, and of her
> 3. Children, Richard, Sara, and Iohn, which she bare to the said Richard
> Brattuph. (474)

Like Humfrey Turner, who erected the adjacent tomb, Richard Leigh
chose not to be buried alongside his wife. Instead, following either his
wife's instructions or his own inclination, he honored the earlier marriage—and the three children from that marriage, who are buried
alongside their parents—assuming for himself only the role of com-
memorator.

A small brass plate at the end of the south aisle marks the grave of
William Cockaine, who lies below with both of his wives:

> Here lyeth the body of the Worshipfull Mr. William Cockaine the elder,
> Citizen and Skinner of London, who departed this life the 18 day of
> November, 1599. Also here lyeth the body of Elizabeth Medcalfe, his first
> wife; by whom hee had 7 sonnes and 4 daughters [she died April 1589]. . . .
> Here also lyeth the body of Katharine Wonton, his second wife, who dyed
> the 19 of September, 1596, by whom he had no issue. (185)

Despite the relative brevity of William's second marriage and its lack
of offspring (compared to the eleven children his first wife bore him),
the epitaph does not privilege one marriage over the other. It registers
simply the basic data of William's life.

Before leaving the southern aisle of the church, we stop before a
rather grand monument tucked away in the corner, with finely carved

effigies of John Walsingham and his wife Elenor. The brass inscription next to the monument reads:

> Here lieth buried the bodies of John Walsingham late of Exhall in ye County of War' Esquire and Elenor his wyfe one of the daughters of Humfrey Ashefield late of Heythropp in the countye of Oxford Esquire. The same John decessed the xxth day of January 1566. And ye said Elenor decessed the _____.[24]

Despite John's expectation of lying with his wife, fate seems to have had it otherwise. E. W. Badger, who recorded this tombstone in his 1895 volume of inscriptions from Warwickshire, notes that Elenor was probably buried elsewhere, although details concerning her fate are unknown. The space on the brass plate reserved for the date of her death is left hauntingly blank, matched in its vacancy by the half-empty tomb below.

Whatever the composition of the tombs' inhabitants, these retrospective epitaphs are generally marked by a tone of emotional detachment; they are above all biographical records, filled with numbers and dates and written in unornamented prose. No mention is ever made of what might await husband or wife after death, nor are any hopes or expectations detailed. Compared to the neighboring prospective tombs that look forward to heavenly reunions, the southern aisle of our church feels overwhelmingly secular.

IV. Earth

We come now to the final group of marital tombs, whose epitaphs fall into neither Panofksy's prospective nor retrospective category, but petition only for the couple to lie side by side in the earth. Although we find these tombs in a Protestant church, they do not adhere to a particular Protestant belief or doctrine. Because Protestantism on the whole regards the flesh as something to be dispensed with as soon as it parts from the soul at the moment of death, the corpse serves no meaningful purpose until it is retrieved and made new at the resurrection. Hence there is no possible theological advantage to lying nearer to or farther from any other person's remains.

The emphasis on the proximity of the spouses' corporeal remains might seem to be rooted in a classical tradition, since joint burial was common in the ancient world, from the Egyptians to the Etruscans to the Greeks and Romans. But there is no pagan philosophy that extols the pleasures of joint burial. Lucretius and his fellow Epicureans may have denied the immortality of the soul, but they did not as a consequence believe that our mortal remains had any significance after death. Cicero similarly argues in the *Tusculan Disputations* that it is not possible "for the man who does not [any longer] exist to "'feel the need of' anything." "It is clearer than daylight," he declares, "that, when soul and body have been made away with, the whole living being destroyed, and complete annihilation has ensued, the creature which has existed has become nothing."[25] Diogenes of Sinope, a skeptic, showed such disregard for the fate of the corpse after death that he asked to be left unburied. When his friends responded with horror, warning that he would surely be devoured by the bird and beasts, Diogenes is said to have replied: "Certainly not, but you must put a stick near me to drive them away with." "How can you," they retorted, "for you will be without consciousness?" To which he answered, with wry amusement, "What harm, then, can the mangling of wild beasts do me if I am without consciousness?"[26]

The desire to lie together seems to have little to do, then, with any particular religious or philosophical tradition. Instead, it can probably best be understood as a deeply human instinct, an urge that pervades different cultures and historical periods without any clear articulation of purpose. There are no major works in either the Christian or pagan tradition that reflect upon the nature of joint burial. Our best early modern source comes in a remarkable antiquarian treatise: Sir Thomas Browne's 1658 *Hydriotaphia, Urne-Buriall, or A Discourse of the Sepulchrall Urnes lately found in Norfolk.* Over the course of his meditation on the relative advantages of cremation versus inhumation, Browne describes the poignancy of pagan lovers who chose to combine their ashes in single urns. "The ashes of Domitian were mingled with those of Julia," he reports, "of Achilles with those of Patroclus." Neither of these examples— the Roman emperor Domitian and his mistress, Julia, nor the two male Homeric heroes—is of marital love. But the conclusion Browne draws about their motives in combining their remains echoes over the centuries in the epitaphs for married couples: "Without confused burnings, they affectionately compounded their bones, passionately endeavouring to continue their living Unions."[27]

Browne's language here is peculiar—he describes the inevitably post-humous act of compounding the lovers' bones together as "affectionate," as if the bones themselves possessed an emotional will—and this peculiarity brings out the paradox at the heart of these joint burials. What can Browne mean by assigning affections, passions, desires to the lovers' material remains? He can mean only that he understands the particularity of our personhood to be continuous with our corpse, that some meaningful part of us lies within our corporeal remains even though the soul has presumably departed (the soul plays very little part in Browne's narrative, and it is equally scarce in the epitaphs desiring joint burial alone). There is no evidence that many ancient Greeks or Romans, let alone early modern Protestants, believed that consciousness persisted in their corporeal remains, so that the subterranean presence of one's lover or spouse would bring real comfort. And yet the simple urge for companionship overwhelmed any rational explanation of its purposelessness.

What Browne imagines the ashes or bones to feel is precisely what people feel in their earthly lives: that sharing a single dwelling, or a single room, is in itself a rewarding form of companionship, comparable to the odd pleasure of sleeping in a state of unconsciousness next to one's husband or wife or lover. Those who were not so lucky as to be buried in a single urn, Browne continues, recovered at least a share of compensatory pleasure in having adjacent urns. "When distance of death denied such conjunctions," he declares, "unsatisfied affections conceived some satisfaction to be neighbours in the grave, to lye Urne by Urne, and touch but in their names" (38). "To lye Urne by Urne" was not so fulfilling as the shared single urn, but it provided "some satisfaction" of a neighborly sort: to know that just nearby, if not within one's own private vessel, was someone beloved. Once again, the projection onto the ashes of rather full emotional lives, replete with "unsatisfied affections" and plans to remedy that dissatisfaction, suggests either that the soul has not in fact left the body (a heresy that Browne elsewhere admits he once believed in, but claims to have left long behind) or, more likely, that the body does not need the soul to experience longing or loneliness.[28] The corpse has, in effect, an emotional life of its own.

The epitaphs that constitute the third and final group of tombs in our church capture exactly the type of longing that Browne describes: a longing simply "to lye Urne by Urne," or corpse by corpse, in the earth. Along the north side of the chancel we come upon the monument for Donne's wife, Ann, who died in 1617. The tomb is engraved with a moving epitaph composed by the poet himself:

Feminae lectissimae, dilectissimaeque,

Coniugi charissimae, castissimaeque,

Matri piissimae, Indulgentissimaeque,

XV. Annis in Conjugio Transactis,

VII. post XII. partum (quorum VII. superstant) dies

Immani febre correptae,

(Quod hoc saxum fari iussit

Ipse, prae dolore Infans)

Maritus (miserrimum dictu) olim charae charus

Cineribus cineres spondet suos

Novo matrimonio (annuat Deus) hoc loco sociandos.

(A woman most choice or select, most beloved/well-read;

A spouse most dear, most chaste,

A mother most loving/merciful, pious, [and] most indulgent,

Fifteen years in marriage completed,

Seven days after the twelfth child [of twelve seven survive]

By a ravishing fever carried off suddenly

Wherefore her husband ordered this stone tablet to speak,

Himself beyond grief made a speechless Infant,

Her husband [most miserably uttered name or designation],

    once dear to the dear,

Pledges his ashes to these ashes

In a new marriage [may God assent] in this place joining together.)[29]

In his poem "The Anniversarie," Donne regrets that he and his mistress are not likely to share a single grave: "Two graves must hide thine and my coarse / If one might, death were no divorce" (11–12). In the epitaph for Ann, he fantasizes about having such a second marriage in the earth. The mingling of their ashes becomes the equivalent of the "plighting of troth" in the Prayer Book service for matrimony; even the optative "annuat Deus" (may God assent) echoes the liturgy's consecration of the union "according to Gods holy ordinance."[30] This marriage is not described in spiritual or eschatological terms. Its pledge is between ashes, not souls.

Whatever his firm intentions at the time of Ann's death, Donne was ultimately buried, some fifteen years later, alone. This was by his own request: in his last will and testament, he directed that he be buried "in the moste private manner that maye be in the church-yard of the Parish where I now live."[31] It is hard not to feel this as a betrayal of his vow, an abandonment of the wife he seems to have deeply loved and whom he wanted to join in the earth. Since Donne never remarried, it is perhaps all the more surprising that he did not honor the sentiments expressed in Ann's epitaph. But for all of the couples whose burial plans remained intact over the decades separating one spouse's death from the other's—and we have seen several examples of such couples already—there were those whose plans changed, whose hopes or expectations moved in different directions. In the case of Donne, as I have argued elsewhere, after years of ever more demanding service to the church and deeper preoccupation with theological matters, it was the reunion of body and soul, and not of husband and wife, that came to obsess him.[32] But the example of Donne speaks more broadly to the human reality of so many of these tombs, where the passage of time alters the urgent longing for further contact that husband or wife feel—and express in brass or stone—at the time of greatest grief.

Near the monument for Ann Donne is the tomb of Elizabeth Brewster, who died in 1609. The stone epitaph erected by her husband, Sir John, describes in terms similar to Donne's the future rekindling of marital vows in the tomb:

> . . . Thou bed of rest,
> reserve for him a roome,
> Who lives a man divorc't

from his deare wife:
And as they were one heart,
so this one Tombe
May hold them neere
in death, as linckt in life.
Shee's gone before,
and after comes her head;
To sleepe with her
among the blessed dead. (425)

Although there is no record of whether John was ultimately buried alongside his wife, the monument was clearly designed to accommodate him. There is no hint, moreover, of a future together beyond the space of the grave: the reunion he desires is in the tomb, which will "hold them neere / in death, as linckt in life."

On the northern wall we come next upon a large stone monument erected for Anne Gibson by her husband, Laurence. This monument is unusually rich in inscriptions, covering nearly all of the space available. The first set of lines falls squarely into Panofsky's retrospective category, recording Anne's pedigree and virtues along with her date of death:

Here lye the bodies of Anne, the wife of Laurence Gibson, Gent. and of their three sonnes. She was a most faithfull and loving wife, and a right-religious, wise, vertuous and modest woman, and adorned with many other such excellent and commendable gifts and qualities, that she is worthy of perpetuall memory. She was of the ancient Family of the *Bamfords* in *Lincolnshire*: and the 29. day of December, 1611 she patiently and Christianly ended this mortall life.

This is followed by a Latin inscription, which shifts its sentiments from commemoration to anticipation of a life together in the earth:

. . . Hoc moestissimus eius maritus, in piam memoriam Uxoris suae, talis, tamq; charissimae construi fecit: eundemq; hic cum illa esse sepulturum sperat & exoptat.

(This saddest husband of hers, in pious memory of his wife, had constructed [this memorial]; he hopes and longs to be buried with her.)[33]

Under the Latin inscription we find this text in English:

> What, is she dead?
> doth he survive?
> No: both are dead,
> and both alive.
> She lives, hee's dead,
> by love, though grieving,
> In him, for her,
> yet dead, yet living.
> Both dead, and living?
> then what is gone?
> One halfe of both,
> not any one.
> One mind, one Faith,
> one hope, one Grave,
> In life, in death,
> they had, and still they have. (309–10)

It is worth noting that the memorial lines on the Gibson tomb are written in prose, whereas the hopes for joint burial are in English verse. English verse, in fact, dominates the tombs in this part of the church: like their counterparts in the first section, these epitaphs are ultimately petitionary. Despite Laurence's elaborate preparations, however, there is no record of his burial here. Because his date and place of death remain unknown, we cannot say with any certainty what his fate was, but once again we are struck with the poignancy of either thwarted or altered intentions.

Just beyond the Gibson monument, under a window, is the tomb for Sir Thomas Blanke and his wife Margaret. Here we find two separate epitaphs side by side. The first, an inscription for Thomas, who died in 1588, does not mention Margaret; it records his impressive service to the city of London as "Sheriffe, Lord Maior, and Alderman," and his long life of seventy-four years. The epitaph for Margaret, by contrast, who lived as a widow for eight years before her death in 1596, focuses on the strength of the couple's marital bond, which extends with apparent ease to their shared burial:

> Death was deceiv'd,
> which thought these two to part:
> For though this Knight
> first left this mortall life,
> Yet till she dyed,
> He still liv'd in her heart.
> What happier husband,
> or more kinder wife?
> Whom foure and forty changes of the Spring,
> In sacred wedlocke,
> mutuall love had linkt:
> The deare remembrance of so deare a thing,
> Was not by death
> in her chaste breast extinct.
> Building this Tombe
> not long before she dy'd,
> Her latest duty
> to his Funerall Rite,
> Crown'd with her vertues,
> like an honest Bride,
> Here lyes at rest
> by her beloved Knight. (227)

Given her probable age at the time of Thomas's death, after forty-four years of marriage, the likelihood of Margaret's remarrying was very low.[34] But the emphasis in the epitaph falls nonetheless on her enduring fidelity to her husband: she kept him alive, we are told, "in her heart" and held his memory dear "in her chaste breast." It also makes clear that the bonds between husband and wife, or husband and widow, were, finally, mortal: they expired if not with his death, then with hers. There is no expectation of a shared life for them beyond the grave. The reward for their "mutuall love" is eternal rest, side by side, in the earth.

Before we leave the church, we come upon a small chapel toward the end of the northern aisle that has two tombs unlike any others. The first is a monument to Thomas Legge, master of Gonville and Caius College at Cambridge University, who died in 1607. The monument—a full-bodied effigy of Legge praying in his academic robes—was erected in 1619 by his friend John Gostlin, who composed the inscription below the effigy: "Iunxit Amor Vivos Sic Inugat Terra Sepultos/Gostlini Reliquum. Cor Tibi Leggus Habes" (Love joined them living. So may the earth join them in their burial. O Legge, Gostlin's heart you have still with you).[35] That Legge and Gostlin understood their earthly union as the equivalent of marriage is confirmed by one of their contemporaries, William More, who said that the two men had lived *conjunctissime* ("qui cum eo conjunctissime vixerat"), employing the superlative of the Latin adjective *conjunctus*, derived from the noun *conjunx*, for "one who is united in marriage."[36]

Across from the Legge monument is a tomb erected in 1684 for Sir John Finch, ambassador to Constantinople, and Sir Thomas Baine, with stone portrait busts of the two men side by side. The epitaph below asks that the two might "in death, at last mingle their sacred ashes" (idem suos defuncti sacros tandem miscerent cineres),[37] a very deliberate echo of Patroclus's request on the eve of his death in the *Iliad*. In an episode also invoked by Browne in *Urne-Buriall*, Patroclus's shade visits Achilles before his body is burned on the pyre in order to make the request: "Lay not my bones apart from yours, Achilles, but let them lie together. . . . let one coffer enfold our bones, a golden coffer with two handles, the one your queenly mother gave you."[38]

As the historian Alan Bray documents in his beautiful book *The Friend*, tombs such as Finch and Baine's and Legge and Gostlin's were not so unusual as we might think: throughout the early modern period men (and more rarely women) either were buried together or erected monuments for one another, commemorating vows that the church did not recognize. The two monuments in this small chapel speak, therefore, on behalf of all of those tombs—the relatively small number actually erected and the many more that were wished for—that brought together lovers who were not formally linked in this world but may have hoped for something more in the next.[39]

The funerary inscriptions that I have surveyed capture the range of expectations that early modern couples had when they thought about their fates after death. These three types of epitaphs represent such divergent understandings of what awaits couples in the afterlife that we might well imagine them to belong to different cultures or historical periods. The fact that such incompatible ideas could coexist in a culture like Renaissance England that closely monitored religious beliefs—and especially monitored the public expression of religious beliefs—deserves our serious attention. This is not to say that the Church of England was uninterested in the fate of couples after death, and certainly some members of its clergy attempted to curtail the hopes and desires of the laity wishing for an afterlife for love. In the next chapter, we will see what Protestants said about our likely company in heaven, and what lines they drew around the extension of human love. The history of the church's attitude toward posthumous love has almost entirely slipped through the cracks of early modern scholarship, but it has important implications for the direction that English poetry took in the century following the Reformation.

1

Love after Death in the Protestant Church

> Death is an absolute diremption, and maketh an vtter dissolution
> of the mariage bond.
>
> —William Gouge, *Of Domesticall Duties* (1622)

According to the Christian scriptures, there is no real possibility for a
shared afterlife between husbands and wives. The idea that marriage
vows would come to an end with the death of one or the other spouse
was common to both Catholicism and Protestantism and was typically
traced to Jesus's response to the Sadducees as reported in the synoptic
gospels. As Matthew relates it, the Sadducees, who did not believe in the
resurrection of the body, asked Jesus what would become of a woman
who had married seven brothers successively. "Now there were with us
seven brethren," they explained, "and the first, when he had married
a wife, deceased, and, having no issue, left his wife unto his brother.
Likewise the second also, and the third, unto the seventh." If all seven
brothers and the single woman meet in the resurrection, whose wife,
they taunted, would she be? Jesus's reply—"For in the resurrection, they
neither marry, nor are given in marriage, but are as the angels of God
in heaven"—became for many the definitive position on posthumous
union in the Christian church (Matthew 22:25-26, 28).[1]

Although the Bible does not specify the boundaries for marital union,

Christian liturgies have always been clear about the limits of the church's jurisdiction. The Latin rite most commonly used in England before the Reformation, known as the Sarum Use, declared wedding vows to be binding "tyl dethe us departe"; even before the adoption of an English-language liturgy in the mid-sixteenth century this so-called plighting of troth was conducted in the vernacular to make certain that there could be no misunderstandings.[2] The Protestant Book of Common Prayer, first published in 1549, made no substantial alterations to the Sarum matrimony service and kept the language of plighting unchanged. According to the Book of Common Prayer, the minister instructs first the man, and then the woman, to say: "I N. take thee N. to my wedded wife [husband], to have and to holde from this day forwarde . . . till death us departe: according to Goddes holy ordeinaunce; And thereto I plight thee my trouth."[3]

The formula "till death us departe" was almost certainly intended to prohibit abandonment or divorce; it was consistent with Jesus's answer to the Pharisees' question, related in Matthew 19, as to whether it is "lawful for a man to put away his wife for every cause," to which Jesus replied, "What therefore God hath joined together, let not man put asunder" (Matthew 19:6). But in the post-Reformation period, the phrase took on a second meaning: it was also used to reinforce the termination of marital vows after death. Far from encouraging the widow (or, less commonly, the widower) to maintain vows of fidelity to the deceased, the emphasis fell on cutting all affective ties with one's deceased husband or wife, in order to encourage remarriage. As William Gouge advises in his 1622 advice manual *Of Domesticall Duties*, surviving spouses should feel no obligation to the deceased but should be free to join "with another yoke-fellow after they are loosed from one." "If they mary againe," Gouge contends, "and manifest such a minde [i.e., by remaining too devoted to the deceased], they plainly shew that they respect [the former spouse] more then Gods ordinance. By Gods ordinance man and wife are no longer bound one to another then [when] they liue together. Death is an absolute diremption, and maketh an vtter dissolution of the mariage bond."[4] "Death is an absolute diremption": the noun *diremption* from the Latin *diripere*, meaning to tear away or violently separate, typifies the uncompromising terms in which certain Protestants imagine the effect of death on marriage. There is no need for continued devotion to the deceased spouse: the role of widow or widower is not disparaged, but it is also not held up as an ideal, especially for women who are still of childbearing age.

The frequency of remarriage during this period in England—Lawrence Stone estimates it at roughly one-quarter of all marriages—as well as the suspicion with which young widows were generally regarded suggests a different cultural orientation from much of medieval Europe, where widows were esteemed as second only to virgins in their piety.[5] As the historian Bernhard Jussen has shown, by around 500 CE the bereaved wife became both a crucial figure for moral order and a metaphor for the church on earth, awaiting the bridegroom Christ.[6] Widowhood, Jussen argues, shifted at this time from a temporary position to a permanent one. It became, in effect, a profession.

There was no comparable system of rewards for widowhood in Protestantism, nor was there ecclesiastical encouragement to remain unmarried as there was in the Catholic tradition.[7] If we compare, for example, a text like Juan Luis Vives's 1523 *De institutione feminae Christianae* (*Instruction of a Christen Woman*), dedicated to the staunchly Catholic Catherine of Aragon, with Gouge's deeply Protestant *Of Domesticall Duties*, the differences in attitude toward remarriage are striking. Vives's Latin manual, which was translated into English by a member of Thomas More's household, lays out characteristically Catholic advice on the subject of widowhood.[8] Although he does not explicitly discourage young widows from remarriage, he reminds them of the life that awaits them in heaven: "This is the true and sure Christian consolation, when they that be alive think and trust, that their friends, which are dead, be not separate from them, but only sent before in to the place, where within short space after they shall meet together full merily." "These things ought Christian priests to show and tell unto young widows," Vives advises, "and not as many do drink to them in the funeral feast, and bid them be of good cheer, saying, they shall not lack a new husband, and that he is provided of one for her already."[9]

Vives's encouragement of the widow to think about her heavenly reunion with her deceased husband, who becomes in this account unavailable to her only temporarily, provides a strong contrast to Gouge's advice to both widows and widowers considering the prospect of re-marriage. Posing the question "Are they who haue buried their husband or wife so free, as they may marie againe?" Gouge answers: "Yea, as free as they who were neuer before maried. The law doth not only permit a widow to marie againe: but if her husband died before he had any children, it commanded the next kinsman that was liuing and free to marie her, that he might raise vp seed to his brother deceased" (186). After citing this crucial passage from Deuteronomy (25:5-6), he refers to Timothy 5:14—"I will therefore that the younger women marry, bear children, guide the house, give none occasion to the adversary to speak reproachfully"—before reaching his conclusion: "We finde no restraint from a third, or fourth, or more mariages, if by the diuine prouidence so many wiues, or husbands one after another be taken away while there is need for the suruiuing partie to vse the benefit of mariage."[10]

The differences between Vives and Gouge capture one of the subtle but important changes wrought by Protestantism in relation to the status of marriage after death. Both religions officially held that marriage was limited to this world, but Protestants tended to draw much stricter lines between earthly and heavenly ties. Nowhere is this more visible than in the writings of John Calvin, who declares in his 1542 work *Psychopannychia* that we should expect no human fellowship whatever in heaven. "To be in Paradise and live with God," he exclaims, "is not to speak to each other, and to be heard by each other, but is only to enjoy God, to feel his good will, and rest in him."[11] This rigid position does not reflect Calvin's feelings about his own marriage or his affection for his wife, Idelette de Bure, who predeceased him by fifteen years. When she died, Calvin expressed his sorrow to his friend Pierre Viret in unusu-ally heartfelt terms. "Truly mine is not common grief," he explains in a private letter; "I have been bereaved of the best companion of my life, who, if any severe hardship had occurred, would have been my willing partner, not only in exile and poverty but even in death."[12] But Calvin does not allow himself the comfort of imagining a possible future with Idelette in heaven. Divine companionship, he argues, is entirely incon-sonant with the companionship of former spouses, and the pleasures of being with Christ should not be compromised or diluted by affection for husbands or wives.

Calvin grounds his argument for the strictly divine nature of heavenly companionship not, as we might expect, on Matthew 22:30 ("For in the resurrection, they neither marry, nor are given in marriage, but are as the angels of God in heaven") but on a later verse from the same gospel: "Then shall two be in the field; the one shall be taken, and the other left" (24:40). The choice of Matthew 24:40 to argue against heavenly companionship between earthly loved ones was entirely idiosyncratic. Unlike the corresponding passage in Luke, for example, which is preceded by a warning that bedfellows will be parted—"I tell you, in that night there shall be two men in one bed; the one shall be taken, and the other shall be left"—the verses in Matthew do not gesture in any way to spouses, nor was there a tradition of biblical commentary that interpreted the two people in the field as a married couple. As Thomas Aquinas shows in his compilation of biblical commentaries, *The Golden Chain*, St. Hilary interprets the verse as the "two people of believers and unbelievers," John Chrysostom as the "masters and servant, they that work, and they that work not," and Remigius of Auxerre as "the order of preachers to whom is committed the field of the Church."[13] In the subsequent verse, moreover, Matthew portrays female laborers grinding at the mill—"Two women shall be grinding at the mill; the one shall be taken, and the other left"—so the division between the sexes in this section of the text is quite explicit, rendering it even more difficult to apply to married couples.

But Calvin saw in Matthew 24:40 a clear articulation of the imperative to separate partners from one another at the moment of death, and he takes this opportunity to warn husbands and wives against any expectations they might have of resuming their ties in the afterlife. As if correcting a false application of Matthew 19:6—"What therefore God hath joined together, let not man put asunder"—Calvin specifies that marital bonds must be severed with the death of one spouse. "Husbands and wives will then be torn apart from one another," he writes, employing the Latin verb *diripere* (to tear to pieces) that lay behind Gouge's noun "diremption," "lest the bonds that connected human beings to one another hinder the pious."[14] The reason for this shattering of human bonds is to ensure that men and women "run with cheerfulness" to their deaths, that they not hold back due to any prior obligations or ties. Christ intended, Calvin concludes, "to cut off every occasion of delay, to enjoin every one to make haste, that those who [are] already prepared may not waste their time in waiting for their companions."[15] Only Calvin could worry about wasting time as he approaches an eternity in heaven.

I. English Heaven

The Church of England never officially adopted Calvin's position. There were no ecclesiastical articles or injunctions issued on the status of marital bonds after death, nor did either the Book of Common Prayer or the Book of Homilies describe what would await deceased spouses after death (in the official "Homily of the State of Matrimony," obligations surrounding the spouse's death are not discussed). Versions of Calvin's position surfaced regularly, however, in English sermons and treatises, where we frequently encounter descriptions of heavenly company stripped of all prior earthly attachments. As Edward Vaughan succinctly puts it in *A Divine Discoverie of Death* (1612), in heaven we will exchange "the company of husband or wife for the company of Iesus Christe himself."[16]

To the extent that English churchmen imagined human company in heaven, this company usually consisted of biblical figures rather than loved ones. The Scottish minister Alexander Hume explains in his 1594 *Treatise of the Felicitie of the Life to Come*:

> We shall haue for our familiar brethren and companions our first progenitor Adam, Noe, Lot, Abraham, Isaac & Iacob, and the twelue Patriarks, the sonnes of Iacob: Likewise wee shall see, by familiar, and contract friendship & brotherhood which never shall be dissolued, with Moses, Aaron, Iosua, and the just judges of Israell, with Samuell, Elias, and Elisha, Esay, Ieremie, Ezechiell, and Daniell, with David, Ezechias, and Iosias, with Iohn the Baptist, Peter, Paul, & Iohn, whome our Saviour loved: with whome wee shal dwell as brethren and Citizens of a Cittie.

Our own families on this earth will be replaced with the likes of Adam and Noah, Peter and Paul. "We shal see them face to face," Hume declares, "which none can behold, nor apprehend in this life, but by faith only."[17]

John Bunyan's description of Christian's reaction to the Evangelist in the opening pages of *The Pilgrim's Progress* provides a vivid illustration of Calvin's message: "So I saw in my Dream, that the Man began to run. Now he had not run far from his own door, but his Wife and Children perceiving it, began to cry after him to return: but the Man put his fingers in his Ears, and ran on crying, Life, Life, Eternal Life."[18] Whatever temptation Christian might feel to remain with his loved ones, he propels himself forward on the journey that will ultimately lead to his salvation, literally plugging his ears so as not to hear the cries of sorrow calling him back. When some pages later Christian is asked by the wavering Pliable "what company shall we have [in heaven]," he replies: "There we shall be with *Seraphims* and *Cherubins*, Creatures that will dazle your eyes to look on them: There also you shall meet with thousands, and ten thousands that have gone before us to that place; none of them are hurtful, but loving, and holy; every one walking in the sight of God; and standing in his presence with acceptance for ever: In a word, there we shall see the Elders with their Golden Crowns: There we shall see the Holy Virgins with their Golden Harps" (13). Christian's vision of heaven is not stripped of humans—there are "thousands, and ten thousands that have gone before us"—but the emphasis is not on the sweet companionship that they will offer. Instead, Bunyan stresses the supernatural creatures that will "dazle your eyes."

Protestant manuals routinely describe one of the central obligations of matrimony as aiding one's spouse in the pursuit of salvation, but these same texts rarely if ever imagine the heavenly afterlife as something the couple will enjoy together. Gouge's *Of Domestical Duties* advises that "it is the greatest good that one can possibly doe for another, to be a meanes of helping forward his salvation. And there is nothing that can more soundly and firmly knit the heart of one to another, then to be a meanes thereof."[19] In his 1619 *Bride-Bush, or a Direction for Married Persons*, Gouge's contemporary William Whately chastises those who worry about their spouses' physical health but neglect their spiritual welfare. "Many husbands and wives have the bodies of their yoke-fellowes so deare unto them," he complains, "that they cannot endure to thinke of their disgrace, poverty, sicknesse, death: but what becommeth of their soules, whether they be sanctified or unsanctified, in the dominion of grace or of sinne, in state of salvation or damnation, going to heaven or to hell: these be in the number of those things, wherewith they are little moved." These men and women, Whately concludes, "love like Heathens, not like Christians, and the Lord is not well pleased, that those which call him Father, should be warmed alone with such carnall affection."[20]

The reward that Whately imagines for those who tend to the salvation of their spouse has no bearing on the status of the marital bond in the afterlife: his vision of heaven is comparable to Calvin's. Hence the role of the husband or wife is merely to facilitate passage from one sphere to the next. "But dost thou often [helpe]," he asks his reader, "with the sanctification and salvation of thy yoke-fellow? Dost thou desire to make thine yoke-fellow, a fellow-heire of Christs Kingdom? Dost thou seeke to helpe thine yoke-fellow to heaven and heavenly benefits, as well as to those earthly? If so, this is to love spiritually: This love beseemes a Christian husband, and a Christian wife" (37). Marriage may be a stepping-stone toward a heavenly future, but that future bears no resemblance to domestic arrangements on earth.

When Donne approaches the topic of heavenly marriage in a 1621 wedding sermon delivered at his parish church of St. Clement Danes—the church in which he had buried his wife Ann only a few years earlier—he declares the impossibility that marital bonds should continue in the life to come. Preaching on Hosea 2:19, "And I will mar[r]y thee unto me for ever [in aeternum]," Donne finds only limited application of this verse to the earthly marriage that he was consecrating that day. For earthly marriages, he explains to the bride and groom, there can be only a limited meaning to in aeternum: it means only that the marriage "can have no end in this life."[21]

In the bulk of Donne's sermon, however, he addresses the two spiritual marriages that Christ makes: on the one hand between Christ and the church, and on the other between Christ and our souls in heaven. These, Donne explains, are the truly "eternall" marriages: "That which ends the secular marriage ends not the spirituall: not death, for my death does not take me from that husband, but that husband being by his Father preferr'd to higher titles, and greater glory in another state, I doe but goe by death where he is become a King, to have my part in that glory" (3:253). Far from describing to the newlyweds the pleasures that await them during their lives together, he shifts to a description of the pleasures that he himself—as a representative Christian soul—will experience once he has ascended to heaven: "I shall see all the beauty, and all the glory of all the Saints of God, and love them all, and know that the Lamb loves them too, without jealousie, on his part, or theirs, or mine, and so be married *in aeternum*, for ever, without interruption, or diminution, or change of affections. Christ himself . . . shall continue a Husband to my soul for ever. Where I shall be rich enough without Joynture, for my Husband cannot die" (255). The monetary compensation of "joynture"—the property a husband sets aside for his wife's use after his death—will be unnecessary, Donne declares, assuming now the position of the heavenly bride, because his marriage with Christ will have no end. This was the eternal marriage Hosea prophesied, and it displaces entirely the marital vows exchanged by mere mortals.

Examples such as these supported the Calvinist notion that spouses will have no further contact after death. English Protestants also frequently gave voice, however, to the opposite position. In his 1592 *Christal glasse for Christian women*, the Elizabethan pamphleteer Philip Stubbes relates that his dying wife Katherine had absolute confidence that she and Philip would be reunited in heaven. Drawing from the parable in Luke 16, which describes "how that the rich man lying in hell, knew *Abraham* and *Lazarus* in heauen a farre off," Katherine "reasoned thus": "If the wicked that be in hell in torments doe knowe those that be in heauen so farre aboue them: how much more shal the godly know one another, being altogether in one place, & fellowe Citizens in the kingdome of heauen?"[22] The idea that the damned should be given something that the blessed are denied clearly struck Katherine as unjust, as did the idea that the blessed would somehow not recognize their heavenly neighbors or "fellowe Citizens." For, she continues, moving now from the rich man in hell to the disciples on earth, if Peter and James and John were able to see Moses and Elias, "the one whereof died almost two thousand yeares before, the other not much lesse," so much the more should the blessed in heaven be able to know one another, "all corruption being taken away, and we in the full fruition and possession of all the ioyes and glory of heauen" (C2r). It cannot be, she reasons, that once we are cleansed of all sinfulness and assume our most perfect state, we will not enjoy the fundamental pleasure of human companionship.

Thomas Gataker, a Protestant clergyman and the author of several treatises on marriage, confirms in his 1620 *Marriage Duties Briefly Couched Togither* the now familiar position that one of the principal duties in marriage is to assist one's spouse in pursuing a virtuous life that will lead to salvation. But unlike Whatley and Gouge, Gataker—who personally lost no fewer than four wives over the course of his life—connects this shared partnership on earth to a comparable partnership in heaven. "Having lived togither for a time as copartners in grace here," he concludes, "they may reigne togither for ever as co-heires in glory hereafter."[23]

Robert Bolton, a fierce Puritan churchman and author of several polemical works against papistry, expands on this idea of continuity between earthly and heavenly partnership in his 1632 *Boltons Last and Learned Worke of the Foure Last Things, Death, Iudgement, Hell, and Heaven.* Bolton contends that one of our principal duties in marriage is to "hel[p] one another towards heaven, and that joyfull forethought of most certaine meeting together in the ever lasting mansions of glory, joy and blisse above."[24] In more or less explicit contradiction of Calvin, Bolton describes why the "glory, joy and blisse above" would not be adequate recompense without the companionship of one's spouse. Since in heaven we shall "enjoy every good thing, and comfortable gift, which may any way increase and inlarge our joy and felicity" (145), it is not possible that we will be denied one of our central sources of happiness.

Bolton directs his reader to a letter written by St. Augustine to a widow, Italica, who had applied to Augustine for comfort following her husband's death. In one of his sermons, Augustine expressed his indifference about the company of loved ones in heaven, declaring that the "temporal" blessing of one's spouse or children will be surpassed in heaven by the "eternal" blessing of "the society of angels." But on this occasion of consoling Italica, he reassured the widow that she would meet her husband again. "We have not lost those of ours who have departed," Augustine writes, "but have sent them on ahead, where they will be dearer to us to the extent that they will be better known and where they will be lovable without any fear of our losing them."[25]

Augustine's letter to Italica offered Bolton a vision of heavenly companionship that did not contradict Jesus's assertion that there would be no marriage in heaven. Whether spouses are actually "married" in heaven is not important, Bolton declares, so long as they can enjoy each other's company. "But meeting there, knowing the[m], and conversing for ever with our old deare Christian friends," he affirms with surprising certainty, "will mightily please and refresh us with sweetest delight." "Society is not comfortable without familiar acquaintance," he concludes. "Be assured then, it shall not be wanting in the height and perfection of all glory, blisse, and joy."[26]

Bolton does not deny that we shall make new acquaintances and mingle with the great Christian figures from the past. But he regards this as compatible with enjoying the company of loved ones. "We shall be able to say," he declares, "this was Father *Abraham*, this King *David*, this Saint *Paul*, this was *Luther, Calvin, Bradford*," but also "this [was] my Father, this my Sonne, this my Wife" (146). For Bolton, heaven is a predominantly social environment, a place to resume, albeit in different form, the relations already familiar to us from our mortal lives. He hastens to add that "our mutuall knowledge one of another in heaven shall not be in outward and worldly respects, but divine and spirituall," making clear that there will be no carnal or material contact with our relations, but the "divine and spirituall" knowledge he anticipates is no less familiar or personal (149).

When Donne writes in 1624 to his recently widowed friend Lady Kingsmill, he dramatically alters the position he took in his 1621 wedding sermon, assuaging her grief with promises that she would meet her husband again: "Madame, Those things which God dissolves at once, as he shall do the Sun, and Moon, those bodies at the last conflagration, he never intends to reunite again; but in those things, which he takes in pieces, as he doth man, and wife, in these divorces, by death, and in single persons, by the divorce of body and soul, God hath another purpose to make them up again."[27] Normally Donne distinguishes between the two separations wrought by death—between husband and wife and between body and soul—as the difference between a union that is mortal and a union that, come the resurrection, will be eternal.[28] On this occasion, however, Donne identifies the two separations as similarly temporary and turns the discreteness of each unit to his advantage. Since both pairings are made up of individual pieces (body, soul; husband, wife) rather than being single indivisible masses like the sun or moon, they can happily be pieced back together again.

In a sermon preached in 1627 at the earl of Bridgewater's house in London for the marriage of his daughter, Donne expands on this possibility of a heavenly reunion between spouses, now completely reversing the position he took in the sermon six years earlier. Having somewhat perversely selected Matthew 22:30—the single verse in scripture most difficult to understand as a defense of posthumous reunion—as his text to preach before the bride and groom, Donne works on this occasion to recover some prospect of hope. He begins by invoking Luke's explanation for Christ's proscription of heavenly marriage, spelled out in Luke's version of the same exchange between Jesus and the Sadducees: "The children of this world marry, and are given in marriage; But they which shall be accounted worthy to obtain that world, and the resurrection from the dead, neither marry, nor are given in marriage; Neither can they die any more" (20:34-36). Christ declared that they shall not marry, Donne begins, "[b]ecause they cannot dy. Because they have an eternity in themselves, they need not supply any defect, by a propagation of children." "But yet," he protests, molding the verse in his hands, "though Christ exclude that, of which there is clearly no use in heaven, Mariage, (because they need no physick, no mutuall help, no supply of children) yet he excludes not our knowing, or our loving of one another upon former knowledge in this world, in the next." "Christ does not say expressely we shall," he admits, "yet neither does he say, that we shall not, know one another there."[29] This is the most that Donne can offer the newlyweds and their guests with any assurance: that although Christ does not affirm, he also does not deny the possibility that we shall be familiar to one another in heaven.

In both wedding sermons that address the subject of posthumous love, Donne makes clear that the issue is not whether couples might technically remain married in heaven. As he preaches in 1621, heavenly

marriage is reserved for the soul's union with Christ. The marriage between man and woman, he argues in that sermon, is unnecessary in
heaven, since none of its three central purposes—the production of
offspring (*in prolem*), the containment of lust or burning (*in ustionem*),
and the provision of mutual help (*in adjutorium*)—will any longer be
required.[30] What Donne (or Bolton or Gataker) stresses is not the importance of heavenly marriage per se but the pleasure of heavenly companionship. It is this prospect of renewed familiarity, with or without
the official bond of matrimony, that characterizes the hopes of many
English men and women for their posthumous lives. And this prospect
was on a continuum with the pleasures of intimacy in their earthly
marriage, pleasures that Protestant writers emphasized to a degree unprecedented in earlier periods.

II. Earthly Companions

It has long been observed that Protestantism stressed the importance of
genuine companionship in marriage.[31] Treatises written for both women
and men drew attention to the spouse's role as a companion and friend,
in addition to that of a procreative partner. None of this, of course, was
an innovation of Protestantism. Centuries of biblical commentary from
both Jews and Christians had discussed the nature of Eve's role as a
"helpmate," often stressing her role as Adam's companion;[32] and in the
Summa contra Gentiles, Aquinas aligns marriage with friendship in a line
of argument traced back to Aristotle's *Nichomachean Ethics*: "The greater
that friendship is, the more solid and long-lasting will it be. Now, there
seems to be the greatest friendship between husband and wife, for they
are united not only in the act of fleshly union, which produces a certain
gentle association even among beasts, but also in the partnership of the
whole range of domestic activity."[33]

What we observe in Protestant texts, however, is a newly pronounced
concern both for the compatibility of husband and wife and for the
strength of their affective bonds. As Edmund Leites has persuasively
argued, English Protestants—and Puritans in particular—regarded the
outward fulfillment of marital duties as inadequate if such duties were
not matched with appropriate inner feelings and intentions. Love, in

short, must complement duty. In the words of Gataker's *Marriage Duties Briefly Couched Togither*, not only should the husband fulfill his obligations to his wife, but it is his duty to "Ioy & delight in her." "Let her brests or her bosome content thee at all times," Gataker instructs, "and delight continually, or . . . even doate on the Love of her."[34]

In his *Bride-Bush, or a Direction for Married Persons*, Whately similarly affirms that "no neighbour, no kinsman, no friend, no parent, no child should be so neere and deare unto the husband as his wife, nor to her as her husband." Such intimacy, he contends, derives from the sheer act of living together: "And if any man finding a want of such love, desire to know how he may get and encrease it, let him understand that love will become such . . . if some naturall meanes be used to confirme it, and some spirituall." "The naturall meanes," he continues, "is cohabitation: let them have one house, one table, one chamber, one bed, so shall they with most ease have also one heart and one soule."[35]

The text that makes the strongest case for compatibility as the essential feature of marriage is, somewhat paradoxically, one that argues in favor of expanding the grounds for divorce. John Milton's 1644 *Doctrine and Discipline of Divorce* defines the purpose of marriage as God's "promising a meet help against loneliness": it is loneliness that God wanted us to avoid above all, and hence any marriage that does not provide fulfilling companionship ought to be terminated. "In the first ordaining of marriage," Milton writes, "God taught us to what end he did it, in words expressly implying the apt and cheerful conversation of man with woman, to comfort and refresh him against the evil of solitary life, not mentioning the purpose of generation till afterwards."[36] The focus of Milton's polemic is to argue that divorces should be granted not merely for problems in sexual relations (whether lack of consummation or adultery) but also for lack of companionship: "How vain, therefore, is it, and how preposterous in the canon law, to have made such careful provision against the impediment of carnal performance, and to have had no care about the unconversing inability of mind so defective to the purest and most sacred end of matrimony" (582). "The unconversing inability of mind" violates the marriage bond, he contends, much more than any lack of carnal relations. "He who affirms adultery to be the highest breach affirms the bed to be the highest of marriage" (590).

The idea of loneliness as a problem that spouses might experience inside and not merely outside of marriage is Milton's particular contribution to this literature: one is never more alone, he maintains, than when married to an unsympathetic husband or wife. "If one's spouse be naturally so of disposition as will not help to remove, but help to increase that same God-forbidden loneliness," Milton contends, "such a marriage can be no marriage" (582). Simply having a spouse with whom to cohabitate does not fulfill God's will that man should have a helpmate. "The ordinance which God gave to our comfort," he concludes, "may not be pinned upon us to our undeserved thralldom, to be cooped up, as it were, in mockery of wedlock, to a perpetual betrothed loneliness and discontent" (618).

Milton's opinions in this tract are hardly conventional: he is explicitly challenging the standard ideas that Protestants held about the necessary conditions for divorce. But his treatise brings out an important strain of thought that appears in different forms throughout the sixteenth and seventeenth centuries, and sheds light on why at least some couples would have imagined the translation from earthly to celestial companionship as potentially smooth. If marriage is defined above all as mutual enjoyment between souls rather than bodies, there need be no significant loss or falling away in those relations when the spouses' souls ascend after death to the heavenly sphere. Why, in other words, should the souls of married couples not continue to enjoy each other in the afterlife as they had on earth? Or, to put it slightly differently, why should the loss of carnal bodies in any way impede posthumous marital bliss? If the model life were the solitary life of the monk or nun, then the companionship of Christ would become the *summum bonum*. But if the bliss of marriage between compatible and spiritually nurturing spouses is the human ideal, the necessity of shifting from the fellowship of the spouse in this world to the exclusive fellowship of Christ in the afterlife becomes harder to understand, and more arbitrary.

III. Poetics of Posthumous Love

The lack of consensus among Protestants about the posthumous fate of married couples; the serious interest that the topic aroused for both religious and secular thinkers; and the widespread desire, as we saw in the introduction, for some form of posthumous connection between earthly spouses or lovers combined to provide remarkably fertile grounds for English poetry. Although connected to issues of salvation and eschatology, posthumous love lay outside any obvious category of jurisdiction; it was something that many people longed to understand but for which there were no coherent or decisive answers. (This was not the case for other questions about the afterlife that may seem to our eyes equally inexplicable: on questions concerning the resurrection of the body, for example, theologians opined with great conviction regarding what will befall us, detailing exactly how body parts will be returned and in what condition.) However confusing or vague theologically, this ambiguity about a subject that was hardly trivial or irrelevant created close to ideal conditions for literary expression. As we shall see, posthumous love offered English poets an unusual opportunity for free play.

Banishing Death
Wyatt's Petrarchan Poems

Se fu beato chi la vide in terra,
Or che fia dunque a rivederla in cielo?
(If he was blest who saw her here on earth
what then will it be to see her again in heaven!)

—Petrarch, *The Triumph of Time*

But though ye have had my heart's cure
Trow ye I dote without ending?
What no, perdie!

—Sir Thomas Wyatt, Rondeaux VII

When the English poet and courtier Sir Thomas Wyatt traveled to Italy in the spring of 1527, he entered a world that was preoccupied with erotic love. In the approximately 150 years between Petrarch's death and Wyatt's arrival in Venice, Italian interest in love had not faded: on the contrary, it had grown only more and more intense. In the scores of sonnets by Petrarchan imitators, the Neoplatonic works of Marsilio Ficino and Pico della Mirandola, the paintings of Botticelli and Raphael, the *trattati d'amore* (treatises on love) by Pietro Bembo and Leone Ebreo, the many medical works on lovesickness—in all of these different discursive and aesthetic forms, Renaissance Italy focused its intellectual energies on the subject of love in a manner unprecedented in any earlier historical period.

The particular focus for male Italian love poets was the idealized female beloved, or *donna angelicata*. Beginning with Dante's *Vita Nuova* if not earlier, the longing that the French troubadour poets of the twelfth and thirteenth centuries had directed toward the *domna*, or lady, assumed a sacred quality.[1] The beloved was not the object of sensual appetite and desire; she was a heavenly character, inspiring goodness and virtue in the poet. Consider, for example, Dante's description of Beatrice as "una cosa venuta / da cielo in terra a miracol mostrare" (a thing that has descended / from heaven to earth to manifest a miracle); or his explanation that "quando truova alcun, che degno sia / di veder lei, quei prova sua virtute / chè gli addivien cio' che gli dà salute" (when she finds someone who would be worthy / of beholding her, that person experiences her virtue, / because what she gives him redounds to his salvation).[2] Although different from Dante in many important respects—not least in his frank acknowledgment on multiple occasions of physical desire for Laura—Petrarch maintains Dante's sense of his beloved as angelic. He refers to Laura's eyes as "un dolce lume / che mi mostra la via ch'al ciel conduce" (a sweet light / that shows me the way that leads to Heaven); he praises her singing as "angelico," and he imagines her as the ideal manifestation of Nature's pattern for heavenly beauty:

In qual parte del Ciel, in quale Idea
era l'esempio onde Natura tolse
quell bel viso leggiadro in ch'ella volse
mostrar qua già quanto lassù potea?

(In what part of Heaven, in what Idea was the pattern from which Nature copied that lovely face, in which she has shown down here all that she is capable of doing up there?)[3]

In the late fifteenth century, Ficino and his followers built from this poetry a Neoplatonic philosophy of love that combined the idealization of the beloved with a belief in the power of beauty to elevate the soul. Despite the equivocations of Petrarch's *Rime sparse*, which are by no means consistently Platonic (Petrarch himself did not know Greek and had never even read the *Symposium*), Florentine philosophers extracted from his poems the materials they needed to support a Neoplatonic model of love, in which the lover is guided from the terrestrial to the heavenly, from the particular to the general.[4] In the interest of promoting their philosophical ends, these authors overlooked Petrarch's reluctance to move beyond Laura to a more abstract, universalized mode of love. They also overlooked the final poems of the *Rime sparse*, where, as we shall see, Petrarch renounced his earthly love and turned exclusively to the divine. Through the pages of Ficino and his followers' treatises on love, Petrarch is cited more often than Plato.[5]

As early as the 1420s, annotated editions of the *Rime sparse* began to appear in which the poems were subjected to a level of scholarly analysis comparable to the treatment theologians gave to the Bible. By the sixteenth century no fewer than ten separate editions with their own commentaries had been published, several with multiple commentaries side by side.[6] On a typical page from one of these volumes, Petrarch's poem was positioned near the left margin of the folio so as to allow the maximum room for extensive commentary, with each line, and sometimes each word, explained in great detail.[7] In their physical design, these Petrarchan editions resembled Italian biblical exegeses done in the fourteenth century.[8]

Although scholarly interest in Petrarch was unrivaled, with the obvious exception of Dante, it was by no means only Petrarch and Dante who received major critical attention. The Italian tendency to take love poetry seriously, to treat it as part of an important intellectual development, manifests itself throughout the period.[9] Among other notable examples: the first of many commentaries on Guido Cavalcanti's late thirteenth-century *canzone* "*Donna mi prega*" was written by a medical doctor who regarded Cavalcanti's poem as an important case history describing the appetitive passion of love;[10] Pico della Mirandola wrote an analysis of a *canzone* by the poet Benivieni as his response to Ficino's commentary on Plato's *Symposium* (*De amore*); and the humanist Benedetto Varchi devoted a lecture at the Florentine Academy to a single sonnet of the poet Giovanni della Casa in order to explicate the "seven doubts" of love.[11] Many more instances could be adduced, but the central point is clear: the Italian poet's depiction of love was deemed a worthy subject of humanist scholarship, as if the poems themselves were the equivalents of philosophical treatises.

When Wyatt traveled to Italy in 1527, he would have been confronted, then, with a culture whose ideas about love were profoundly different from those of his own. In early sixteenth-century England, love poetry was not treated as a potential source for philosophical or medical or even literary inquiry. The issue was not only that England's vernacular lyric was not considered an elevated form, although this was certainly part of the problem. Even as late as the 1580s, Thomas Watson worried that writing sonnets in English would suggest a lack of seriousness as a poet, and he referred to his poems repeatedly as "toyes." In a dedicatory poem to Watson's sonnet series *Hekatompathia*, his friend George Peele tried to reassure him by offering this odd advice, which only confirmed the love sonnet's poor status: "If graver headdes shall count it overlight / To treate of Love: say thou to them: A staine / Is incident unto the finest die."[12]

The lack of stature of English love poetry was connected to a larger issue: the subject of love itself did not occupy an important place in England's intellectual landscape. To the extent that Italian philosophers like Ficino were read by the English, they were read not for their commentaries on the *Symposium* but for their religious works. For example, John Colet, dean of St. Paul's in the early sixteenth century, admired Ficino's theological treatises and even exchanged several letters with him, but there is no evidence that Colet ever read, or expressed any interest in, Ficino's *De amore*.[13]

Plato himself had very little circulation in early Tudor England: there was no copy of his works in the university library at Cambridge through most of the sixteenth century, and there is no evidence that Plato was being read in any sustained fashion until well into the Elizabethan period, when his works arrived on English soil dressed in Protestant trappings.[14] The most popular translation of Plato at this time was not Ficino's but that of a French Calvinist, Jean de la Serre, whose 1578 text was published by the Protestant printer Henri Estienne.[15] Plato may have been admired by some Protestants, but only for the compatibility of his ideas with certain strands of Christianity. Luther, for example, declared in his Heidelberg disputation of 1518 that Plato was much preferable to Aristotle because he studied the divine and immortal.[16] But Plato's *Symposium* was not the text that Protestants embraced, and his metaphysics of love had no real following among Englishmen until the final decades of the sixteenth century.[17] During the Tudor period, the most widely disseminated and quoted dialogue of Plato's was not the *Symposium* but the *Laws*.[18]

Petrarch's fame in Tudor England was likewise derived from his moral writings, not his love poems. In northern Europe he was often referred to as "Franciscus Patriarcha," as if he were a medieval church father.[19] His Latin treatises were widely known and imitated, and his long didactic poem written in Italian, the *Trionfi*, was immensely popular in the Henrician court.[20] This work, which consists of six terza rima poems cycling through the triumph of love, chastity, death, fame, time, and eternity, was translated into English sometime before Henry VIII's death by Henry Parker, Lord Morley, and inspired multiple translations over the course of the century. Queen Elizabeth herself translated the first 88 lines of *Il Trionfo della Eternità* (*The Triumph of Eternity*), and Mary Sidney translated all 190 lines of *Il Trionfo della Morte* (*The Triumph of Death*). The *Trionfi* also fared well as a subject for pictorial representation: an inventory of Henry VIII's tapestries lists eleven depictions from the *Trionfi*, and Cardinal Wolsey is known to have commissioned a full set of *Trionfi* tapestries for his chambers.[21]

Despite the success of the *Trionfi*, however, Petrarch's other great vernacular collection, the *Rime sparse*, had little circulation in early sixteenth-century England. The only known translation of a Petrarch sonnet before Wyatt's was a single poem of Chaucer's, incorporated into *Troilus and Criseyde*.[22] Known as the "Canticus Troili," or Song of Troilus, this version of Petrarch's *Rime sparse* 132 was written in three seven-line stanzas of the native English verse form, rhyme royal, and not in the fourteen-line Italian form of the sonnet. Chaucer himself represented the "Canticus Troili" as a foreign borrowing, a text that he ascribes to the unknown (and almost certainly fictional) author Lollius rather than claim as a work of his own.

Between Chaucer's adaptation of this poem in the 1380s and Wyatt's sonnets in the 1520s and 1530s, there are no significant examples of English poets translating Petrarch. Moreover, there is no evidence outside of Chaucer's adaptation of *Rime sparse* 132 that Petrarch's love sonnets circulated in England before the end of the fifteenth century. Although some English men and women must have read Petrarch's poems in the original Italian (a complete translation of the *Rime sparse* in English was not available until the middle of the nineteenth century), the poems did not occasion any attention comparable to the kind that Petrarch's moral treatises and poems received.[23] Love was not, in short, regarded as a serious matter for philosophical and humanistic inquiry in England as it was in Italy, and there was no equivalent cultural importance attached to the production of erotic verse.

The fact that Wyatt was writing from within a culture in which erotic love was not a celebrated subject of contemplation needs to be fully accounted for when we consider the changes he made to Petrarch's poems. That Wyatt bothered to translate the poems at all speaks to his having a sense of their importance—no doubt he would have gathered this from his time on the Continent, where Petrarch's influence was widely felt—but the changes he made in adapting the poems reflect a very different understanding of love and its boundaries. These changes are perhaps most apparent if we consider some of his most important innovations in negative terms—what Wyatt's sonnets, compared to Petrarch's, strikingly do not do:

1. Whereas Petrarch famously idealizes Laura's virtues in a manner comparable to Dante's depiction of the heavenly Beatrice in *La Vita Nuova*, Wyatt is reluctant to praise his mistress, either physically or spiritually. There are almost no descriptions of Wyatt's mistress in any of his poems—no blazons or paeans to her beauty—and she is certainly not treated as a flawless angelic creature.

2. Whereas Petrarch, following the path of Dante, depicts the death of his mistress as the central episode in his narrative, the mortality of Wyatt's mistress plays no real role in his poems. The relationship is threatened by unfaithfulness and inconstancy, not by death.

3. Whereas Petrarch's sonnets transcend Laura's death, depicting a love that continues in its intensity and passion once her soul has ascended to heaven, Wyatt never imagines an afterlife for love.

Much has been said in the critical literature about the first of these differences, but very little attention has been paid to the second and third, both of which address the role that death plays in the poems.[24] This is a surprising and consequential oversight, for the fact that Wyatt never imagines an afterlife for love represents one of his most significant alterations to the Petrarchan tradition. When Wyatt translated Petrarch's poems, he stripped from them one of their most fundamental features: the idea that erotic love could transcend the beloved's death.

There are certainly biographical explanations for Wyatt's rejection of posthumous love. Wyatt's own romantic history was far from paradisaical: regardless of whether he and Anne Boleyn were actually lovers (as recent biographers have shown, the evidence in fact is flimsy), they certainly had some kind of relationship that ended in feelings of bitterness and mistrust; and his only marriage, to Elizabeth Brooke, was nothing short of catastrophic.[25] After six years of living together, Thomas and Elizabeth separated, and he subsequently accused her of adultery. In a letter written to their only child, also named Thomas, some ten years after the marriage ended, Wyatt advises his son to "[l]ove well and agree with your wife, for where is noyse and debate in the house, there is unquiet dwelling"; he then confesses that he knows this only too well, for "the fault is both in your mother and me, but chiefly in her."[26] Later in his life Wyatt formed a long-term attachment to a woman named Elizabeth Darrell, with whom he lived for some years and fathered a son (both Darrell and her son are bequeathed property in Wyatt's will). He was forced, however, to separate from Darrell and resume conjugal relations with his wife as one of the conditions of his pardon from the Privy Council, which had imprisoned him in the Tower of London on accusations of treason.

None of this personal history would have inspired Petrarchan desires for an eternity spent with his beloved, except perhaps Wyatt's relationship with Darrell, which was the source for the most loving of his Petrarchan translations, "In Spayne."[27] The larger court in which Wyatt lived, moreover, hardly provided positive examples of long-lasting erotic bonds. Henry VIII was no role model for erotic steadfastness, and Wyatt describes the Henrician court as one of slipperiness and change.[28] Hence the Petrarchan paradigm of unconsummated love was routinely transformed, as Gordon Braden has persuasively argued, into episodes of "promiscuous sexual love," and the aftermath of these affairs was not envisioned in terms of Neoplatonic transcendence.[29] This was a crowded, fickle, unreliable world, far from the solitude of Petrarch. One need only compare Wyatt's sonnet "Who so list to hounte" with its Petrarchan original (*Rime sparse* 190) to gauge the profound differences in the two poets' mental landscapes. Whereas Wyatt's poem is filled with mention of male competitors, who join him in the "vain travail" of the hunt, Petrarch describes an entirely solitary experience in which he finds himself alone with a white doe in an idyllic landscape.

There are certainly aspects, then, of both Wyatt's personal history and the culture of the Henrician court that influenced his reaction to Petrarchan ideas of transcendent love. But Wyatt's reaction to Petrarch's attitude toward both love and love's duration was by no means unique to him. On the contrary, in sixteenth-century English poetry it is a nearly universal response. Wyatt's rejection of posthumous love was conditioned, that is, not only by the accidents of his own personal situation but also by the theological and philosophical beliefs of the world in which he lived. In particular, the various conditions considered in chapter 1—the strong resistance among some Protestants to the idea of love's persisting after death; the church's hardening of boundaries between the living and the dead; the culture's distaste for Neoplatonic ideas about transcendent love that were so widely disseminated in fifteenth-century Italy—all helped to enable a mode of poetry that understood love as limited to this world alone.

I. Petrarch's in morte *Poems*

Wyatt probably encountered the 366 poems that make up Petrarch's *Rime sparse* during his 1527 diplomatic mission to Venice. Many of the late fifteenth- and early sixteenth-century editions of Petrarch were printed in Venice, and there is evidence that Wyatt used the heavily annotated edition of Petrarch published in 1525 by Alessandro Vellutello as the basis for his own translations.[30] Whether he used this particular Petrarch edition or not, he is likely to have had an edition accompanied by extensive commentary. He also would almost certainly have found

the poems divided into two crucial categories: those that were written
in vita di madonna Laura, when Laura was alive, and those that were
written in morte di madonna Laura, that is, after she died. This was not a
division that Petrarch himself introduced to his sequence, and it is not
necessarily a division that he would have embraced, so continuous were
his feelings for Laura before and after her death. He did, however, leave
seven blank pages after poem 263—the last poem written when Laura
was still living—in the manuscript of his poems now at the Vatican
library in Rome, and this extravagant gesture of emptiness strongly suggests the author's desire to mark a decisive break between the two parts
of his series.[31] As early as 1472, an edition of Petrarch's poems based on
the Vatican manuscript added "Finit vita amoris" and "Incipit de morte
amoris" to the transition from one section to the next.[32] Several decades
later, in 1501, the categories in vita and in morte appear in the important edition overseen by Bembo and published by Aldus Manutius, and
nearly all subsequent sixteenth-century editions adopted this design.

What does it mean for Petrarch to have written over 100 of the 366
poems in the Rime sparse after Laura has died? As anyone who has read
through the Rime sparse can testify, it does not mean that the in morte
poems are strictly elegiac, filled with longing for someone who is irre-
parably lost.[33] To be sure, Petrarch elaborately mourns Laura's death, but
this mourning is tempered almost immediately by his anticipation of a
reunion on the other side. No sooner has the poet declared that Laura
is dead than he expresses his hope to join her as soon as possible: "Madonna è morta et à seco il mio core, / et volendol seguire, / interromper
conven quest'anni rei" (My lady is dead and has my heart with her, /
and if I wish to follow it / I must break off these cruel years [268.4-6]).
Laura's possession of his heart creates a bond between his earthly self
and her heavenly one: it is ostensibly his heart, and not his beloved, that
he longs to follow, although the two (his heart, his beloved) are completely intertwined. The pattern Petrarch establishes here—declaring a
seemingly absolute end ("Madonna è morta") only to soften its finality
with the hope of some future reunion—repeats itself in the poem's very
next lines. Petrarch asserts that he will never see Laura again, but then
qualifies this "never" through the enjambment "perché mai veder lei / di
qua non spero" (for I never hope to see her [/] on this side [7-8]).

In this early *in morte* poem, Petrarch negotiates his future with Laura, wavering between the seeming finality of their separation and the prospect of their reunion. As the sequence continues, the absoluteness of this separation disappears as a serious possibility. To return to the question of what it means for so many poems to have been written to Laura after her death, one obvious answer is that it allows Petrarch to embark upon an entirely new phase of the relationship in which he speaks to Laura's spirit on a more or less regular basis. In poem 279, for example, he describes Laura's response from heaven to his heavy sighs; she instructs him in this poem not to weep for her: "ch' e' miei dì fersi, / morendo, eterni" (for my days became / eternal by dying [12–13]). Or in poem 282, Petrarch addresses Laura as "Alma felice che sovente torni / a consolar le mie notti dolente / con gli occhi tuoi" (Happy soul who often comes back / to console my sorrowing nights / with your eyes [1–3]). Lest we imagine that her posthumous form has been reduced merely to a set of eyes, he proceeds to describe her as if she were still fully embodied: "che quando torni te conosco e 'ntendo / a l'andar, a la voce, al volto, a' panni" (When you return I know you / by your walk, by your voice, by your face, by your dress [13–14]).

Readers of Petrarch have long observed that Laura has no voice in the *Rime sparse*, but as Diana Vickers has noted, she is much more present in death than in life.[34] It is only in the *in morte* poems, moreover, that Petrarch describes something like mutuality in their affections and suggests their ultimate destiny together. In poem 302, he lifts his thoughts "in parte ov' era / quella ch' io cerco et non ritrovo in terra; / ivi fra lor che 'l terzo cerchio serra / la rividi più bella et meno altera" (to where she was / whom I seek and do not find on earth; / there, among those whom the third circle encloses, / I saw her more beautiful and less proud [1–4]). Laura's placement in the third circle of heaven—the sphere of Venus, where the souls of love poets are said to dwell—implies already that her posthumous fate is bound up with, even determined by, his own.[35] This is what Laura herself assures him:

> Per man mi prese et disse: "In questa spera
> sarai ancor meco, se 'l desir non erra;

i' so' colei che ti die' tanta guerra
et compie' mia giornata inanzi sera.
Mio ben non cape in intelletto umano;
te solo aspetto, et quel che tanto amasti
et là giuso è rimaso, il mio bel velo." (5–11)

(She took me by the hand and said: "In this sphere you will be with me, if my desire is not deceived; I am she who gave you so much war and completed my day before evening. My blessedness no human intellect can comprehend. I only wait for you and for that which you loved so much and which remained down there, my lovely veil.")

Petrarch uses the metaphor of the veil (*il velo*) to many different effects over the course of his sequence, but in this poem it clearly refers to Laura's flesh, which shall be returned to her at the resurrection.[36] This is an interesting example of Petrarch representing his love in starkly non-Neoplatonic terms, elevating the flesh to something worthy of continued affection. The sonnet ends with both frustrated longing, as Laura releases her hand from his, and a sense of possibility: "Deh, perché tacque et allargò la mano? / ch' al suon de' detti sì pietosi et casti, / poco mancò ch' io non rimasi in Cielo" (Ah, why did she then become still and open her hand? / for at the sound of words so kind and chaste, I almost remained in Heaven [12–14]).

Rime sparse 328 provides a similar mingling of conviction, hope, and loss, as Petrarch contemplates his own death and subsequent reunion with Laura. "L'ultimo, lasso, de' miei giorni allegri / (che pochi ò visto in questo viver breve) / giunto era, et fatto, 'lcor tepida neve" (The last, alas, of my happy days / [of which I have seen but few in this short life] / had arrived and had turned my heart to melting snow [1–3]), he begins, anticipating his own imminent demise. Then, turning toward Laura, he receives the beams of her *occhi belli*:

Li occhi belli, or in Ciel chiari et felici
del lume onde salute et vita piove,
lasciando i miei qui miseri st mendici,
dicean lor con faville oneste et nove:

"Rimanetevi in pace, o cari amici;
qui mai più, no, ma rivedremne altrove." (9–14)

(Her beautiful eyes, now in Heaven bright and happy in the Light that
rains salvation and life, leaving my eyes here wretched and poor, with
chaste, strange shining said to my eyes: "Peace be with you, dear friends;
never again here, no, but we shall see each other again elsewhere.")

In this final line, we glimpse the very core of Petrarch's aspirations for
his posthumous future. Here, on earth, never again. But there, yes.

Perhaps the strongest articulation of posthumous reunion in the *Rime
sparse* comes in poem 359, a canzone in which Laura's spirit explains,
with alternating patience and irritation, what would await the poet if
only he could abandon the mortal world to which he still seems to cling:

"A che pur piangi et ti distempre?
Quanto era meglio alzar da terra l'ali,
et le cose mortali
et queste dolci tue fallaci ciance
librar con giusta lance,
et seguire me . . ." (38–43)

("Why still weep and untune yourself? How much better it would have
been to raise your wings from earth and to weigh with an accurate balance mortal things and these sweet deceptive chatterings of yours, and to
follow me . . .")

Laura gently dismisses Petrarch's poems as "dolci tue fallaci ciance"
(your sweet deceptive chatterings), one of the "cose mortali" (mortal
things) that he needs to leave behind. In heaven, she reassures him, she
will be even more beautiful than he imagines her in her earthly guise:

"Spirito ignudo sono e'n Ciel mi godo;
quel che tu cerchi è terra già molt'anni.
Ma per trarti d'affanni
m'è dato a parer tale, et ancor quella

sarò più che mai bella,
a te più cara, sì selvaggia et pia,
salvando inseme tua salute et mia." (60–66)

(I am a naked spirit, and I rejoice in Heaven; what you seek has been dust
for many years now. But to help you from your troubles it is given to me
to seem such, and I shall be so again, more beautiful than ever, and more
loving to you, once so wild and kind, saving at once your salvation and my
own.)

Here Petrarch reimagines Laura's distance from him on earth as a deliberate strategy to save them from earthly sins that would have marred
their chances of heavenly bliss.

Petrarch's confident expression of Laura's waiting for him in the
afterlife, and his fantasy that she intentionally avoided him in this world
to guarantee their being together in the next, also shapes his depiction
of her death in the *Trionfi*. In *Il Trionfo della Morte* (*The Triumph of Death*)
that constitutes the third poem in this work, Petrarch describes his noc-
turnal vision of the deceased Laura and the conversation that ensued
between them. Laura confesses to Petrarch that she had in fact reciprocated his love all along:

. . . Mai diviso
da te non fu 'l mio cor, né già mai fia;
Ma temprai la tua fiamma col mio viso,
Perché a salvar te e me null'altra via
Era e la nostra giovenetta fama.

(Never was my heart
From thee divided, nor shall ever be.
Thy flame I tempered with my countenance
Because there was no other way than this
To save us both, and save your youthful fame.)[37]

At the end of this poem, Laura warns him that it will be a long time before he follows her to heaven: "Tu serai in terra senza me gran tempo"

(Thou wilt be long without me on the earth). But there is no ambiguity about her expectation that they will ultimately be joined together.

There are times when Petrarch is less sanguine about his posthumous relationship to Laura. In *Rime sparse* 22, for example, one of the only overtly sexual poems in the collection, he pleads to the heavens to give him just one night ("sol una notte") with his beloved wrapped in his arms before he departs from this world: "Prima ch' i' torni a voi, lucenti stelle, / o tomi giù ne l'amorosa selva / lassando il corpo che fia trita terra" (Before I return to you, bright stars, or fall down into the amorous wood, leaving my body which will be powdered earth [25-26]). This is the closest Petrarch comes to a *carpe diem* poem, and it is set entirely against his dread of an afterlife without the company of his beloved.[38] The "amorosa selva" (amorous wood) into which he imagines himself falling is an allusion to Virgil's "silva magna"[39] of mourning lovers in book 6 of the *Aeneid*; this is where Aeneas encounters those shades "whom bitter love consumed with brutal waste."[40]

In *Rime sparse* 82, another *in vita* poem in which Petrarch anticipates his own death, he actively refuses a posthumous life of loving Laura. This sonnet begins with the very uncharacteristic declaration that Petrarch's love—so long as it remains unrequited—must come to an immediate end:

> Io non fu' d'amar voi lassato unquanco,
> Madonna, né sarò mentre ch' io viva;
> ma d'odiar me medesmo giunto a riva
> et del continuo lagrimar so' stanco,
> et voglio anzi un sepolcro bello et bianco
> che 'l vostro nome a mio danno si scriva
> in alcun marmo ove di spirto priva
> sia la mia carne, che po star seco anco. (1-8)

(I have never been weary of loving you, my Lady, nor shall I be while I live, but I have come to the end of hating myself and am weary of my constant weeping, and I would rather have a blank tombstone than your name should be accounted to my loss on marble, when my flesh is deprived of my spirit, which now dwell together.)

Not only does the poet want to bring to an end his self-loathing and despair. He also wants to ensure that his death will have no relationship to his abject condition of loving.[41]

The belief that unrequited love could cause the lover's death was not simply a poetic fancy. European physicians treated *Amor heroes*, or lovesickness, as a serious disease: following the views of the eleventh-century Persian philosopher and physician Avicenna, which were largely derived from Galen, medieval and early modern doctors recommended some combination of baths and topical ointments, defamation of the beloved, and, in extreme cases, coitus with an aim toward evacuating seed.[42] There is a large body of medical literature on this subject in Italy and France, with testimonials from physicians who claim their patients have indeed died of erotic love. (There is tellingly very little of this literature written in England, where Rosalind's verdict in *As You Like It* seems generally to have been accepted: "the poor world is almost six thousand years old, and in all this time there was not any man died in his own person, *videlicet*, in a love-cause. . . . Men have died from time to time, and worms have eaten them, but not for love.")[43]

In *Rime sparse* 82, Petrarch not only declares his resistance to dying of love, which was understood as a real, not imaginary, threat. He also makes clear his preference not to be *remembered* as having died of love—his particular concern pertains to what gets inscribed on his tombstone. As someone who never married and had no legitimate children, Petrarch does not anticipate that his tombstone will name a beloved wife or offspring left behind. But he does anticipate, and reject, the idea that Laura's name will be engraved in marble as the cause of his death. This fantasy does not draw upon any actual Italian funerary practice. There is no tradition of Italian gravestones that record a broken heart as the cause of death, let alone name the deceased's mistress. Nor would Petrarch have been likely to be buried alongside Laura even if they had been married: as I shall discuss in chapter 4, it was not nearly so common for couples to be buried in shared tombs in Renaissance Italy as it was in Renaissance England. It is altogether conventional, then, that the substantial funerary monument to Petrarch in the town of Arquà erected six years after his death makes no mention of Laura, nor of any woman besides the Virgin Mary.[44]

The idea, however, that Petrarch would not only die of love but spend his afterlife brokenhearted is entirely compatible with his Virgilian *amorosa selva* depicted in *Rime sparse* 22, and it is this vision of his future that he rejects in poem 82. The poem ends with a relatively stern ultimatum:

> Però s' un cor pien d'amorosa fede
> può contentarve senza farne strazio,
> piacciavi omai di questo aver mercede;
> se 'n altro modo cerca d'esser sazio
> vostro sdegno, erra, et non fia quell che crede;
> di che Amor et me stesso assai ringrazio. (9–14)

> (Therefore if a heart full of faithful love can satisfy you without your torturing it, let it please you to have mercy on it; and if your disdain seeks to glut itself in any other way, it errs and shall not have what it seeks; for which I greatly thank Love and myself.)

These lines reveal something that otherwise has very little presence in the *Rime sparse*: Petrarch's desire for immediate resolution in one direction or another, his desire that his love be reciprocated now or cease to be.

The most significant instance of Petrarch's imagining his fate after death as separate from Laura's comes at the very end of the *Rime sparse*, when he actually renounces his love and turns in repentance to God. In these final poems he rejects the idea that loving Laura elevated him to higher things, and declares his own weariness after years of wasting his time. In poem 364, he exclaims: "Omai son stanco, et mia vita reprendo / di tanto error che di vertute il seme / à quasi spento; et le mie parti estreme / alto Dio, a te devotamente rendo" (Now I am weary and I reproach my life for so much error, which has almost extinguished the seed of virtue; and I devoutly render my last parts, high God, to you [5–8]); and the next poem begins: "I'vo piangendo i miei passati tempi / i quai posi in amar cosa mortale / senza levarmi a volo" (I go weeping for my past time, which I spent in loving a mortal thing without lifting myself in flight [1–3]). In the sequence's final lyric, a long hymn of over one hundred lines addressed to the Virgin Mary, Petrarch beseeches the Vir-

gin for mercy—"fammi, che puoi, de la sua grazia degno" (make me, for
you can, worthy of [God's] grace [37])—and refers to his loving Laura
only as his *error* (111).

This sudden shift in mood and spirit is hard to take entirely seriously,
however, given both the collective weight of the hundreds of poems that
precede it and the convention of ending collections of love poems with
such retractions. This was a tradition that dates back to Ovid's *Remedia
amoris* and was widely practiced in the medieval period. It is certainly
the case that Petrarch's retraction was largely ignored by both Neoplatonists and poets who wanted to see in his series a model for building transcendent love. For them, as for many centuries of subsequent readers,
the *Rime sparse* reaches its appropriate ending with poem 362, which
serves as a more or less exact illustration of the Neoplatonic principle:

> Volo con l'ali de' pensieri al Cielo
> sì spesse volte che quasi un di loro
> esser mi par ch'àn ivi il suo tesoro,
> lasciando in terra lo squarciato velo . . .
> Menami al suo Signor; allor m'inchino,
> pregando umilemente che consenta
> ch' i' stia a veder et l'uno et l'altro volto.
> Responde: "Egli è ben fermo il tuo destino,
> et per tardar ancor vent'anni o trenta
> parrà a te troppo, et non fia però molto." (1–4; 9–14)

> (I fly with the wings of thought to Heaven so often that it seems to me
> I am almost one of those who there possess their treasure, leaving on
> earth their rent veils. . . . She leads me to her Lord; then I incline myself,
> humbly begging that He permit me to stay to see their two faces. He re-
> plies: "Your destiny is certain, and a delay of twenty or thirty years will
> seem much to you, but it will be little.")

Here we see Laura as Petrarch's Beatrice, guiding her lover straight to
the Lord, who reassures him of his ultimate salvation and asks him to
be patient. Another twenty or thirty years of longing, God advises, is not
too much, so long as your reunion is *ben fermo*, or fully settled.

II. Wyatt's Limits

Of the twenty-five poems that Wyatt translated from Petrarch's *Rime sparse*, very few address the afterlife of love.[45] Wyatt was on the whole noticeably uninterested in the *in morte* poems: from the 103 poems in this part of the sequence, he translated only two. But from the *in vita* section—the source, therefore, for nearly all of his Petrarchan translations or adaptations—he was especially drawn to those poems that imagined love's ending. At times this ending is pictured as a result of his mistress's indifference or cruelty, which may lead the poet to his death. Wyatt translated more or less verbatim *Rime sparse* 153, in which Petrarch declares: "et se prego mortale al ciel s'intende / morte o mercé sia fine al mio dolore" (and if mortal prayers are heard in heaven, let death or mercy end my torment [3–4]). In Wyatt's hands, these lines became "if that mortal prayer / In heaven be heard, at least yet I desire / That death or mercy end my woful smart."[46] At other times, as we shall see, the ending might come through a rare assertion of self-resolve. But regardless of whether the poems imagine a causal relation between love and death, Wyatt avoided sonnets like *Rime sparse* 122, which begins, "Dicesette anni à già rivolto il cielo / poi che 'mprima arsi, et giamai non mi spensi" (The heavens have already revolved seventeen years since I first caught fire, and still my fire is not extinguished). This vision of love as long lasting, without an end in sight, has no place in Wyatt's poetic repertoire.

The first important thing to say, then, about Wyatt's translations of Petrarch is that he generally chose poems whose views about love were more or less compatible with his own (this is no doubt one reason why he translated only twenty-five, and not several hundred, of these lyrics). Wyatt's version of *Rime sparse* 82, "Was I never, yet, of your love greeved," provides a good introduction to the kinds of changes he tended to make. If Wyatt found Petrarch's refusal in this poem to imagine Laura as the cause of his death worthy of his attention, he also found Petrarch's formulation of this refusal weaker than he would have liked. Wyatt's poem is on the whole one of his more faithful translations, but it departs from the original in the spitefulness of its tone.

Beginning with its address of Laura as "Madonna," *Rime sparse* 82 is for the most part polite and loving; only in the last lines does the poet convey an unusual frustration or impatience with Laura's "disdain" (*sdegno*). Wyatt, by contrast, assigns a much stronger degree of agency to his mistress as the willful instigator of his potential demise, and he assumes a more defensive position as he protects himself from her vengeful strikes. His poem begins:

> Was I never, yet, of your love greeved:
> Nor never shall, while that my liff doeth last:
> But of hating myself that date is past:
> And teeres continuell sore have me weried. (1–4)

Petrarch's "Io non fu' d'amar voi lassato unquanco" (I have never been weary of loving you, my Lady) becomes Wyatt's "Was I never, yet, of your love greeved," and the substitution of "greeved" for the Italian *lassato* (weary) is far from straightforward. Wyatt's line could mean that he is not yet weary, as Petrarch suggests, or that he has not yet suffered from loving her, or that he has not yet suffered from her way of loving (or not loving) him. Whatever Wyatt means by substituting "greeved" for *lassato*, he fundamentally alters the line by adding the "yet," which sounds a kind of warning that this weariness or grievance might come on at any time.

Lest the force of Wyatt's "yet" go unnoticed, he repeats it at the beginning of the second quatrain, where it serves not as a warning but as a signal of defiance against his mistress's murderous intentions:

> I will not yet in my grave be buried:
> Nor on my tombe your name yfixed fast:
> As cruell cause, that did the sperit sone hast
> Ffrom th'unhappy bonys, by great sighes sterred. (5–8)

Recall Petrarch's declaration "et voglio anzi un sepolcro bello at bianco / che 'l vostro nome a mio danno si scriva" (I would rather have a blank tombstone than that your name should be accounted to my loss), and consider what Wyatt does with this. First, he declares his outright resistance to his mistress's killing him—"I will not yet in my grave be buried"—and then he describes a second, separate act of resistance: her name will not be "yfixed" on his tomb as his death's "cruell cause." (Wyatt, as it happens, was buried in an uncertain location inside a small chapel in Sherborne Abbey, where a simple commemorative stone was laid on the floor with no mention of either his wife or Elizabeth Darrell.)[47]

Petrarch's spirit parts quietly from his flesh, and he places no blame on Laura for this rupture of the self. He simply refers to the future time "ove di spirto priva / sia la mia carne, che po star seco anco" (when my flesh is deprived of my spirit, which now dwell together). Wyatt, by contrast, describes his "unhappy bonys" robbed of their spirit as a result of his mistress's cruelty, which in turn caused his "great sighes," which in turn led to his death.

Excessive sighing was no laughing matter in early modern medical discourse—it was imagined to shorten one's life span by either releasing too much of the spirit or doubling the pace of breathing, as the physician Jacques Ferrand explains in chapter 18 of his *Treatise on Lovesickness* (1623):

> Sighs come to melancholy lovers because they forget to breathe due to the absorbing fantasies they feed upon. . . . Once the lack [of the desired object] is realized, nature is constrained to draw in the quantity of air in a single gasp that is taken in normally in two or three breaths: that form of respiration is called a sigh, which is in fact a doubling of the breath.[48]

Hence Donne, for example, is not merely using a poetic conceit when he warns his beloved in "Sweetest love: I doe not goe" against sighing too vigorously during his absence—"When thou sigh'st," he cautions, "thou sigh'st not wind / But sigh'st my soule away."[49] Wyatt, it seems, has not had Donne's opportunity to exchange souls with his mistress, and the sighs that Wyatt's mistress "sterred" hasten only him to the grave.

Wyatt's hostility to imagining his death as an expression of his love emerges even in his more subtle adaptations of Petrarch's poems. In "The long love, that in my thought doeth harbar," his translation of *Rime sparse* 140, Wyatt maintains the basic narrative of Petrarch's sonnet, in

which the beloved angrily dismisses Love, and Love subsequently re-
treats into the poet's heart:

Amor, che nel penser mio vive et regna
e 'l suo seggio maggior nel mio cor tene,
talor armato ne la fronte vene;
ivi si loca et ivi pon sua insegna.
Quella ch'amare et sofferir ne 'nsegna
e vol che 'l gran desio, l'accesa spene
ragion, vergogna, et reverenza affrene,
di nostro ardir fra se stessa si sdegna.
Onde Amor paventoso fugge al core,
lasciando ogni sua impresa, et piange et trema;
ivi s'asconde et non appar più fore.
Che poss'io far, temendo il mio signore,
se non star seco infin a l'ora estrema?
Ché bel fin fa chi ben amando more. (1–14)

(Love, who lives and reigns in my thought and keeps his principal seat
in my heart, sometimes comes forth all in armor into my forehead, there
camps, and there sets up his banner. She who teaches us to love and to be
patient, and wishes my great desire, my kindled hope, to be reined in by
reason, shame, and reverence, at our boldness is angry within herself.
Wherefore Love flees terrified to my heart, abandoning his every enter-
prise, and weeps and trembles; there he hides and no more appears outside. What can I do, when my lord is afraid, except stay with him until the
last hour? For he makes a good end who dies loving well.)

The loyalty that Petrarch feels towards Love is represented less as an expression of fidelity towards his "lord" (il mio signore) than as a desire for
the affective experience—the experience of loving—that such loyalty
produces. His poem concludes with the aphoristic declaration "ché bel
fin fa chi ben amando more": to die of love is to die well indeed.

In Wyatt's sonnet, the emphasis shifts from the desirability of dying
through loving to the desirability of serving his (male) lord with total
fidelity:

The longe love, that in my thought doeth harbar
And in myn hert doeth kepe his residence
Into my face preseth with bold pretence,
And therin campeth, spreding his baner.
She that me lerneth to love and suffre
And will that my trust, and lustes negligence
Be rayned by reason, shame, and reverence
With his hardines taketh displeasure.
Wherewithall, vnto the hertes forrest he fleith,
Leving his entreprise with payne and cry
And there him hideth and not appereth.
What may I do when my maister fereth,
But, in the felde, with him to lyve and dye?
For goode is the liff, ending faithfully.

The poet's pledge to the figure of Love trumps his commitment to his mistress—"she that me learns to love, and to suffer"—and in place of Petrarch's dying through "ben amando" (loving well), he imagines dying by "ending faithfully." What Wyatt conspicuously avoids is Petrarch's notion that dying of love is the desired end; for Wyatt, it is faithfulness between lord and servant, and not between lover and beloved, that reflects the life well lived.

Wyatt's lack of attraction to the idea of dying from love connects to a far more overarching resistance to the idea that his love that would extend without limits across time. Where Petrarch seeks continuity, Wyatt seeks rupture. This is best captured, perhaps, by the short rondeaux "But though ye have had my heart's cure / Trow ye I dote without ending? What no, perdie!" To "dote without ending" is what Wyatt wants least of all. However often he affirms his constancy in love—and he affirms this quite routinely—he is also very quick to stress its mortal bounds. Thus in the sonnet that begins, "Eche man me telleth I chaunge moost my devise," Wyatt informs his mistress that he shall remain steadfast in his affection so long as his body and soul remain together:

But you that blame this dyvernes moost,
Chaunge you no more, but still after oon rate

Trete ye me well, and kepe ye in the same state;
And while with me doeth dwell this weried goost,
My word nor I shall not be variable,
But alwaies oon, your owne boeth ferme and stable. (9–14)

To declare his love will last while his spirit ("goost") dwells in his flesh might seem to be nothing more than a formulaic articulation of his fidelity: what more, one might ask, could he pledge than this? But given the Petrarchan model against which Wyatt composed so many of his poems, his insistence on the terminal nature of his love—on its lasting only until the wearied ghost might be liberated from its body—takes on a different inflection. Far from fantasizing that his love would last for all eternity, he repeatedly seeks the moment of his release.

At the end of the short poem "Madame, withouten many wordes," a translation from a very un-Petrarchan madrigal by the sixteenth-century Neopolitan poet Dragonetto Bonifacio, Wyatt offers an ultimatum that reveals something important about the allure of the possible rupture:[50]

Yf it be yea, I shalbe fayne;
If it be nay—frendes as before;
Ye shall an othre man obtain,
And I myn owne and yours no more. (9–12)

However much he wants the answer to be "yea," he seems equally if not more drawn to the "nay." It is the "nay" that frees him from his beholdenness, that leads him back to himself.[51]

In this respect, one of the most revealing moments in all of Wyatt's Petrarchan poems comes in his sonnet "I fynde no peace and all my warr is done," an adaptation of *Rime sparse* 134. Petrarch's sonnet, which is structured around a series of paradoxes, culminates with his declaration "et ò in odio me stesso et amo altrui" (and I hate myself and love another [11]). In Wyatt's hands, the order of feelings is reversed, and the two sentiments are represented as causally linked. In place of Petrarch's "I hate myself and love another," Wyatt writes: "I love an othre and thus I hate my self." "And thus I hate my self": love of his mistress and love of self are for Wyatt mutually exclusive. This mutual exclusivity helps to explain what attracted Wyatt so much to ending love. Within his erotic relationships, self-possession was unattainable.

III. Continental Examples

From the entire *in morte* sequence in Petrarch's *Rime sparse*, Wyatt chose to translate only two poems. In one of these—"The piller pearisht is wheareto I lent," his version of Petrarch's poem 269—Wyatt dropped all reference to the deceased beloved, focusing exclusively on the death of his patron, Thomas Cromwell (Petrarch's poem mourns the death of both Laura and his patron, Cardinal Giovanni Colonna, who died a few months after Laura in 1348). Wyatt did not engage directly, then, with Petrarch's endless imaginings of his relationship to Laura after her death. This was an important and conscious decision, as he almost certainly had full access to Petrarch's poems and was free to pick and choose among them. But Petrarch's depiction of his love for Laura after her death was obviously not what Wyatt found compelling about the *Rime sparse*.

In choosing not to represent the death of the beloved, Wyatt makes an important departure from many of his contemporary poets on the Continent.[52] To put Wyatt's decision in perspective, let us briefly consider a number of the prominent sonnet sequences written in the early or middle decades of the sixteenth century that addressed the deceased beloved in their poems. Bembo's immensely popular *Rime* (1535, 1548) provides a good starting point. This volume includes a sequence of poems that Bembo's secretary, Goro Gualteruzzi, titled *Rime in morte di Messer Carlo suo fratello e di molte altre persone* (Poems on the death of his brother Mr. Carlo and many other people), but the poems are in fact centered on Bembo's beloved companion Morosina. In poem after poem, Bembo describes his soul's longing to depart this world following Morosina's death in 1535, and begs his beloved to help. The very first of these sonnets, *Rime* 161, sets the tone for the rest: the poet's soul wants to abandon the body and urges his tired limbs to follow the soul's path to heaven, where the now blessed Morosina dwells.[53] The next poem begs Morosina to intervene in this passage, to bring him through celestial flight to her feet. *Rime* 166 bemoans his fate to remain on earth and exclaims that if Morosina does not untie the knot of soul and body, freeing his spirit to join her, he will spend the rest of his days in tears ("piango et son per pianger sempre"), and *Rime* 170, composed on the first anniversary of Morosina's death, reaffirms his longing to depart in order to see her again in heaven ("la rivegga in cielo"). In poem 171, the poet gets some reassurance from his beloved, who tells him that they will be together once again ("Tu pur qui sarai meco anchora"); and in *Rime* 172 and 173, the poet laments his not having followed his beloved immediately to heaven. The sequence ends, in *Rime* 174, with a canzone that Bembo began on the occasion of his beloved's death but finished some five years later.[54] Here he once again asks her to intervene on his behalf so that he may join her in heaven: "Please importune God to release me from my ties to the world, and allow my soul, which should have left before you, to follow you" ("Impetra dal Signor non più ne' suoi / lacci mi stringa il mondo et possa l'alma / che devea gir inanzi, homai seguirti" [7–9]).

In the Neapolitan poet Berardino Rota's *Rime* (1561), the poet begins his *in morte* sequence with the announcement in sonnet 129 of the death of his wife, Portia Capace, whom he had praised in verse while she lived ("gia' viva in rime").[55] Rota declares that he will spend his days crying until they are reunited by a single stone, just as one single key closed both of their hearts ("chiuda inseme un sasso come ne chiuse il cor sola una chiave" [9–11]). This idea of lying together under a single stone—presumably in the earth—shifts in subsequent sonnets to a heavenly register. In sonnet 139, he asks Portia to come to him in her heavenly splendor in the night and to beg God to take him to her sooner ("più rapido e chino ne corra il tempo, e più veloci l'hore" [7–8]). Later poems repeat the nightly visitations of her blessed spirit and his self-reproaches for not departing sooner to meet her.[56] These poems continue through the fifth anniversary of Portia's death, commemorated in poem 190; this sonnet is followed by two sacred poems, which conclude the *in morte* section of the *Rime*.

A third example of the *in morte* tradition in early sixteenth-century Italian poetry is the verse of Vittoria Colonna, the first woman poet ever to have her own book of poems published in Italy; her *Rime* first appeared in 1538 and were issued in twelve subsequent editions in the next ten years. Following the death of her husband, Ferrante Francesco d'Avalos, in 1525, Colonna composed over one hundred sonnets to her deceased spouse. These poems, categorized in modern editions as her *rime amorose*, begin with the poet's declaration that she will write elegiac poetry filled with grief ("Amaro lacrimar, non dolce canto"), but following Petrarch's example, she quickly moves from the retrospective to the prospective, from the elegiac to the anticipatory. In sonnet 44, she begs Ferrante to hasten her path to him in heaven ("Sgombri le spesse nebbie d' ogn' intorno / sì ch' io trovi a volar spedite l' ali / nel già preso da voi destro sentiero"). In sonnet 10, "Chi puo' troncar quel laccio che m'avinse?" she describes her desire to exchange her life on this earth for the happy bond awaiting her in heaven ("onde tanto obligò lo spirto interno / ch' a cangiar vita fermerò la voglia; / soave in terra, in Ciel felice nodo"); and in sonnet 45, she declares that time will never alter her bond to him and that the knot they tied remains just as tight as ever ("Tempo non cangiò mai l' antica fede; / il nodo è stretto ancor com' io l' avolsi"). In her greatest moments of despair, she writes that she is held back from taking her own life by the knowledge that this sinful act would separate them forever: "Pushed over the edge many times, near death / by my own hand: prevented only by / this intense urge to be restored to him ("La propria man dal duol più volte spinta / fatto l' aria, ma quell' ardente zelo / di trovar lui fa pur ch' a dietro io torni").[57] Toward the end of her *in morte* poems, Colonna affirms the reciprocity of her longing from her husband's spirit, describing the desire she feels emanating from him: "And, while he sees my life withdrawn and fearful / Holding a bridle on my mortal flesh, / I feel his spirit still desires my love" ("e mentre il viver mio raccolto e schivo / scorge ei, col fren in man del mortal velo, / sent'io lo spirto suo del mio amor vago").[58]

There are other Italian poets we might consider: Bernardo Tasso, for example, the father of the more famous Torquato, wrote sonnets to his deceased wife (*in morte della moglie*), published in 1560, and Gian Giorgio Trissino lamented the deaths of not one but two beloved women in his 1529 *Rime*. In France, the great sixteenth-century poet Pierre Ronsard composed a sequence of poems on the death of Marie ("Sur la mort de Marie") as part of his *Amours* (1578).[59] In one of the more celebrated poems from this sequence, he despairs:

Soit que tu vives pres de Dieu,
Ou aux champs Elisez, adieu,
Adieu cent fois, adieu Marie:
Jamais Ronsard ne t'oublira,
Jamais la Mort ne deslira
Le nœud dont ta beauté me lie.

(Whether you live near God or in the Elysian fields, good-bye, good-bye one hundred times, good-bye Marie; never will Ronsard forget you, never will death untangle the knot that ties me to your beauty.)[60]

Ronsard may lack Petrarch's confidence in a Christian afterlife—he is willing to imagine his beloved either in the heavens above or in a pagan Elysium—but what matters is not where Marie will be but that she shall not be forgotten. The possibility of rupture or disentanglement runs counter to the deepest spirit of this sequence, as expressed in his epigraph from the great Latin poet Propertius: "Trajicit et fati littora magnus amor" (Great love leaps over the shores of fate).[61] Death is no boundary for love.

IV. Wyatt's Exceptionalism

Although by no means an exhaustive survey, these examples from the Continent help to draw attention to the particular, if not peculiar, nature of Wyatt's decision to abandon what many of his contemporaries clearly regarded as a compelling poetic mode. In the second of the two *in morte* poems that Wyatt adapted from Petrarch, "Myne olde dere En'mye, my froward master," the full extent of his struggle to impose a temporally bounded understanding of love onto the Italian poet's idea of transcendence comes to the surface. This poem, a translation of *Rime sparse* 360, a long canzone, gave Wyatt his greatest opportunity to articulate the differences between Petrarch's understanding of love and his own.

Rime sparse 360 comes after the canzone that I have already briefly considered in which Laura's spirit chastises Petrarch for not letting go of "le cose mortali" (his mortal things) in order to follow her directly to heaven: "A che pur piangi et ti distempre? / Quanto era meglio alzar da terra l'ali / Et le cose mortali . . . et seguire me" ("Why still weep and untune yourself? How much better it would have been to raise your wings from earth and to weigh with an accurate balance mortal things . . . and to follow me" [38–43]). In poem 360, Petrarch stages a mock trial of Love in which "la reina / che la parte divina / tien di nostra natura" (the queen who holds the divine part of our nature [2–4]) serves as the judge and Petrarch plays the role of chief prosecutor. Both he and Love deliver their opposing arguments to this queen, who has traditionally been understood as the personification of reason, regarding the effect that loving Laura has had on Petrarch's life. When Love makes his case, he emphasizes the ways in which he has improved Petrarch's spiritual and moral worth through his love for Laura:

"Ancor, et questo è quel che tutto avanza,
da volar sopra 'l ciel li avea dat' ali
per le cose mortali,
che son scala al Fattor, chi ben l'estima:
ché mirando ei ben fiso quante et quali
eran vertuti in quella sua speranza,
d'una in altra sembianza
potea levarsi a l'alta cagion prima." (136–43)

(Again, and this is all that remains, I gave him wings to fly above the heavens through mortal things, which are a ladder to the Creator, if one judges them rightly; for if he looked fixedly at how many and how great virtues were in that hope of his, from one likeness to the next he could have risen to the high First Cause.)

Through the mouthpiece of Love, Petrarch delivers what in the fifteenth century became the conventional Neoplatonic account for how love ought to work, an account that Petrarch elsewhere endorses. Consider, for example, *Rime sparse* 306, where he describes Laura as "Quel sol che mi mostrava il cammin destro / di gire al Ciel con gloriosi passi" (That sun which showed me the right way to go to Heaven with glorious steps, returning to the highest Sun [1–2]). "Her I do not find," he concludes, "but I see her holy footprints all turned toward the road to Heaven" (lei non trov'io, ma suoi santi vestigi / tutti rivolti a la superna strada / veggio, lunge da' laghi averni et stigi [12–14]). This is also Petrarch's position in the *Secretum*, where, in response to Augustine's accusation that Petrarch has replaced his love for God with his love for Laura—"she has distracted your mind from the love of heavenly things and has attracted it from the Creator to a desire for created things"—Petrarch demurs: "[L]ove of her was indeed responsible for my love of God."[63]

In *Rime sparse* 360, Love contends that Laura's beauty and virtue were but a stepping stone to rise "d'una in altra sembianza" (from one likeness to the next) until Petrarch could have reached "l'alta cagion prima" (the high First Cause). Employing the metaphor (derived from Diotima's speech at the end of the *Symposium*) that was most conspicuously associated with Neoplatonic accounts of love even before Plato's text was available, Love blames him for wasting the opportunity to climb this *scala* or ladder.[62] Petrarch replies in anger that Love may have given him this exceptional woman to love but "ma tosto la ritolse" (soon took her back), away from the land of the living. Love replies, "Io no, ma chi per sé la volse" (Not I, but One who desired her for Himself [149–50]). The clear implication is that "One" is none other than God, who has already been invoked on multiple occasions in the poem. This interpretation corresponds to that of the Vellutello commentary that Wyatt may have used, where the line is glossed "intendendeno d'Iddio' [meaning God]."[64] Given the poem's placement, moreover, toward the very end of the sequence and long after Laura's death, there can be little uncertainty as to either why Laura is no longer present or who has taken her away.

When Wyatt approaches this material, he confronts that aspect of Petrarch's poetry that was most alluring to Italian Neoplatonists: the idea that the love of one ideal being is not an end in itself but serves as a vehicle for reaching the divine. What made the poem bearable for his purposes, we might imagine, is that on this occasion Petrarch opposes the Neoplatonic position espoused by the figure of Love. Nor does Petrarch ever come around, as it were, to Love's side: the poem does not end with Love's victory; instead, the trial is left unresolved. The queen has the last line, and it is entirely inconclusive: "Piacemi aver vostre questioni udite, / mia più tempo bisogna a tanta lite" (it pleases me to have heard your pleas, but more time is needed for so great a lawsuit [156–57]).

Wyatt's distaste for the Neoplatonic argument that Love makes in canzone 360 is hardly ambiguous, however, and his alterations to the poem make abundantly clear where his sympathies lie. He denies the figure of Love the most powerful argument that he makes in Petrarch's poem: namely, that the poet's love of Laura sets him on the path toward the Creator. Instead, Wyatt's Love emphasizes only the temporal nature of his gifts:

> But oon thing there is above all othre:
> I gave him wynges wherewith he myght flye
> To honour and fame, and if he would farther
> By mortall thinges above the starry skye. (127–30)

These lines strikingly omit any reference to the staircase or ladder, and they omit as well any discussion of ascending upward until reaching the Creator. (They also only obliquely acknowledge that Love's gifts took the form of poetry, as Braden has rightly observed; here as elsewhere, Wyatt has little interest in the poetic ambition that runs so powerfully through Petrarch).[65] In place of the Petrarchan wings that carry him to the divine, Wyatt's wings deliver only the human rewards of "honour and fame." There is the vague suggestion of something more "above the starry skye," but it is a strangely discontinuous image: a place marked apart, somewhere "above," rather than a continuous flow upward.

Wyatt's most decisive gesture of resisting the Petrarchan narrative of heavenly transcendence through love comes at the end of the poem, when he obfuscates the explanation that Love gives for why Laura has been taken away. In Petrarch's poem, as we have seen, Love tells the speaker that someone, presumably God, has taken Laura for himself: "Io no, ma chi per sé la volse" (Not I, but One who desired her for Himself). In place of this more or less transparent account of Laura's absence, Wyatt provides a rather opaque alternative:

"Thou gave her me," quod I, "but, by and by
Thou toke her streight from me, that wo worth thee!"
"Not I," quod he, "but price, that is well worthy." (138–40)

The force of these lines turns on the substitution of *price* for Petrarch's
chi, indicating what, or who, has taken Wyatt's mistress from him.

Price has a number of possible meanings in the early sixteenth century, and they pull in somewhat antithetical directions. In Catholic theology it could refer to the currency of spiritual exchange through which
grace might be purchased: good works, meditative exercises, or another
form of piety.[66] But given Wyatt's fervent Protestantism, and given more
specifically his aggressive refusal to associate his mistress with the
heavens above, it seems unlikely that he meant to suggest her "worthy"
adoption by God. The more common meaning of the term *price* would
have suggested the beloved's earthly "honor" or "praise"; this possibly
also connects to the term *pretz* frequently used in Occitan love poetry
to describe the transcendent quality of the ideal lady (derived from the
Latin *premium*, *pretz* is etymologically tied to both *price* and *prize* in English).

Price also carries potentially negative connotations, and within
Wyatt's canon there is precedent for using the term in a pejorative sense.
In his song "Alas, the greiff and dedly wofull smert," Wyatt describes his
mistress's leaving him for a rival of presumably greater wealth and stature:[67]

I have wailed thus weping in nyghtly payne
In sobbes and sighes, Alas! and all in vayne,
In inward plaint and hertes wofull torment;
And yet, Alas, lo! crueltie and disdayn
Hath set at noght a faithfull true intent
And price hath priuilege trouth to prevent. (19–24)

"And price hath privilege trouth to prevent": "price" and its privilege
have come before truth, Wyatt has been "prevent[ed]" from keeping his
mistress because someone else has offered her more.

This idea of being trumped by wealthy, powerful rivals also calls to mind the ending of Wyatt's "Who so list to hounte," in which the diamond necklace worn by the hind declares her to be the property of Caesar:

Who list her hount I put him owte of dowbte,
As well as I may spend his tyme in vain:
And graven with Diamondes in letters plain
There is written her faier neck rounde abowte:
"Noli me tangere for Cesars I ame,
And wylde for to hold though I seme tame." (9–14)

To return to the translation of *Rime sparse* 360: when Love declares "Not I . . . but price that is well worthy," Wyatt seems deliberately to complicate, and compromise, Petrarch's idea that his mistress has returned to God following her death. Wyatt's mistress has not died. She has simply been taken away by someone with a stronger claim.[68]

V. English Love

Why is it that, exposed to a tradition in which mortality posed no obstacle to the intensity of erotic bonds, Wyatt chose to depict an exclusively earthly and transient mode of love? Recent critics have not posed this question; it reveals something about the state of the topic that the answers we have date back more than fifty years and are either meteorological or racial in nature. According to J. W. Lever, author of *The Elizabethan Love Sonnet* (1956), the English climate was to be blamed for the lack of transcendence in the English love lyric. "The elemental foe," Lever opined, "persisted in the northern imagination. . . . Despite occasional touches of gaiety, the great majority of surviving lyrics view love as pitiable and frail, at the mercy of wind and weather."[69] "Perhaps we have to do with a matter of racial temperament rather than of creed," E. K. Chambers and F. Sidgwick proposed in their 1907 *Early English Lyrics*, "and it is the Anglo-Saxon melancholy that inspires so keen a sense of the transitoriness and uncertainty of all mortal things."[70] If we take these explanations at all seriously, we are left with the idea that

Wyatt's rejection of Petrarchan transcendence had little or nothing to do with his reaction to the Italian love sonnet. It was merely a result of the damp northern air that he and other English poets breathed.[71]

Putting aside its racial and climatological assumptions, there is something fundamentally mistaken about an argument that regards Wyatt's rejection of transcendent love as simply his adherence to medieval English traditions. First, there are medieval English lyrics that directly contradict this characterization of the poetry. In Chaucer's "Complaint unto Pity," for example, the speaker declares his everlasting love for his deceased mistress:

> I wol be youres evere,
> Though ye me slee by Crueltee your foo,
> Algate my spirit shal never dissevere
> Fro youre servise, for any peyne or woo.
> Sith ye be ded—alas that hyt is soo!—
> Thus for your deth I may wel wepe and pleyne
> With herte sore and ful of besy peyne.[72]

This is a poem that Wyatt surely would have known, and it is much closer to the Petrarchan model than to the melancholic, nontranscendent lyrics that Lever or Chambers and Sidgwick describe.

Second, and more important: any account of Wyatt's poems that simply absorbs his position as a continuation of certain prevalent English attitudes fails to recognize the ways in which he responded forcefully and directly to the Italian poems he was imitating. Wyatt's representation of love as insistently this-worldly needs to be understood as an active decision on his part, and this decision reflects less on the dreariness of the English weather or the English temperament than on Wyatt's desire to write love poems—in response to the Petrarchan tradition—that would not look beyond the confines of this world.

Such a desire stemmed in part from Wyatt's Protestantism, a religion that may not have taken an official position on posthumous love but in other important ways rejected the Catholic belief in sustaining relations with the dead. Indeed, the Protestant suspicion of speaking to the dead became a central part of the Reformers' agenda, which was codified in the church's Thirty-Nine Articles and the 1552 Book of Common Prayer. Although Wyatt did not live to see the full articulation of these doctrinal positions, he was exposed to the theological arguments made by his contemporaries who criticized the Catholic concept of purgatory for (among other reasons) collapsing the necessary boundaries between this world and the next.[73] And when reading a poem like *Rime sparse* 126, in which Petrarch expresses his hope that if he dies before Laura, he might be buried where she makes her usual walks so that she might intervene on his behalf at his graveside—"Amor l'inspiri / in guisa che sospiri / sì dolcemente che mercé m'impetre / et faccia forza al cielo" (Love will inspire her to sigh so sweetly that she will win mercy for me and force heaven [35–38])—Wyatt was confronted with a Catholic eschatology that his religion was determined to overthrow.

Wyatt's desire to forgo the posthumous component of Petrarch's poems did not derive only from his Protestantism. It also stemmed from his related lack of sympathy for Neoplatonism. Neoplatonism and Protestantism are not by definition opposed to each other, and later in the 1500s English Protestants became more attracted to aspects of Neoplatonic philosophy. On the topic of posthumous love, however, there is a clear incompatibility between the two sets of belief. When Wyatt wants to write about love of God, he does not move through the vehicle of loving an earthly woman. Instead, in a pattern that becomes typical of sixteenth- and seventeenth-century English poets, he shifts decisively from erotic to devotional poetry. Hence in the prologue to his translation of the penitential psalms—his most explicitly Protestant text—Wyatt emphasizes David's turn to God as a turn away from women. David's feelings for Bathsheba do not lead him to heavenly contemplation, but instead to "Withdrawyng hym into a dark Cave / Within the grownd, wherein he myght hym hyde, / Fleing the lyght, as in pryson or grave" (108.60–62). To love God, in other words, is not on a continuum with loving one's mistress: it requires an act of repentance, a denunciation, a dramatic break. (Wyatt's source for his psalm translations, the Italian author Pietro Aretino, shared Wyatt's distaste for Petrarchan love: in his *Ragionamenti*, Aretino openly parodied Neoplatonic love treatises in general, and Bembo's *Asolani* in particular, setting his dialogue inside a whorehouse.)

Taken as a whole, Wyatt's alterations to Petrarch represent an attempt to liberate the love lyric from what he perceived to be Neoplatonism's shackles. In its description of love as an experience of transcendence, moving the lover, through the beloved, closer to the divine, Neoplatonism denied the possibility that the poet might ever free himself from the burdens of love—that he might conclusively, and irreversibly, say goodbye. This possibility for closure was immensely important to Wyatt, and his poetry returns repeatedly, as we have seen, to the prospect of regaining self-possession on the other side of his erotic entanglements.

Wyatt's desire not to luxuriate in the bittersweet agonies of love helped to spawn a lyric mode that drew its power from the urgency and intensity of representing love as temporally bound. Whatever ambivalence we find in the culture of Protestant England—and I have noted such ambivalence in both the epitaph tradition and the sermons and treatises of the church—there is no comparable equivocation in English poetry. Although there were plenty of poets during this period who praised their beloved in extravagant terms, and who suffered from the agonies of unrequited love, there were very few lyrics written that described an erotic attachment that extended beyond the mortal world. (When such attachments are imagined, they take the most spiritually reduced and insistently corporeal forms: once again we might invoke Donne's "bracelet of bright hair about the bone" as his greatest hope for a shared afterlife with his beloved.) What began with Wyatt resulted in a poetic mode that both systematically avoided posthumous love and emphasized the emotional and aesthetic power that such avoidance might bring. Renaissance English poetry evolved through an understanding of love as finite.

3

Dead Ends
The Elizabethan Sonnet

O haste thee gentle death I linger for thee
> —Anon., *Teares of Fancie* (1593)

Toward the end of the sixteenth century, English love poets began for the first time to write lengthy sonnet sequences modeled on Petrarch's *Rime sparse*. These sequences typically idealize the poet's mistress and bemoan her refusal to requite his love, but they depart from Petrarch's model in rejecting the central feature of his narrative: the death of the beloved. Although the Elizabethan sonneteer does not imagine his mistress's death, he does routinely imagine his own demise. He does so, moreover, not to lament the termination of his love but rather to effect that very termination.

The poet's wishful anticipation of his own death in order to end his suffering from love does not figure prominently in the celebrated examples of the English sonnet sequences—it is missing from the poems of Sidney and Daniel and Spenser and Shakespeare—but it recurs quite routinely in the minor sequences, those poems that are rarely read or studied because they seem to be uninspired imitations of the Petrarchan genre. In studying these minor poems, however, we learn something important about the tradition that evolved in England over the course of the sixteenth century, a tradition that at its very core broke from the Petrarchan paradigm by representing death as the final blow to love.

In *The Origin of German Tragic Drama*, Walter Benjamin considers how ordinary works of literature often reveal more about the nature of their genre than extraordinary works. Benjamin writes:

> It is one thing to incarnate a form; it is quite a different thing to give its characteristic expression. Whereas the former is the business of the poetic elect, the latter is often done incomparably more distinctly in the laborious efforts of minor writers. The life of the form is not identical with that of the works which are determined by it, indeed the clarity with which it is expressed can sometimes be in inverse proportion to the perfection of a literary work; and the form itself becomes evident precisely in the lean body of the inferior work, as its skeleton so to speak.[1]

In the scores of relatively undistinguished sonnet series that Elizabethan poets wrote in the 1580s and 1590s, we glimpse the consequences of dropping posthumous love from the poetic repertoire with a clarity that is missing from the more inventive examples of English sonnets. The sonnets in this chapter represent, in effect, a dead end: they show what English love poetry looked like before it found the means to build, on the very ruins of transcendent love, something powerful and new. The remainder of this book is devoted to those more ambitious, and more successful, poetic edifices: literary works that do not simply welcome death as an escape from love but understand love's mortality as a source for alternative forms of pleasure. Before turning to those works, let us briefly consider the skeletal articulation of mortal poetics: a body of poems that, building on the conviction that love will not cross the grave, longs for death as a means of erotic extinction.

I. Petrarch's Death

To understand the radical departure that the English sonnet series made from the Petrarchan model in its conception of death as terminating love, I want to return to a few resonant examples from the *Rime sparse* in which the poet anticipates predeceasing Laura. These poems occur, needless to say, in the *in vita* section of the sequence, where Petrarch tries to imagine what will happen to his love once he has left this world. In the last chapter, we saw Petrarch's rare attempt to negotiate a post-humous future that would not be defined by loving Laura. That poem—*Rime sparse* 82—is an exception to the general rule: Petrarch typically imagines his death as a direct result of his suffering in love, and also imagines that even after death, his love for Laura will persist with the same frustrating intensity as before.

The absolute futility of dying as a means to escape love is clearly articulated in *Rime sparse* 36:

> S'io credesse per morte essere scarco
> del pensiero amoroso che m'atterra,
> colle mie mani avrei già posto in terra
> queste membra noiose, et quello incarco;
> ma perch'io temo che sarebbe un varco
> di pianto in pianto et d'una in altra guerra,
> di qua dal passo anchor che mi si serra
> mezzo rimango, lasso, et mezzo il varco. (1–8)

(If I thought that by death I would be lightened of this amorous care that weighs me down, with my own hands by now I would have consigned to earth these burdensome members and that weight; but because I fear that it would be a passage from weeping into weeping and from one war to another, still on this side of the pass that is closed to me I half remain, and half pass over).

S'io credesse: if I believed that death might bring me relief from love, he reasons, I might even take my own life—*ma* (but), of course, I do not. Far from relieving him of his *pensiero amoroso* (amorous care), death will only perpetuate his state of misery: it will move him simply *di pianto in pianto, et d'una in altra guerra* (from weeping into weeping and from one war into another).

In *Rime sparse* 86, Petrarch laments that none of the arrows with which Cupid has struck him have proved to be mortal:

Io avrò sempre in odio la fenestra
onde Amor m'aventò già mille strali,
perch'alquanti di lor non fur mortali:
ch'è bel morir mentre la vita è destra. (1–4)

(I shall always hate the window from which Love has by now shot a thousand arrows at me, because none of them has been mortal: for it is good to die when one's life is fortunate.)

Even if he were to receive a mortal wound, he quickly adds, it would do nothing to end his suffering:

[M]a 'l sovrastar ne la pregion terrestra
cagion m'è, lasso, d'infiniti mali;
et più mi duol che fien meco immortali
poi che l'alma dal cor non si scapestra. (5–8)

(but my staying longer in my earthly prison is a cause of infinite evils to me, and it pains me the more that they will be immortal along with me, for the soul is never disentangled from the heart.)

The verb *scapestrare* (8) means literally "to slip one's head out of the halter": this is what the soul cannot do in relation to the emotions of the heart, and this is why Petrarch's sufferings in love will be, like his soul, immortal.

Petrarch returns to the idea that the soul will experience no liberation from love at the moment of death in *Rime sparse* 256, near the end of the *in vita* poems, in which he marvels that "L'alma, cui morte del suo albergo caccia, / da me si parte; et di tal nodo sciolta / vassene pur a lei che la minaccia" (My soul, which Death drives from its dwelling, leaves me, and loosed from that knot goes off still to her who menaces it [9–11]). Freed from the knot that binds soul to body—what Donne will describe as "that subtile knot, which makes us man"—Petrarch's soul does not travel to the heavens but clings to his mortal beloved.[2]

This stubbornness in his soul's attachment thwarts any straightforward claim for Petrarch's Neoplatonism: he describes his soul as stuck in its earthly affections in a manner that Ficino and his followers certainly would not have admired. (Had Laura not died, the *Rime sparse* would probably have surfaced very rarely in their treatises and lectures.) Petrarch's refusal to imagine any kind of transformation between the longings of his soul before and after death is also incompatible with standard Christian ideas about the afterlife, as such a refusal denies his soul the experience of both transcendence and heavenly joy (both of which are absolutely central features in his portrayal of Laura's afterlife). What is significant for our purposes, however, is not Petrarch's indifference in these *in vita* poems to Christian metaphysics but his complete rejection of the notion that death might bring erotic change. It is this idea of continuity that is completely missing from the Elizabethan sonnet series, in which mortality represents an unequivocal severing of the poet's emotional ties.

II. Courting Death

For Elizabethan sonneteers, the appeal of death was the certainty that it would eliminate their erotic woes forever. So the anonymous poet of *The Teares of Fancie* (1593) declares:

> Long have I swome against the wished wave,
> But now constrained by a lothsome life:
> I greedilie doe seeke the greedie grave,
> To make an end of all these stormes and strife.
> Sweete death give end to my tormenting woes,
> And let my passions penetrate thy brest:
> Suffer my hart which doth such griefes inclose
> By timelie fates inioie [enjoy] eternall rest.
> Let me not dwell in dole sith thou maist ease me,
> Let me not languish in such endles durance:
> One happie stroke of thy sad hand will please me,
> Please me good death it is thy procurance.
> To end my harts griefe (heart shee did abhorre thee)
> O hast thee gentle death I linger for thee.[3]

"I greedilie doe seeke the greedie grave": this is not a passive acceptance of death but rather its active pursuit. Death becomes the lover whom the poet wants to seduce: it is death whom he wants to "penetrate," and who might "ease" him from his pain. Unlike the cycles of sexual desire, however, this desire for death is clearly terminal. The poet wants above all to "make an end" and "[enjoy] eternall rest."

Later in *The Teares of Fancie*, the poet explains that his particular disease—lovesickness—is unlike other ailments of mind or body in that the only possible cure is his mistress's love:

> For natures sickenes sometimes may have ease
> Fortune though fickle sometime is a friend:
> The minds affliction patience may appease,
> And death is cause that many torments end.
> Yet I am sicke, but shee that should restore me,
> Withholds the sacred balme that would recure me. (5–10)

Over the course of the sonnet, the possibility of reciprocated love is abandoned, however, and the poet shifts only to the solution offered by death—a solution that is also, at least for the moment, denied him:

> And fortune eke (though many eyes deplore me,)
> Will lend such chance that might to ioy procure me.
> Patience wants power to appease my weeping,
> And death denies what I have long beene seeking. (11–14)

The desire for immediate death that runs through the *Teares of Fancie* corresponds to Robert Burton's description in the *Anatomy of Melancholy* (1621) of the consequences of love melancholy: "It is so well knowne in every village, how many have either died for love or voluntary made away themselves, that I need not much labor to prove it; *Nec modus aut requies nisi mors reperitur amoris*: Death is the common *Catastrophe* to such persons."[4] The governing assumption is that dying for love eradicates all symptoms of lovesickness; once the lover is dead, Burton does not imagine that he or she could possibly continue to suffer. His Latin quotation, which translates literally as "she can find neither way nor rest from love, except for death," bears this out. This easy severing of erotic passion is subtly compromised, however, by the source for Burton's quotation: the story of Myrrha from book 10 of Ovid's *Metamorphoses*. Myrrha, who is consumed with desire for her own father, Cinyras, ends up transformed into a tree, while her tears take the form of myrrh dripping from her bark. The irony of Burton's quotation is that Myrrha does not die but lives a strange form of immortal life, forced to reenact her grief for all eternity. This is what English poets clearly want to ward off at all costs: an eternity of continuous, unreciprocated longing.

The fear of suffering forever the pain of unfulfilled desire; of being in a state of permanent misery caused by the cruelty or indifference of the beloved; of having an unrequited love that spans from this world to the next: these are the anxieties that plague the Elizabethan sonneteers and lead them to hope desperately that death might eliminate all aspects of their sentient experience. Thus in Thomas Lodge's *Phillis* (1593), the shepherd Damon entreats death to release him at once from his mistress's cruelty:

> Burst burst poore heart thou hast no longer hope,
> Captiue mine eyes vnto eternall sleepe,
> Let all my sences haue no further scope,
> Let death be lord of me and all my sheepe.
> For *Phillis* hath betrothed fierce disdaine:
> That makes his mortall man[s]ion in hir heart,
> And though my tonge haue long time taken paine,
> To sue deuorse and wed hir to desart.
> She will not yeeld, my wordes can haue no power,
> She scornes my faith, she laughes at my sad layes,
> She filles my soule with neuer ceasing sower,
> Who filt the world with volumes of hir praise:
> In such extreames what wretch can cease to craue
> His peace from death, who can no mercy haue.[5]

In the abstract, Damon's petition for "eternall sleepe" might seem to invoke the everlasting rest associated with Christian salvation. But in this sonnet "eternall sleepe" is not connected to any vision of a Christian afterlife, nor is it suggestive of an afterlife elsewhere. Damon craves only an annihilating peace that would move through all of his "sences," leaving him incapable of further feeling.

Here as elsewhere in these poems, the soul plays no role in the poet's conception of death: Damon never describes his possession of an eternal part that would be spared the fate of his flesh. This connects to an emphasis on the corporeal nature of the beloved, articulated in one of the eclogues interspersed among Lodge's sonnets, in which the character Demades warns Damon that once Phillis is dead, he will finally recognize how fleeting his love for her was:

> How large a scope lendes *Damon* to his moane,
> Wasting those treasures of his happy-witte:
> In regestring his wofull woe-begone?
> Ah bende thy Muse to matters farre more fitte:
> For time shall come when *Phillis* is interd,
> That *Damon* shall confesse that he hath erd.
> When natures riches shal (by time dissolued)
> Call thee to see with more iudiciall eye:
> How *Phillis* beauties are to dust resolued,
> Thou then shalt aske thy selfe the reason why
> Thou wert so fond, since *Phillis* was so fraile,
> To praise her giftes that should so quickly faile? (115–26)

Reminding Damon that Phillis is made purely of matter and thus, once dead, will be "to dust resolued," Demades reasons that there will be nothing left of Phillis to love. In different hands, as we shall see with Marvell, this insistent materialism will serve as the basis for a *carpe diem* message: since Phillis will be reduced to dust, Damon might urge her to take advantage of her present "beauties" and "giftes." In Lodge's poem, however, there is no manipulation of the dreary future for present gains. Damon must either cure himself of his passion or terminate that passion through death.

It is tempting to connect the sentiments expressed in *Phillis* or *Teares of Fancie* with the ancient belief that death brought an absolute termination of all human experience, that on the other side of this world there was nothing but a *nox perpetua* of eternal darkness. As Seneca puts it in his tragedy *Troades*: "There is nothing after death, and death itself is nothing, the final goal of a course full swiftly run" (397-98). This sentiment is also famously given voice in Lucretius's Epicurean masterpiece *De rerum natura*: "Death is nothing to us," Lucretius writes, and so "when we shall be no more . . . nothing by any hazard will happen any more at all."[6]

Whether many Elizabethan poets actually thought that there would be no sentient or meaningful afterlife is difficult to prove. According to Robert Watson, there was a strong "annihilationist" bent in Renaissance England, and many more people believed in the absolute finality of the self than we have generally been led to think. "The traditional assumption that Jacobeans would automatically have believed in an afterlife," Watson argues, "is at best an exaggeration."[7]

It is also possible that English poets imagined the far less radical but still unorthodox idea of "psychopannychism"—the idea that the soul would sleep with the body until the time of the resurrection—which would allow them to retain belief in the immortality of the soul while still envisioning a long period of inert dormancy in which mortal affections would be erased.[8] But putting aside the nature of the poets' underlying beliefs, the attraction of the annihilationist position, at least as a poetic conceit, seems irrefutable: it offered the easiest way to imagine a final and irreversible escape from the erotic unhappiness evoked in their poems.

To imagine death as permanently severing erotic affections, however, by no means necessitated the elimination of the afterlife altogether, and there are plenty of sonnets that allow for a posthumous future so long as that future is free from erotic ties. In his 1596 series *Fidessa*, for example, Bartholomew Griffin begs the fates to release him from this world and allow his passage to the heavens:

Worke worke apace you blessed Sisters three,
In restles twining of my fatall threed:
Oh let your nimble hands at once agree,
To weaue it out, and cut it off with speed.

Then shall my vexed and tormented ghost
Haue quiet passage to the Elisian rest:
And sweetly ouer death and fortune boast,
In euerlasting triumphs with the blest.
But ah (too well I know) you haue conspired
A lingring death for him that lotheth life:
As if with woes he neuer could be tyred:
For this you hide your all-diuiding knife.
One comfort yet the heauens haue assign'd me,
That I must dye and leaue my griefes behind me.[9]

The poet regards the "lingring" nature of his death—the slow unraveling of his "fatall threed"—as a form of further punishment, and urges the pagan "Sisters three" to hasten his passage to the next world. There is no coherent vision of what this next world will be: the poem alternates between conjuring up the ghosts of the Elysian fields and the Christian company of "the blest." But Griffin is not interested in theological consistency; he simply wants to be reassured that he will carry none of his pains to the next world, that the heavens will be a place of "rest."

In *Parthenophil and Parthenophe* (1593), Barnabe Barnes similarly longs for death to disperse—and in so doing erase—each symptom of his lovesickness:

Long wish't for death, sent by my mistresse doome
Hold take thy prisoner full resolu'd to dye,
But first as cheefe, and in the highest roome
My soule to heauen I doe bequeath on hye,
Now readie to be seuer'd from thy loue:
My sighes to ayer, to Christall springes my teares,
My sad complaintes (which thee could neuer moue)
To mountaines desolate, and deafe, my feares
To Lambes beset with Lyons, my dispare
To night, and irksome dungeons full of dread:
Then shalt thou finde (when I am past this care)
My tormentes which thy cruelties haue bredde

In heauens, clouds, springs hard mountaines, lambes, & night.
Here once vnited, then disseuer'd quite.[10]

To die in this poem means not simply that the poet's soul will ascend to heaven but that he will "be seuer'd from [his mistress's] loue." In a manner more or less consistent with Calvin's account of what happens at the moment of death that we saw in chapter 1—that "husbands and wives will then be torn apart from one another"—Barnes defines heaven as a place free of all mortal attachments: "Here once vnited, there disseuer'd quite."[11]

This is not to suggest that Barnes has a strictly Calvinist vision of heaven; on the contrary, his poems are strikingly varied and inconsistent in their religious orientation. Later in the series, Barnes turns his prayers to Cupid and Venus, begging them to free him from love's tortures by killing him now:

Oh take my life, and after death torment mee,
Then (though in absence of my cheefe delight)
I shall lament alone, my soule requires,
And longes to visite sweet Elizian fieldes:
Then that I lou'd it neuer shall repent me,
There (till those dayes of Iubile shall comme)
Would I walke pensiue, pleas'd, alone and dumme. (Elegy 9, 18–24)

Although he invokes the pagan idea of the Elysian fields, he suggests that his time there will be temporary, lasting 'till those dayes of Iubile," a reference to the emancipation described in Leviticus 25 to be held every fifty years and proclaimed by a blast of trumpets. The poem therefore mixes pagan and Judeo-Christian conceptions of the afterlife, with the intervening period of suffering between Elysium and the Jubilee suggestive in particular of Catholic purgatory. But whatever its religious affiliations, the defining characteristic of the afterlife Barnes imagines is one of complete solitude: the adjective *alone* occurs twice in the space of five lines.[12]

Perhaps the most extreme articulation of the idea of an afterlife shorn of erotic love comes in Henry Constable's series *Diana*. Sonnet 2 of Constable's "Eighth Decade" concludes with the couplet "For if I die, and thou repent t'have slain me / T'will grieve me more, then if thou didst disdain me," and Sonnet 3 begins by repeating, and reframing, this final line:

> T'will grieve me more then if thou didst disdaine me,
> that I should die, and thou because I dye so:
> and yet to die, it should not knowe to paine me,
> if cruell Beauty were content to bid so.
> Death, to my life: life, to my long dispaire,
> prolong'd by her: given to my love and dayes:
> are meanes to tell how truly she is faire,
> and I can die to testifie her praise:
> Yet not to die though fairenes mee despiseth,
> is cause why in complaint I thus persever,
> though Death mee and my love imparadizeth,
> by interdicting mee, from her for ever:
> I doe not greeve that I am forst to die,
> But die, to think upone the reason, Why.[13]

In a poem whose conceits are for the most part conventional, two lines stand out for their counterintuitive, and fiercely anti-Petrarchan, sentiment: "though Death mee and my love imparadizeth, / by interdicting mee, from her for ever" (11–12). Read on its own, the first of these lines suggests that death will bring the lovers together in heaven, and conjures up images familiar to us not only from Petrarch but also from some of the English epitaphs considered in the introduction. In those inscriptions, located in the first section of our imaginary church, death was the conduit to the lovers' forging eternal bonds.

But Constable does not affirm that death propels the lovers upward to be "imparadized" together (the *OED*, incidentally, cites this poem as the first usage of this verb). On the contrary: death may imparadise the two lovers, but it does so by separating them for all eternity. Paradise is not a dwelling place for lovers; it does not resemble Luca Signorelli's beautiful fresco in the Cathedral of Orvieto of couples embracing, or Giovanni di

Paolo's Siennese predella now at the Metropolitan Museum of Art show-ing pairs of the blessed (along with angels and saints) warmly greeting one another. To be in paradise is to be "interdicted" from one's earthly beloved, to be released forever from the chains of love.

III. Alternative Solutions

If the sonnets in this chapter represent a dead end for posthumous love, how did English love poetry find its way onto a more affirmative and empowering path? One obvious solution would have been to adopt the idea of the poetic retraction, in which the poet renounces his secular love in order to embrace the idea of sacred love in heaven. This was, as we have seen, how Petrarch ends his sonnet sequence; there is also a strong English precedent for such a retraction in Chaucer's *Troilus and Criseyde*, which concludes with several different repudiations of mortal love in favor of the divine. Once Troilus has died at the hands of Achilles and ascends to the eighth sphere in heaven, he looks down with disdain upon the "wrecched world" (bk. 5, 1817) and "lough[s] right at the wo / Of hem that wepten for his deth so faste" (1821–22).[14] Troilus's laughter leads to the most moralizing of Chaucer's multiple conclusions:

> O yonge, fresshe folkes, he or she,
> In which that love up groweth with youre age,
> Repeyreth hom fro worldly vanyte,
> And of youre herte up casteth the visage
> To thilke God that after his ymage
> Yow made, and thinketh al nys but a faire,
> This world that passeth soone as floures faire.
> And loveth hym the which that right for love
> Upon a crois, oure soules for to beye [redeem]. (1835–43)

Adopting an absolutely standard Christian position on the perils of earthly love, the narrator warns his "yonge, fresshe" readers to re-nounce human passion in favor of loving Christ.[15] The posthumous realm remains affectively charged, but the nature of the affect under-goes a profound—and religious—transformation.

Within Renaissance English love poetry, however, there is no equivalent moment of transforming secular to sacred love. Even when a poet imagines that his earthly passion might come to an end without having to die to effect this ending, as is the case in Thomas Watson's *Hekatompathia*, the poet does not describe transferring his passion to the heavens. The last twenty poems of Watson's series, subtitled "My Love Is Past," provide a perfect occasion for such a shift, but the poems retain a largely pagan context in which the speaker disputes with Cupid and Venus rather than embracing a Christian world of heavenly love.

Only the devotional sonnet series, and not its erotic counterpart, shifts love from the secular to the divine. It is no coincidence that the devotional sonnet emerged so forcefully as a genre in the years immediately following the explosion of the love sonnet sequences: the lack of accommodation within the erotic poems for heavenly love and the perceived incompatibility of loving an earthly mistress and loving the divine made room for a new poetic mode that took up, as it were, the other half of the equation. Authors of erotic poems often subsequently wrote explicitly devotional sonnets that announced a shift of affection from one sphere to the other: Barnes's *A Divine Century of Spirituall Sonnets*, published only two years after *Parthenophil*, opens by declaring, "No more lewde laies of Lighter loves I sing," and declares Christ's "love my theame and holy Ghost my Muse"; and John Donne similarly recasts his poetic voice in his devotional sonnet that begins: "O might those sighes and teares returne againe / Into my breast and eyes, which I have spent / That I might in this holy discontent / Mourne with some fruit, as I have mourn'd in vaine."

This anonymous sonnet from the collection appended to Sir Philip Sidney's *Astrophil and Stella* neatly captures the English poet's perception of the necessity of abandoning love poetry in order to aspire toward the divine:

> Leave me, O love! which reachest but to dust!
> And thou, my mind! aspire to higher things!
> Grow rich in that, which never taketh rust!
> Whatever fades, but fading pleasure brings.
> Draw in thy beams, and humble all thy might

To that sweet yoke, where lasting freedoms be!
Which breaks the clouds, and opens forth the light
That doth both shine, and gives us sight to see.
O take fast hold! Let that light be thy guide!
In this small course which birth draws out to death:
And think how evil becometh him to slide,
Who seeketh heaven, and comes of heavenly breath!
Then farewell, world! Thy uttermost I see!
Eternal Love, maintain Thy love in me![16]

There is no connection between mortal and immortal love, no path that leads from one to the other. To move from earth to heaven requires not a ladder, but a leap.

If, then, Renaissance English love poets accepted neither the idea of earthly love transcending the mortal world nor the idea of a continuum between earthly and heavenly love, how did they ultimately create an affirmative poetic mode that embraced love's mortality? What, in short, differentiates the largely nihilistic poetry of the Elizabethan sonnets we have looked at in this chapter from the immensely powerful celebrations of mortal love that we will find in Shakespeare and Spenser and Donne, to name only a few? In some cases, the answer lies in a new understanding of what kind of afterlife was available for love: if the lovers themselves could not remain together for all eternity, at least their love, preserved in the poem, could have an immortal life of its own. In other cases, the answer comes from a new appreciation of the fleetingness of love as that which renders the erotic experience more precious. Rather than willingly hasten toward the end, these poets take pleasure in what precedes mortality, fully inhabiting the idea of *carpe diem*. Chapters 5 and 6, respectively, will consider the lyric expression of each of these modes. But before turning to these two groups of poems, let us first explore a dramatic work that was certainly the most positive, if also the most tragic, expression in the Elizabethan period of the idea that love is mortal: Shakespeare's *Romeo and Juliet*.

4

The Capulet Tomb

Then love-devouring death do what he dare—
It is enough I may but call her mine.

—*Romeo and Juliet* 2.5.7–8

The most famous tomb in Shakespeare's works contains his lovers from Verona, Romeo and Juliet. Romeo and Juliet's tomb is not, in fact, devoted to the young couple. It is an Italian family tomb, filled with the remains of the Capulets. Romeo and Juliet lie buried together inside the Capulet monument, but their names are not inscribed on its walls. The commemoration of Romeo and Juliet takes place elsewhere, in the golden statues erected by their fathers, which record their tragic love for all of Verona to see. Shakespeare does not supply an epitaph for Romeo and Juliet's statues, as some of his sources do, but his play makes clear what kind of epitaph there would have to be. It would not look forward to a reunion in heaven, nor would it ask for prayers for the lovers' souls. Shakespeare's epitaph for Romeo and Juliet, should it have been written, would simply petition for them to lie side by side in the earth. This would be a version of the inscriptions we found in the third section of our imaginary English church in the introduction, an inscription that declared the couple's wish to be buried together without any mention of heaven.

Why Romeo and Juliet end their lives together in a tomb is at the center of the story that Shakespeare inherited from his Italian, French, and English predecessors, who told this tale in multiple versions over the course of the sixteenth century.[1] But how Romeo and Juliet understand the fate of their love is entirely Shakespeare's invention. Here the playwright introduced a new conception of the relationship between Romeo and Juliet's love and their mortality; here he gave new shape to what might or might not await them on the other side of the grave. In Shakespeare's sources, the tragedy of Romeo and Juliet's deaths was softened by the idea, articulated by the lovers themselves, that their souls would share some form of meaningful, sentient afterlife. Shakespeare removed any such transcendent vision of posthumous love from his play. In doing so he created his most potent expression of what it meant for love to be mortal.

The sixteenth-century English exploration of the mortal boundaries of love is already familiar to us: from Wyatt's rejection of Petrarch's *in morte* poems to the Elizabethan sonnets embracing death as a desirable and irreversible exit from love, English poetry is marked by a surprisingly widespread understanding of love's inherent limits. These limits find new expressive power in Shakespeare's play, which captures both the enormous loss and the enormous gain of binding love to this world. If *Romeo and Juliet* is English literature's most celebrated depiction of tragic love, the explanation for the tragedy's success lies to no small degree in the play's refusal of a transcendent future for the lovers, in its willingness to say, along with Romeo, "Here, here, will I remain." Shakespeare did not develop this refusal of transcendence from the Continental sources for his play. Instead, as the last few chapters have shown, his attitude toward posthumous love emerged from within the English tradition. The English turn to a mortal understanding of love made possible, that is, the story that Shakespeare wanted to tell.

I. Romeo and Giulietta

Shakespeare's *Romeo and Juliet* was the latest version of a tale that had been circulating widely on the Continent since the early 1500s.[2] In all of its incarnations, it involved two young lovers from feuding families and ended with the lovers' joint suicide and subsequent burial together. The origins of the story can be traced to two different tales from Giovanni Boccaccio's *Decameron*, both of which involve the mistaken burial of live persons who are then rescued from their tombs.[3] These tales otherwise have nothing to do with the ill-fated lovers Romeo and Giulietta, nor do they include characters with these names. Boccaccio's tales of live burials were adapted, however, by Masuccio Salernitano, in his *novella* "Mariotto e Ganozza," which begins to resemble the story we know. Masuccio's tale involves two lovers from Siena who both die tragically after a mistaken report of the woman's (Ganozza's) death. This *novella* involved Mariotto's opening Ganozza's tomb secretly in the night, only to find that the friar had already removed her body.

It was in Luigi da Porto's 1530 *Istoria novellamente ritrovata di due nobili amanti* that the story assumed a shape roughly similar to the narrative of Shakespeare's play. Da Porto's novella, which preceded the more popular and influential *novella* of Matteo Bandello by some twenty years, describes two young lovers from Verona, Romeo and Giulietta, and establishes the plot of the warring families, the secret marriage, and the joint suicide. Underlying the plot of da Porto's tale—and all subsequent versions until Shakespeare's—is the hope that the love between Romeo and Giulietta is not bound by temporal constraints but is immortal. This hope of immortal love emerges in the very first private meeting of the two lovers. When da Porto's Giulietta urges Romeo to leave her bedroom before he is seen, Romeo replies:

> My lady, it is true that I could easily lose my life, and I surely shall one night, if you do not help me. But since I am as near to death everywhere else as I am here, I am striving to die as close as I can to your person, with which I yearn to live forever, should you and heaven so please.[4]

This may sound like an extravagant expression of affection rather than a genuine hope for a shared afterlife. But given the story's denouement, there are good reasons to take Romeo seriously. From its earliest articulation, the love between Romeo and Giulietta is expressed as a desire to share not only this world but also the next.

Da Porto's depiction of Romeo and Giulietta's love as a desire to be together both in heaven and on earth played a more central role in Bandello's expanded *novella* from 1554, in which the lovers' death scene is framed by mutual pledges to join each other in the afterlife. When Romeo hears from his servant Pietro of Giulietta's supposed death, he berates himself for not taking his own life immediately, imagines that her spirit is already in heaven, and grows impatient with his delay: "Marry, she goeth yonder wandering and waiteth for thee to follow her."[5] His final words to Giulietta before his poison takes full effect assure her of his intention to remain with her in the grave:

> Since it hath not pleased God that we should live together, may it please Him at the least that I abide ensepulchred with you; nay, you may rest assured that, come now what may, I will nevermore depart hence without you. (164)

Giulietta's last words address the imminent reunion of their souls, in this case without any concern for their bodies. Allowing for no delay, she expresses her urgent desire to meet her husband's spirit forthwith:

> Do I not feel that thy spirit goeth wandering hereabout and already marvelleth, nay, complaineth, that I tarry so long? Seignior mine, I see thee, I feel thee, I know thee and I know that thou awaitest no other than my coming.[6] (166)

"I see thee, I feel thee, I know thee" ("Signor mio, io ti veggio, io ti sento, io ti conosco"): already before her death, Giulietta converses with Romeo's spirit—like Petrarch conversing with Laura—and affirms their continued intimacy.

The mode of the lovers' burial further establishes their intended companionship in both the celestial and earthly spheres. The prince, Bandello relates, allows the couple to "abide ensepulchred in that same tomb" rather than moving Romeo to the tomb of the Montecchi (this is presumably what Romeo feared in declaring his determination "nevermore [to] depart hence without you"). Although Bandello does not specify the details of the burial arrangements, the lovers seem to be placed

inside a single casket or tomb, upon which an epitaph commissioned by
Romeo's father is engraved:

> Romeo believing that his lovely bride
> Was dead, his life with water did away,
> That folk call serpent-water, not a day
> After her choosing in the world to bide.
> Whenas she knew the sore chance, weeping-eyed,
> She turned her to her husband, as he lay,
> And mourned as most she might his life's decay,
> Nor spared at heaven and all the stars to chide.
> Then, when his life, alack, at end she knew,
> More dead than he, "Ah God," uneath she sighed,
> "Grant me my dearest husband to ensue,
> So where he goeth I may go abide
> With him; for this alone I seek and sue";
> And saying this, for stress of dole she died. (168)

The epitaph reaffirms Giulietta's dying words spoken over Romeo's
corpse. It also confirms the shared understanding of the tomb as a container only for the lovers' bodies, not for their souls.

The idea that the couple's joint epitaph would declare their hope to
transcend the tomb in a heavenly reunion has little foundation in Italian burial practice during the fifteenth and sixteenth centuries. Unlike
their English counterparts, Italian funerary inscriptions rarely refer
to expectations for the afterlife, and even less often speak of heavenly
expectations that spouses might share. Spousal tombs were much less
common in Renaissance Italy than in England; the majority of Italian
couples were not buried in shared tombs, or even in the same church,
graveyard, or city. Unlike in England, where marital bonds seem to
have been privileged above all other ties in determining where (or with
whom) to be buried, the Italian priority seems to have been proximity
to the natal, not conjugal, family. As Stanley Chojnacki has shown in
his study of Renaissance Venice, the relationship between the strength
of marital bonds and the desire for joint burial was surprisingly thin.

Among other examples, Chojnacki summarizes the wills of the couple Valerio Zeno and Vittoria Vitturi, which follow a typical pattern. Valerio and Vittoria leave almost all of their property to each other, and their wills convey their mutual affection in multiple ways. When it comes to their burial, however, each expresses the desire to be buried with his or her family of origin: Valerio requests burial "in our [family] tomb of Ca'Zeno," and Vittoria asks to be buried "in the tomb where my father, *dominus* Andrea [Vitturi], and my mother are buried."[7]

Epitaphs from churches in Renaissance Rome reflect the same pattern. It is very rare to find shared inscriptions for married couples among the roughly seventeen thousand epitaphs recorded by the nineteenth-century antiquarian Vincenzo Forcella, although it is common to find expressions of great sorrow for the loss of the deceased spouse.[8] The overwhelming impression that these volumes convey is of spousal isolation in death. Husbands and wives mourn each other; they testify to the other's good character; they affirm the joys of the years they have shared. But they do not declare a desire to lie with each other in the ground, nor do they affirm the hope of meeting again in the next world. The inscriptions we do find for shared tombs are almost exclusively for blood relatives, not married couples. Paolo Cortesi is buried under a single stone with his sister Lisandra; Lazaro Archangelo, his brother Iacobo, and their kinsman Nicolao are commemorated on a single stone erected by Lazaro's wife, Faustina Paluzella; Augustina Stella, a married woman, and her umarried sister Adriana are buried together by their mother; and the list goes on and on (1.157; 5.47, 53).

When Bandello and da Porto describe, then, the joint burial of Romeo and Giulietta, they describe an arrangement that was far from ordinary within Italian Renaissance culture. In da Porto's story, in fact, Romeo begs the Friar to keep his and Giulietta's death secret "so that our bodies may remain together for ever in this tomb"; the assumption, of course, is that should their deaths become known, their corpses would be separated from each other, with Romeo's returned to his family and Giulietta's remaining in her family vault. The joint burial of Romeo and Giulietta represents the ultimate triumph of the couple against the natal family. Loyalty to family is trumped by loyalty to spouse not only in the choice of husband or wife, as readers and audiences have long under-stood. It is also trumped in the choice of burial site.

Before the story of Romeo and Giulietta reached Shakespeare's hands, it underwent several modest reworkings, first by the French author Pierre Boaistuau and then by two English authors, Arthur Brooke and William Painter, who worked directly from Boaistuau's French text. Al-though Shakespeare almost certainly knew both of the English versions, Brooke's 1562 *The Tragicall Historye of Romeus and Juliet* is widely believed to have been his primary source. Brooke's poem, a faithful translation of Boaistuau, is not significantly different from Bandello's novella, but it introduces a more explicitly Christian emphasis to the lovers' expec-tations for the afterlife and intensifies the transcendent nature of their love. When Romeus comes to the tomb and discovers Juliet, whom he believes already to be dead, his first instinct is to pray to Christ for for-giveness:

> Lord Christ, that so to raunsome me descendedst long agoe
> Out of thy fathers bosome, and in the virgins wombe
> Didst put on fleshe, O let my plaint out of this hollow toombe,
> Perce through the ayre, and graunt my sute may favour finde;
> Take pity on my sinnefull and my poore afflicted mynde.
> For well enough I know, this body is but clay,
> Nought but a masse of sinne, to frayle, and subject to decay.[9]

Rehearsing the traditional language of Christian metaphysics, Romeus dispenses altogether with his flesh, which he relegates to the earth, while he petitions God to pardon his "poore afflicted mynde."

Brooke's Juliet similarly divides the fate of her body from the fate of her soul as she addresses the dagger before her:

> Feare not to darte me nowe, thy stripe no longer stay,
> Prolong no longer now my lyfe, I hate this long delaye,
> For straight my parting sprite, out of this carkas fled,
> At ease shall finde my Romeus sprite, among so many dead. (2775–78)

Once again, the body is dismissed as a worthless "carkas," whereas the soul is a source of concern. Or rather, in Juliet's case, the soul is not so much a source of concern as it is a source of comfort. Unlike Romeus, who petitions Christ for his salvation, Juliet asserts with seeming confidence that her soul will ascend to heaven, where she anticipates she will "[at] ease . . . finde my Romeus sprite."

The very last words that Brooke's Juliet utters make absolutely clear that she understands herself to be exchanging a lesser world for a greater one, that she is gaining more than she has lost. Having just declared her intention to find Romeus in heaven, she explains her expectations for what will await them: "That so our parted sprites, from light that we see here / In place of endlesse light and blisse, may ever live yfere" (2787–88). The compromised pleasures of earth are replaced with "endlesse light and blisse"; the separations that the lovers have endured are erased by an eternity of life "yfere," an archaic English word for "together." In their affirmation of a shared posthumous life, these lines not only shift our focus from one world to the next. They also diminish the force of the tragedy. The love between Romeus and Juliet has not expired; it has merely moved to another sphere.

The version of the story written closest to the date of Shakespeare's play is also the only other surviving dramatic version: Luigi Groto's 1578 Italian tragedy La Hadriana. The names of the characters and some details of the plot have been changed (the Romeo and Juliet figures, for example, expend a great deal of energy worrying about how their two mothers will react to their deaths), but Groto's play shares with its predecessors a depiction of the lovers' bond as eternal. Early in the play, in act 2, Latino (Romeo) affirms his intention to love Hadriana (Juliet) not only in this life but also, if possible, posthumously: "And if after death one can still love / Then after death I swear to love you too."[10] This uncertainty about the continuity of love after death disappears as the play evolves. In the death scene in act 5, Latino holds what he believes to be the corpse of Hadriana in his arms and declares that his corpse will accompany hers to heaven. When she awakens and they exchange their final words before dying, he laments: "How very little we have been able to enjoy each other on this earth," to which Hadriana replies: "We will enjoy each other for all eternity in the next world." Her last words echo those of Bandello's Giulietta: "Aspettatemi, Sposo, ch'io vi seguo" (Wait for me, husband, so that I may follow you).

II. Violent Delights

When Shakespeare came to write *Romeo and Juliet*, he inherited a story in which love had no mortal limits. As we have seen, the Italian sources and their subsequent iterations in France and England all maintained the idea that love could transcend the grave, positing a strict division between the lovers' mortal remains, which would rest together in the ground, and their souls, which would be joined in heaven. In Shakespeare's play, this interest in the lovers' spiritual afterlife finds no place whatsoever. Instead, he gives us a relentlessly materialist view of both love and death.

It has long been observed that love and death are inseparable in *Romeo and Juliet*.[11] From the opening description of the chorus, which announces that "[a] pair of star-crossed lovers take their life" and declares their love "death-marked," the play concentrates our attention on the tragic destiny of the protagonists.[12] It has also been noted that love in *Romeo and Juliet* is not so much compromised as conditioned by the shadow of mortality—in Julia Kristeva's terms, the play shows how "erotic expenditure is a race towards death."[13] But what has not been adequately explored is how Romeo and Juliet understand the future of their love after death and, more specifically, how little either of the lovers imagines anything like the heavenly transcendence that awaits their counterparts in Shakespeare's sources. What emerges between Shakespeare's Romeo and Juliet is a distinctly mortal conception of love governed by two central premises: first, that love is fleeting, brief, and restricted to this world; and second, that this temporal restriction intensifies the nature of erotic experience, and renders it more precious. This is an important modification of the Italian sources: it moves the story from the sentimental toward the tragic.[14] The tragedy of *Romeo and Juliet* is built to no small degree upon thwarting the desire to sustain posthumous intimacy. As a result, the play's orientation becomes overwhelmingly focused on the present: it is neither forward- nor backward-looking in its erotic energy.

It is Romeo who first articulates the link between love and death in this play. As he awaits Juliet before their clandestine marriage, he responds to the Friar's supplication—"So smile the heavens upon this holy act / That after-hours with sorrow chide us not" (2.5.1–2)—with an outright dismissal of the Friar's concern:

> Amen. Amen. But come what sorrow can,
> It cannot countervail the exchange of joy
> That one short minute gives me in her sight.
> Do thou but close our hands with holy words
> Then love-devouring death do what he dare—
> It is enough I may but call her mine. (2.5.3–8)

What begins as a seemingly conventional expression of enthusiasm for his impending nuptials quickly becomes an unexpected defiance of death. This defiance is in fact rather more like an invitation to death: an expression at once of anticipated satisfaction with the present, here reduced to "one short minute," and a willingness to forgo any future pleasures.

Romeo's words are sometimes compared to those of Othello, who declares upon his reunion with Desdemona in Cyprus:

> If it were now to die
> 'Twere now to be most happy, for I fear
> My soul hath her content so absolute
> That not another comfort like to this
> Succeeds in unknown fate. (2.1.186–90)

But in several respects the two speeches are importantly different. First, Romeo does not articulate anything like the fear that Othello articulates—he is not warding off future anxieties, nor is he declaring himself at the limit of something that he can accommodate no further. He is merely stating that "one short minute" of joy is enough to counter either sorrow or death, that the joy of this present moment is itself profoundly satisfying.

Second, the phrase Romeo uses to describe death—"love-devouring"—supposes a very different relationship between love and death from what Othello seems to have in mind. Romeo does not strive to sustain love through death, which is how we might characterize Othello's perverse hope in murdering Desdemona: "Be thus when thou art dead, and I will kill thee / And love thee after" (5.2.21–22). Here the wish is that death will return Desdemona to her original purity and hence render her lovable once again; the "monumental alabaster" of her skin that Othello wants to keep intact is the equivalent of the marble effigy that will grace her tomb, preserving her beauty for his posthumous adoration. For Romeo, by contrast, "love-devouring death" means that there will be no more love after death. By describing death in this manner, he overturns the very premise of the Petrarchan tradition that underlies the sources for Shakespeare's play. In place of the idea that the bond between Romeo and Giulietta might transcend the mortal world, Shakespeare gives us a clear, irreversible ending for love. In *Romeo and Juliet*, death is not something that love can overcome. It is what kills love, or brings it to closure.

The threat that Romeo's words pose to the longevity of his love is immediately grasped by the Friar, whose response assumes that Romeo will want his love to endure for as long as possible:

> These violent delights have violent ends,
> And in their triumph die like fire and powder,
> Which as they kiss consume. The sweetest honey
> Is loathsome in his own deliciousness,
> And in the taste confounds the appetite.
> Therefore love moderately. Long love doth so.
> Too swift arrives as tardy as too slow. (2.5.9–15)

This warning falls on deaf ears, of course, as there has been nothing in the play to suggest that Romeo wants to "love moderately." On the contrary, the relationship that the Friar fears between "violent delights" and "violent ends" is one that Romeo seems to embrace. The consummation of a passionate love, "like fire and powder," will be a magnificent and short-lived combustion.

One conclusion we might draw from this exchange is that Romeo actively seeks death as a way out of love—that, like many of the Elizabethan sonneteers we encountered in the last chapter, he is motivated by a death-drive. This sense of Romeo as a melancholic lover resonates with Montague's description of Romeo in the very first scene of the play. "Away from light steals home my heavy son," he complains to Benvolio, "And private in his chamber pens himself, / Shuts up his windows, locks fair daylight out / And makes himself an artificial night" (1.1.130–33). The melancholy that Romeo experiences in his unrequited love for Rosaline, however, does not carry over to his entirely reciprocated love for Juliet. In his exchange with the Friar, it seems less productive to say that Romeo is driven by a desire for death than to imagine that his love for Juliet carries with it the recognition of that love's inevitable ending. Romeo recognizes, that is, the shape or arc of their love—its beginning and its end—from the very start. And in this respect he is matched, or even outdone, by Juliet. Although it is Romeo who is identified early in the play as having melancholic leanings, whereas Juliet has no prior history of lovesickness, it is nonetheless Juliet who relentlessly pairs death and love together and who almost always conceives of their love in terms of its eventual rupture.

From the minute Romeo and Juliet meet, Juliet connects her sudden passion, or "violent delight," to her death. Even before learning Romeo's name, she remarks to the Nurse at the ball: "If he be married / My grave is like to be my wedding bed" (1.5.131–32). This is the first of several links that Juliet makes between her grave and her wedding bed—it replaces, in fact, the far more common metaphorical link in the early modern period between graves and wombs (which Romeo himself will make in act 5). The particular sentiment that Juliet expresses at this early moment is more conventional, however, than what she gives voice to thereafter. At the ball, she measures the strength of her feelings in terms of her inability to live without Romeo. The grave would become the repository of her feelings if she were *not* able to marry him, so that death represents the alternative to fulfilling her love.

This conception of the grave as the site where Juliet will find herself should Romeo be unavailable quickly shifts to her conception of the grave as the very destiny of their reciprocated passion. When she believes Romeo to have been killed in the brawl with Tybalt, she exclaims in despair:

> O break, my heart, poor bankrupt, break at once!
> To prison, eyes; ne'er look on liberty.
> Vile earth, to earth resign; end motion here,
> And thou and Romeo press one heavy bier! (3.2.57–60)

After commanding the different parts of her body to desist or cease to be—she wants her heart to break, her eyes to stop seeing, her flesh to begin the process of decomposing, her whole person to stop its "motion"—Juliet can imaginatively assume the position to which she aspires: that of a prostrate corpse. Her mind turns specifically on the shared funerary litter that she and Romeo will occupy, the marital bed that will carry their remains to the grave. Upon thinking that Romeo is dead, in other words, Juliet does not respond by praying that their souls may quickly be reunited in heaven; she never mentions their souls at all. Instead, she prays for an "end" to her vitality in order to join her husband on a single "heavy bier."

When Juliet prepares the next morning to part from Romeo, her imagination similarly turns toward the grave. When she asks whether they are likely to meet again, he replies with uncharacteristically hopeful reassurance: "I doubt it not, and all these woes shall serve / For sweet discourses in our times to come" (3.5.52–53). Juliet's response, however, is in an altogether different key: "O God, I have an ill-divining soul! / Methinks I see thee, now thou art so low / As one dead in the bottom of a tomb" (3.5.54–56). What is striking here is less the pessimism itself than the form that her pessimism takes. Juliet does not fear that Romeo will soon be dead in an abstract sense. Rather, she sees him as a corpse: he is "low" in the ground, at the "bottom" of a plummeting grave.

Hence Juliet's reaction later in this scene to her mother's plan to have Romeo murdered is not necessarily so duplicitous as it might seem. Lady Capulet declares:

> . . . I'll send to one in Mantua
> Where that same banished runagate doth live,
> Shall give him such an unaccustomed dram
> That he shall soon keep Tybalt company;
> And then I hope thou will be satisfied. (3.5.88–92)

To this plan of poisoning Romeo with an "unaccustomed dram"—foreshadowing, of course, Romeo's means of suicide—Juliet answers:

> Indeed, I shall never be satisfied
> With Romeo till I behold him, dead,
> Is my poor heart so for a kinsman vexed. (3.5.93–95)

Juliet's declared wish to "behold him, dead" serves a perfect casuistical turn. To her mother, she seems to wish Romeo killed, and "dead" therefore modifies "him." Inwardly, however, she enjambs, so that "dead" begins the next clause and describes not Romeo but her heart: "Dead / Is my poor heart so for a kinsman vexed." This is in fact how the line is printed in both the Folio and three of the four Quartos, with a period following "him." It was not until the eighteenth century that em dashes or commas were put on either side of "dead," rendering ambiguous what is actually being modified.

It is clear why Juliet would imagine her heart to be dead, and this requires no further glossing (although it is worth noting that Romeo has in effect become her "kin," since at this moment she is clearly mourning not Tybalt's death but the absence of her husband). But it is not so clear that the alternative reading—that she wishes Romeo dead—is meant solely for her mother, and therefore that there is so decisive a divide between what she intends Lady Capulet to understand and what some part of herself wants as well. If we read the line with an end stop—"I shall never be satisfied / With Romeo till I behold him, dead."—we are in fact eerily close to what Juliet has told Romeo that she feared a mere forty lines earlier. In that conversation, her "ill-divining soul" envisions him "dead in the bottom of a tomb." Now, the fear is expressed as wish.

The distinction between what Juliet pretends to want and what she in fact desires becomes even more blurred in her final petition to her mother:

> Madam, if you could find out but a man
> To bear a poison, I would temper it
> That Romeo should, upon receipt thereof,
> Soon sleep in quiet. (3.5.96–99)

Once again, the hope that Romeo should "sleep in quiet" is not only the wordplay that critics often assume it to be—namely, that Juliet seems to reassure her mother that they want the same result, when she really means to say that she will "temper" or soften the mixture so that it produces sweet sleep, ideally with herself on Romeo's bosom. The problem with this explanation is that Lady Capulet's bloodthirsty call for murder is not adequately answered by Juliet's call for restful sleep. The peaceful rest Juliet calls for, in other words, is not the vengeful "satisfaction" that would match her mother's sense of the crime. Juliet's desire that Romeo might "soon sleep in quiet" seems instead to originate from another place within her, a place altogether free of the double-entendres with which she tricks her mother, and it serves an altogether different purpose. Like Horatio's parting words to Hamlet—"Good night sweet prince, and flights of angels sing thee to thy rest"—Juliet's wish for Romeo comes out of the language of consolation given to the dying.[15] It is a benediction, not a curse.

Juliet's prayer that Romeo might "sleep in quiet" would for Shakespeare's audiences have conjured up ideas of the "good death" rehearsed in devotional tracts and sermons, which regularly described the posthumous life of the dead as comfortably at rest; these descriptions echoed as well across churchyards on spousal epitaphs. The phrase also may have had a more sinister echo for Shakespeare's literary contemporaries. An invitation to "sleep in quiet" is the bait that Edmund Spenser's figure of Despaire dangles before the Red Crosse Knight in book 1 of *The Faerie Queene*, published in 1590 (seven years before the first Quarto of *Romeo and Juliet*):

He there does now enioy eternall rest
And happie ease, which thou doest want and craue,
  And further from it daily wanderest:
What if some litle paine the passage haue,
That makes fraile flesh to feare the bitter waue?
Is not short paine well borne, that brings long ease,
And layes the soule to sleepe in quiet graue?[16]

Despaire offers this "sleepe in quiet graue" as the reward for suicide, urging Red Crosse to take his own life, in violation of Christian doctrine. Despaire's promise of "eternall rest," "happie ease," and "sleepe in quiet graue" closely resembles, however, the way both Juliet and Romeo envision the experience of being dead: as a liberation from the mortal world without any sense of another world awaiting them.

These resonances between Despaire's seduction to suicide and Juliet's wish for Romeo help to bring out what may lie behind her words to her mother, something that Romeo has perhaps already intuited earlier in the scene. "Come, death, and welcome," he remarks, "Juliet wills it so" (3.5.24). On the surface of things, this is meant to provoke her acknowledgment that it is morning and he indeed must leave. But it is also potentially a deeper perception about Juliet's will. This is not to suggest that Juliet imagines a life for herself after Romeo, as his widow. It is to suggest that the future she is most capable of imagining is one in which both she and Romeo are dead. Kristeva has argued "that Juliet's jouissance is often stated through the anticipation—the desire?—of Romeo's death," and she connects this to the "intrinsic presence of hatred in amatory feeling" (221). I would propose that Juliet's feelings for Romeo are tied up with the relationship not between love and hatred but between love and death. "Violent delights" and "violent ends" are for Juliet, as for Romeo, inextricably mingled.

Juliet's mingling of delights and ends is perhaps most fully visible in her rhapsodic invocation to night, earlier in act 3, as she awaits Romeo's arrival to consummate their marriage. Even at this moment of ecstatic anticipation, her imagination focuses centrally on their deaths. The soliloquy that begins with her coaxing appeal for the day to hurry itself

along, so that night—and with night, Romeo—might join her, turns un-
expectedly to her hopes for their posthumous state:

> Come, gentle night; come, loving, black-browed night,
> Give me my Romeo, and when I shall die
> Take him and cut him out in little stars,
> And he will make the face of heaven so fine
> That all the world will be in love with night
> And pay no worship to the garish sun. (3.2.20–25)

Critical attention to these lines has focused on their obvious sexual resonances, grounded in Juliet's use of the verb *to die*, a common expression
for experiencing orgasm. In this respect, Juliet's desire for her own or-
gasmic experience to be matched by Romeo's scattering himself through
the cosmos becomes an instance of her sexual generosity. "It seems no
paradox," Edward Snow declares, "that the desire for Romeo she expresses in her apostrophe to night should culminate in an image that
sublimates an experience of orgasm"; in a footnote, he explains further
that "she identifies what she experiences at the moment of sexual cli-
max as *his* transformation, and hence posits at the extreme limit of privacy ('when I shall die') a paradoxical sharing of experience."[17]

But Snow's quick translation of Juliet's fantasy of a celestial afterlife
into a sexual experience and his unwillingness to read "die" as anything
other than a metaphor for orgasm blind him to the peculiar turn her
imagination takes. For Juliet, the first night of their marriage is already,
in effect, the last: the epithalamion is already the *Liebestod*. There is no
imagining anything other than what Romeo described in the preceding
scene as the pleasure of "one short minute" of joy, as Juliet moves in-
stantly, within a single line, from "Give me my Romeo" to "when I shall
die." The orgasm, in other words, not only is an alternative meaning for
dying but is identical to it. Death becomes the full, explosive experience
of love.

If we recall the emphasis in Shakespeare's sources on the shared
afterlife that the lovers anticipate for their souls, Juliet's account of
what will happen to Romeo after her death becomes all the more strik-

ing. Rather than imagining a spiritual reunion between them in heaven, she envisions a cosmos scattered with little Romeos, a collection of stars to be admired by all, and not a single, intact creature whom she alone would enjoy. We could regard this, too, as a symptom of her bounteous generosity—she wants to share Romeo with the entire world—or we could see it, as Kristeva does, as a symptom of her "unconscious desire to break up Romeo's body."[18] But it seems more tellingly to be a symptom of her materialist, and mortal, sensibility, her inclination toward redistribution rather than resurrection as the body's posthumous fate. Romeo's transcendence to the position of stars may be a form of apotheosis, but it is an apotheosis that is exclusively physical.

III. Worms, Cords

The materialism that Juliet manifests in her invocation to night does not belong to her alone: it is deeply embedded in the play. None of the characters in *Romeo and Juliet* offers a compelling account of Christian or Neoplatonic metaphysics to counter the lovers' resistance to the idea of a spiritual afterlife. On the contrary: any gestures toward such explanations are immediately rejected or compromised, so that the play leaves us with nothing but the mortal world as its sphere of reference. *Romeo and Juliet* is one of Shakespeare's strongest expressions of monism rather than dualism; it affords no role for the soul whatever.

The first example of this strain of materialism comes from Mercutio, whose "Queen Mab" speech early in the play includes one of the only explicit mentions of atoms in Shakespeare's works. Describing the "fairies' midwife" who "gallops night by night / Through lovers' brains" to produce dreams of love, Mercutio declares that this tiny creature travels in a chariot "drawn with a team of little atomi" (1.4.55; 71–72; 58). It is not, however, Mercutio's elaborate explanation for the mechanics of dreams but his curt account of his death that warrants our attention. After receiving a mortal wound in his battle with Tybalt, Mercutio explodes with rage to Romeo: "A plague o' both your houses. They have made worms' meat of me" (3.1.101–2). This entirely unsentimental assessment of his posthumous fate, anticipating Hamlet's account of Polonius's whereabouts ("Not where he eats, but where a is eaten. A certain convocation of politic worms are e'en at him") is by no means reversed or even tempered by Benvolio's attempt to impose a conventional Christian explanation upon his friend's death.[19] "O Romeo, Romeo, brave Mercutio is dead!" Benvolio declares. "That gallant spirit hath aspired the clouds" (3.1.111–12). As they have just witnessed Mercutio's pointless murder in an unheroic brawl, Benvolio's claim for both gallantry and heavenly aspiration rings hollow, and fails altogether to console Romeo.

A similar tension between materialism and metaphysics governs the exchange between Romeo and his servant Balthasar, when Balthasar returns to Mantua with news of Juliet's supposed death. In response to Romeo's question "How doth my Juliet?" Balthasar replies: "Her body sleeps in Capels' monument / And her immortal part with angels lives" (5.1.18–19). This division of Juliet into mortal body and immortal soul functions entirely as euphemism, a formulaic attempt to soften the blow of the news he is delivering. Romeo is not comforted by Balthasar's words, nor does Balthasar seem to imagine he would be; there is no further Christian wisdom offered in the scene, which turns immediately to Romeo's plans to join Juliet in the Capulet tomb. Moreover, given that neither Romeo nor Juliet nor any of their survivors mentions that the souls of the lovers are in heaven, Balthasar's explanation that Juliet's "immortal part with angels lives" seems to issue from an ontological universe completely foreign to the play.

Even the Friar, the play's one representative of the church, is denied the opportunity to offer the pastoral comfort of Christian dualism to the lovers' families following Romeo and Juliet's deaths. Or rather, the occasion on which he offers such consolation is a fraudulent one. During the funeral he stages for Juliet while she lies fast asleep from the effect of his potion, he reassures her family that her soul has ascended to heavenly bliss:

> Your part in her you could not keep from death,
> But heaven keeps his part in eternal life.
> The most you sought was her promotion,
> For 'twas your heaven she should be advanced,
> And weep ye now, seeing she is advanced
> Above the clouds as high as heaven itself? (4.4.96–101)

The Friar, who not only is aware that Juliet still lives but is responsible for arranging her feigned death, gives this theological explanation with a wink to the audience, and presumably with a casuistic exemption for himself. We are not for a moment meant to take his words seriously, and this complicity on our part cannot help but render the words suspect. By rehearsing the Christian justification of death as an "advancement" of the soul at this point in the play—and not at the end of act 5, when Juliet is in fact dead—Shakespeare ironizes the idea of spiritual transcendence.

Perhaps the strongest example of Shakespeare's resistance to spiritual transcendence comes in his treatment of the Platonic idea of the ladder of love. As we have already seen in chapter 2, the ladder of love was the metaphor derived from the *Symposium* and used by Ficino and fellow Neoplatonists in the fifteenth century to explain the way in which love of a human being not only was compatible with love of the divine but was itself the vehicle to lead from one sphere to the next. English poets were less taken with this model of the mechanics of love than were many of their Italian counterparts. But the idea that one might begin by loving someone's physical beauty and then ascend to love of spiritual beauty was certainly familiar to Elizabethan authors; if they did not read the Italian sources directly, they were exposed to these ideas in the 1561 English translation of Baldessar Castiglione's *Il cortigiano*, whose fourth book spells out this Neoplatonic philosophy very clearly.[20]

Shakespeare completely eschews this explanation for love in *Romeo and Juliet*, and he does so quite explicitly by transforming the ladder from something metaphorical to something real. What transports Romeo from the ground to Juliet's bedroom is an actual ladder made of cords, and this ladder is described in terms that are meaningfully nonplatonic. "Within this hour my man shall be with thee," Romeo tells the Nurse,

> And bring thee cords made like a tackled stair,
> Which to the high topgallant of my joy
> Must be my convoy in the secret night. (2.3.169–72)

"[C]ords made like a tackled stair" describes the heavy ropes of a ship's ladder, weighed down by the sailor's foot as he climbs up the mast; the "topgallant of my joy" similarly invokes the highest point on the mast from which the sail was flown. What Romeo describes is simultaneously the acme of his joy and the relatively modest height that it represents: he is not soaring through the heavens but climbing a delimited, earthly distance. The ladder of love becomes a physical means to a physical end. It does not transport the lovers to a celestial sphere but brings them together to consummate their love.

It is no coincidence that the task of obtaining such a ladder passes from Romeo to the Nurse, whose understanding of love is shown throughout the play to be emphatically corporeal. After reporting to Juliet the plans Romeo has made for their clandestine marriage, the Nurse declares:

> Hie you to church. I must another way,
> To fetch a ladder by the which your love
> Must climb a bird's nest soon, when it is dark.
> I am the drudge, and toil in your delight,
> But you shall bear the burden soon at night. (2.4.71–75)

This clear opposition between the path that leads to church and the path that leads to the ladder is reinforced in the clean break of the line, "Hie you to church. I must another way." The Nurse's description, moreover, of both the labor involved in obtaining the ladder ("[I] toil in your delight") and the labor that the ladder will make possible (Juliet's "burden") pointedly lacks any transcendent veneer. The ladder is stripped of any higher metaphysical purpose: it is simply the stepping-stone to Juliet's "nest" of sexual pleasure.

It is not only the Nurse but also Juliet who regards the ladder of cords as an integral part of realizing her love. The Nurse, in other words, is not represented in this case as having a vulgar conception of love in order to serve as a foil to Juliet's more elevated position. On the contrary, Shakespeare makes no distinction here between the attitudes of the two women. When the Nurse returns to Juliet's chamber, she enters with the ladder in her hands, and Juliet comments on its presence immediately: "Now Nurse, what news? What, hast thou there / The cords that Romeo bid thee fetch?" (3.2.33–34). "Ay, ay," the Nurse responds, "the cords." Given that Juliet's next question assumes the Nurse has suddenly two free hands—"why dost thou wring thy hands?"—most editors include a stage direction here, "Throws the cords down," or "putting down the cords," indicating that the cords now lie in a heap on the ground as a symptom of their new purposelessness.[21] The cords also quite conspicuously become a phallic substitution, erected when Romeo is meant to arrive, slack in his absence.

Having learned of Romeo's banishment, Juliet bemoans her new peculiar status as "maiden-widowèd" and instructs the Nurse to take away the cords that would have brought her husband to consummate their marriage.[22] In an act of projected (and misplaced) sympathy, she next turns to address the cords themselves, which she imagines to be suffering from their own tragic fate:

> Take up those cords. Poor ropes, you are beguiled,
> Both you and I, for Romeo is exiled.
> He made you for a highway to my bed,
> But I, a maid, die maiden-widowèd.
> Come, cords; come, Nurse; I'll to my wedding bed,
> And death, not Romeo, take my maidenhead! (3.2.132–37)

Both she and the cords are "beguiled" from their intended purpose; both are unused, wasted objects. In calling to the cords again, in conjuring them back up from their discarded place on the ground—"Come, cords; come Nurse; I'll to my wedding bed"—Juliet intimates as well another use for the "tackled stair" that would have transported Romeo to her.[23] This time the cords would bring death, not love, to her chamber. The potential use of the cords as a vehicle for suicide is by no means explicit, but the suggestion is certainly there, and it conveys the demotion of the cords from a means of ascent to one that leads underground.

The cords are not mentioned again in the play, although Romeo does both "ascend to [Juliet's] chamber," as the nurse had instructed him to do, and later descend when morning comes; stage directions typically indicate the use of the ladder for both (3.4.145–46; 3.5.42). The motions, in other words, of not only ascending but also descending the ladder are accomplished, so that Romeo is returned finally to the earth, and the ladder, like other props no longer needed, vanishes from the stage. There is no possibility in the play of any further climbing upward, either literal or metaphorical; the direction of love at this point turns decisively downward. The love between Romeo and Juliet is not meant to climb to the heavens in the manner of Petrarch ascending to Laura or Dante to Beatrice. It is distinctly bound to the earth.

IV. The Capulet Tomb

We have already seen that Juliet's imagination inclines not only toward death but specifically toward the grave. This inclination becomes more pronounced as the pressure of the play intensifies, so that it is she, and not the Friar, who introduces the idea of hiding from her family inside an actual tomb. In response to the Friar's general offer to "give thee remedy" to escape from the proposed marriage to Paris, Juliet releases the full force of her dark imaginings:

> O, bid me leap, rather than marry Paris,
> From off the battlements of any tower,
> Or walk in thievish ways, or bid me lurk
> Where serpents are. Chain me with roaring bears,
> Or hide me nightly in a charnel house,
> O'ercovered quite with dead men's rattling bones,
> With reeky shanks and yellow chapless skulls;
> Or bid me go into a new-made grave
> And hide me with a dead man in his tomb—
> Things that, to hear them told, have made me tremble—
> And I will do it without fear or doubt,
> To live an unstained wife to my sweet love. (4.1.77–88)

To communicate the full extent of her dread, Juliet moves through a series of comparisons—she would prefer to leap from a high tower, or walk through a den of thieves, or be surrounded by serpents, or be chained up alongside vicious bears. These random or unrelated evocations of danger then crystallize around a single nightmare: to be hidden with the remains of the dead.

Before she will marry Paris, Juliet declares her willingness to lie in a charnel house, with "reeky shanks and yellow chapless skulls" for her companions, the smells and colors of the deceased oddly present to her mind. Or, she continues, she would rather lie in a "new-made grave" with a fresh corpse, a possibility whose horrors she cannot bear even to describe. Only at this point does the Friar introduce the idea of giving Juliet a poison to render her "stiff and stark and cold," a "borrowed likeness of shrunk death," and then bury her alive in "that same ancient vault / Where all the kindred of the Capulets lie" (4.1.103, 104, 111–12). In Bandello's tale, Giulietta asks Fra Lorenzo to dress her like a boy so that she can escape Mantua; when he refuses, she simply requests poison to end her life rather than "break my wifely faith to Romeo." Shakespeare, by contrast, represents the plan for live burial as Juliet's: she plants the idea in the Friar's head.

Juliet's imagination now returns to what it had earlier resisted— "things that, to hear them told, have made me tremble." Before taking the potion the Friar has prepared, she gives free rein to a macabre vision of what might await her:

How if, when I am laid into the tomb,
I wake before the time that Romeo
Come to redeem me? There's a fearful point.
Shall I now then be stifled in the vault,
To whose foul mouth no healthsome air breathes in,
And there die strangled ere my Romeo comes?
Or, if I live, is it not very like
The horrible conceit of death and night,
Together with the terror of the place—
As in a vault, an ancient receptacle
Where for this many hundred years the bones
Of all my buried ancestors are packed;
Where bloody Tybalt, yet but green in earth,
Lies fest'ring in his shroud; where, as they say,
At some hours in the night spirits resort—

Alack, alack, is it not like that I,
So early waking—what with loathsome smells,
And shrieks like mandrakes torn out of the earth,
That living mortals hearing them run mad—
Or, if I wake, shall I not be distraught,
Environed with all these hideous fears,
And madly play with my forefathers' joints,
And pluck the mangled Tybalt from his shroud,
And, in this rage, with some great kinsman's bone
As with a club dash out my desp'rate brains?
O, look! Methinks I see my cousin's ghost
Seeking out Romeo that did spit his body
Upon a rapier's point. Stay, Tybalt, stay!
Romeo, Romeo, Romeo! Here's drink. I drink to thee. (4.3.29–57)

The initial fear of death through suffocation quickly shifts to an even worse fear of living among the dead. The old dead, her Capulet ancestors who have been buried for hundreds of years; the new dead, her cousin Tybalt, who still lies bloody in his shroud: this is the company she will keep. Like Eurydice, Juliet enters an underworld from which only her husband can retrieve her. And yet, unlike Eurydice, she is not actually dead, but this is in effect the only death from which Romeo can rescue her: a half-death, or fake death, without real metaphysical consequences. (The idea that Juliet is in fact semidead inside the Capulet monument is reinforced by the Friar's description of her as a "poor living corpse, closed in a dead man's tomb!" [5.2.29].)

From the static tableau of rotting flesh and bones that Juliet initially conjures up, she moves in the next phase of her imaginings to animate the scene, anticipating her own horrific interactions with the corpses' remains. The consequence of living with the dead, in Juliet's mind, is nothing short of complete madness: she will "madly play" with the bones of her ancestors; she will violate Tybalt's corpse; she will "dash out [her] desp'rate brains." In her morbid fantasies Juliet breaks one of the most ancient commandments, repeated on tombs throughout the ancient world: *ossa tibi bene quiescant*, may your bones rest well.[24] She also breaks, of course, the Christian prohibition of self-slaughter.

At more or less the same time that Juliet envisions being alive in a tomb, Romeo dreams of being dead. But unlike Juliet's nightmarish imaginings, which end with her using the remains of her kinsman to shatter her skull, Romeo's dream ends with his miraculous revival:

> If I may trust the flattering truth of sleep,
> My dreams presage some joyful news at hand.
> My bosom's lord sits lightly in his throne,
> And all this day an unaccustomed spirit
> Lifts me above the ground with cheerful thoughts.
> I dreamt my lady came and found me dead—
> Strange dream, that gives a dead man leave to think!—
> And breathed such life with kisses in my lips
> That I revived and was an emperor. (5.1.1-9)

The irony of these lines in relation to the play's tragic conclusion— Romeo's horribly mistaken sense of hopefulness as he anticipates "joyful news"; the transformation of the kiss of life to a kiss of death, as Juliet does not revive him but seeks poison from his lips; his imagining himself an emperor and not a lifeless corpse—has been noted before.[25] But there is one further irony, or poignancy, which returns us to Juliet's staging of her own mini-death in the tomb. The resurrection Romeo envisions is as fleeting as the dream from which he has already awakened, a vision of revival within this world, and not in the next. This is the only type of rebirth made available to either of the lovers, and its rewards are not eternal, but temporary. There is no expectation of real redemption, only the illusion of such metaphysical phenomena within the all too physical world.

Once Romeo learns of Juliet's death, all fantasies of extending this mortal life fall away, and his only concern is with entering—and remaining within—the Capulet tomb. If the central prop of act 3 is the ladder of cords that transports Romeo up to Juliet's chamber, the central prop of act 5 is the "wrenching iron" that Romeo uses to pry the monument open.[26] The bedroom and the tomb are the two homes that the couple inhabits, the two places where they lie together. Like Juliet's bedroom, the tomb belongs to the Capulet family, but it is transformed into a marital dwelling.

When Romeo arrives at the monument, he addresses it as if confronting a living foe:

> Thou detestable maw, thou womb of death,
> Gorged with the dearest morsel of the earth,
> Thus I enforce thy rotten jaws to open,
> And in despite I'll cram thee with more food. (5.3.45–48)

No longer a passive receptacle, the tomb becomes an active and monstrous personification of death, gorging on bodies that fill its already "rotten jaws." Like Mercutio's description of his flesh as meat for worms, Romeo describes the Capulet corpses as food, differentiating Juliet's from the others not in kind but only in degree: she is the "dearest morsel" but substantially no different from the rest. There is no mention of a soul that has recently departed and that he wishes to join. His only concern is with protecting her corpse.

At this point Shakespeare's insistence on a strictly materialist explanation for death and its aftermath reaches new heights, and the play assumes the tragic gravity that its sources lack. The final scene begins, however, not with the death of Juliet or Romeo but with the death of Paris. The presence of Paris in the graveyard is entirely Shakespeare's innovation; he makes no similar entrance in any of the sources, nor does he meet his death. By introducing Paris to this scene, Shakespeare intensifies the sense of lives wasted by adding another body to the newly dead. He also intensifies the already powerful sense in the play that love has no meaningful future. As Paris lies dying, he neither turns to God in prayer nor expresses any hope that his soul will ascend to heaven. His focus is only on his corpse and where its burial shall be. Having come to the Capulet tomb to perform his solemn obsequies to his intended bride—"Sweet flower," he exclaims, "with flowers thy bridal bed I strew" (5.3.12)—he requests from Romeo that he might join Juliet in the grave. "O, I am slain!" he exclaims. "If thou be merciful / Open the tomb, lay me with Juliet" (5.3.72–73). Like many of Shakespeare's contemporaries, he wants nothing more than to mingle his remains with those of his beloved. These are the final words that Paris speaks.

"In faith, I will." So Romeo responds to Paris's request, and Shakespeare makes clear that Romeo is as good as his word. "I'll bury thee in a triumphant grave," Romeo declares. "A grave—O no, a lantern, slaughtered youth / For here lies Juliet" (5.3.74; 83–85). Paris's burial inside the Capulet tomb is then confirmed in the exchange between the Friar and Juliet: when Juliet awakens from her sleep and asks, "Where is my Romeo?" the Friar responds, "Thy husband in thy bosom there lies dead / And Paris, too" (5.3.155–56). This is a strange response, in several different respects. First, the Friar describes Romeo as lying dead "there," in Juliet's bosom, as if her bosom were in effect not "here," part of her body, but somewhere else instead. Second, the location of Paris's corpse is entirely ambiguous: "And Paris, too" either indicates simply that Paris is also dead or that Paris is also dead in her bosom.

"Thy husband in thy bosom there lies dead" could also simply mean "thy bosom husband" or "the husband thou lovest" lies "there," but this still leaves the problem of the "there," which contains the bodies of both men, somehow set apart from Juliet. Juliet makes clear, however, that she awakens next to Romeo, from whose lips she takes a final kiss, and the Chief Watchman informs us that the three bodies (Romeo, Juliet, and Paris) are all entangled together. In fact, when he first describes the scene, he forgets to mention Romeo, exclaiming: "Pitiful sight! Here lies the County slain / And Juliet bleeding, warm, and newly dead"; some twenty lines later, he expands this description in his account to the prince: "Sovereign, here lies the County Paris slain / And Romeo dead, and Juliet, dead before / Warm, and new killed" (5.3.173–74, 194–96).

Why does Shakespeare have Romeo bury Paris with Juliet? One possible answer is that however brutal and unnecessary Paris's killing may have been, Shakespeare wants to make clear that Romeo retains basic civility: he fulfills Paris's final petition out of respect for the wishes of the dead. But for Romeo to bury Paris with Juliet is also to negate the intimacy that such a burial might seem to afford. In this sense, Shakespeare's decision to include Paris not only in the scene but also in the tomb upsets whatever consolation the joint burial of the lovers—alone, not with other company—might have offered to his audience. In burying Paris alongside Juliet, Romeo reveals his fundamental skepticism about the possibility of posthumous love even for the couple's physical remains. The presence of Paris, or Tybalt or anyone else, does not seem to affect Romeo's hopes, because these other corpses, like his own and Juliet's, will not experience passion in the grave. The craving of lovers to lie side by side—which, we will recall, Browne describes in *Urne-Buriall* as an attempt to keep earthly affections alive even in the bones of the dead—simply does not apply to Romeo, who strips from their burial all traces of sentimentality.

It is not as a rival of Paris but as a rival of Death—the only sentient, living creature he imagines in the tomb—that Romeo declares his intention to lie beside his beloved:

> . . . Ah, dear Juliet,
> Why art thou yet so fair? Shall I believe
> That unsubstantial death is amorous,
> And that the lean abhorred monster keeps
> Thee here in dark to be his paramour?
> For fear of that I still will stay with thee,
> And never from this pallet of dim night
> Depart again. (5.3.101–8)

Romeo perceives Death at once as "unsubstantial" and yet hungry for matter; he resolves this paradox by imagining Death to be "lean" and hence in need of nourishment. But the problem he has fallen upon is one that haunts his conception of death in general. It is always material and never metaphysical.

Romeo already made clear his plan to join Juliet in his response to the news of her supposed death reported by Balthasar: "Well, Juliet, I will lie with thee tonight" (5.1.34). But the perceived threat of Death as a necrophiliac preying on his bride is what propels him forward and prompts his decision never to "depart again":

> Here, here will I remain
> With worms that are thy chambermaids. O, here
> Will I set up my everlasting rest,

And shake the yoke of inauspicious stars
From this world-wearied flesh. Eyes, look your last.
Arms, take your last embrace, and lips, O you
The doors of breath, seal with a righteous kiss
A dateless bargain to engrossing death. (5.3.108–15)

Although Romeo invokes the terms of a Christian afterlife—he asks for "everlasting rest" or *requiem eternam*, the formula used on countless epitaphs to describe the repose of the blessed dead—he immediately qualifies this request, indicating that he means nothing more than the "everlasting rest" the vermiculated earth will provide.[27] The sentimental interpretation offered by the German Romantic critic August Wilhelm Schlegel, that Romeo "cheers himself with a vision of everlasting marriage," shows the extent to which readers over the centuries have resisted the very bleak terms of Romeo's wish.[28] Romeo does not, moreover, turn to God, nor does he mention his soul's imminent liberation from his flesh. In Brooke's poem, we will recall, Romeus's immediate wish is to leave his body behind: "For well enough I know, this body is but clay," he declares, "Nought but a masse of sinne, to frayle, and subject to decay." For Shakespeare's Romeo there is only the desire—repeated three times in the space of two lines—to remain "here."

When Juliet awakens to find Romeo dead beside her, she likewise makes no mention of their posthumous heavenly prospects. Gone are the words given to her by Brooke, whose Juliet petitions, as we have seen, for an eternal life together: "That so our parted sprites, from light that we see here / In place of endlesse light and blisse, may ever live yfere." In Shakespeare's hands, Juliet makes no mention of either a heavenly reunion or the possibility that the couple might enjoy each other's company in the tomb. Instead, she concerns herself exclusively with bringing her life to a quick end before the Friar might take her away; she longs for death itself, and not what might follow upon it. Juliet dies with an apostrophe not to the heavens above, nor to the husband lying in her bosom, but only to the knife that she thrusts into her breast: "O happy dagger / This is thy sheath! There rust, and let me die" (5.3.168–69).[29]

V. Afterlife

In nearly all of the sources for *Romeo and Juliet* the bodies of the lovers are removed from the Capulet monument in order to be buried together in a private tomb.[30] Da Porto describes the display of their corpses on rugs inside the Church of St. Francis, and their subsequent burial together in a newly commissioned monument. Brooke similarly has the two lovers' corpses taken out of the Capulet tomb in order to be placed upon a stage for viewing; following this theatrical display of their bodies, he recounts that they are put "in a stately tombe, on pillers great, of marble rayse they hye." In da Porto and Brooke, the new tomb for Romeo and Juliet is both an earthly reminder of what has passed and a symbolic representation of the union that awaits their spirits in the heavenly sphere. To return once again to Panofsky's distinction, it is simultaneously a retrospective and a prospective tomb.

Shakespeare's treatment of Romeo and Juliet's burial delivers a double blow. Not only are the lovers denied any hint of a transcendent afterlife, but they are also denied the intimacy of a private tomb. As we have seen, the couple lies in some complicated tangle with the corpse of Paris, and the remains of Tybalt and other Capulet kinsmen are in close proximity. Moreover, unlike all of his sources, Shakespeare's description of the commemoration of Romeo and Juliet's love has no connection to the burial itself; the funerary statues that the fathers propose to erect are described not in terms of a new tomb for the two corpses but as a separate monument. "I will raise her statue in pure gold," boasts Montague, "That whiles Verona by that name is known / There shall no figure at such rate be set / As that of true and faithful Juliet." Capulet, not to be undone, replies: "As rich shall Romeo's by his lady's lie / Poor sacrifices of our enmity" (5.3.298–303). The statues are in effect, a form of cenotaph: literally an empty (*kenos*) tomb (*taphos*) that honors the bodies in their absence. There is no relationship established between the sculptures recording their love and the lovers' physical remains.

That the statues erected in their names would mean nothing to Romeo and Juliet seems entirely obvious; whatever the monument may offer to future lovers warned by this tragic tale, not even Montague and

Capulet imagine that it will preserve their children's love. There is nothing in the play to suggest, moreover, that Romeo and Juliet want to be either memorialized or, as it were, eternized. This is a couple that resists all of the conventional forms of consolation available for spouses confronting their mortality, a couple that will stake everything on the pleasures of "one short minute" without anticipating anything more. In this respect, the intensity of the young lovers matches the intensity of the play itself, a play that is singularly obsessed with the pressure of time, the urgency of the moment, the incandescent experience of its "two-hours' traffic of our stage" (prol. 12). It is not a coincidence that it is here and nowhere else in his works that Shakespeare draws our attention to the specific duration of the performance, emphasizing the nature of the theater itself as something to be experienced live, in the here and now. *Romeo and Juliet* becomes, in the end, Shakespeare's greatest expression of *carpe diem*.

Coda: Antony and Cleopatra

Some twelve years after *Romeo and Juliet,* Shakespeare returned to the idea of ending a play with the deaths of two lovers in *Antony and Cleopatra.* There is much in common between the death scenes in the two plays. In both cases, the man does not realize the woman's death has been faked, and therefore initiates his own death. In both cases, the lovers have their final meeting inside a private funereal monument. By the end of each play, the two lovers have taken their lives. In his revision of the scene of lovers' suicides in *Antony and Cleopatra,* however, Shakespeare included what he had stripped from *Romeo and Juliet:* the couple's anticipation of a posthumous life together.

The context for the deaths of Antony and Cleopatra is not Christian but pagan; this is a story that Shakespeare inherited from Plutarch, inflected by whatever additional knowledge he may have had about ancient attitudes toward the afterlife. In his Roman plays, Shakespeare had the opportunity to imagine things in a world remarkably different from his own, and in the case of the lovers' suicides, he seems to have embraced these differences without any adjustment or accommodation to the culture in which he lived. He could imagine crocodiles and eunuchs and love after death in a time before Christ declared that there would be no marriage in heaven.

The shift from a mortal to an immortal vision of love is nothing less than a shift from tragedy to romance, and *Antony and Cleopatra* in this respect embodies the playwright's transition from one genre to the other. As has often been observed, at the center of the romance genre is the prospect of recovery, in place of the gravity of loss. In *Antony and Cleopatra*, this generic ideal is not fulfilled on the ground, as it is in the later romances (*The Winter's Tale, Pericles*); it is projected onto the world to come. Upon hearing of Cleopatra's supposed death, Antony prepares to meet her anew in the afterlife:

Unarm, Eros. The long day's task is done,
And we must sleep.
. . . I will o'ertake thee, Cleopatra, and
Weep for my pardon. So it must be, for now
All length is torture. Since the torch is out,
Lie down, and stray no farther. . . .
Eros!—I come, my queen.—Eros!—Stay for me.
Where souls do couch on flowers we'll hand in hand,
And with our sprightly port make the ghosts gaze.
Dido and her Aeneas shall want troops,
And all the haunt be ours. (4.15.35-36, 44-47, 50-54)

Antony's anticipation of being "where souls do couch on flowers" refers to the Elysian fields; with his invocation of Dido and Aeneas he conjures up more specifically the *lugentes campi*, or fields of mourning, where the victims of love forever dwell. As Virgil relates in book 6 of the *Aeneid*,

And here, concealed by secret paths, are those
whom bitter love consumed with brutal waste;
a myrtle grove encloses them, their pains
remain with them in death.[31]

Antony's allusion to Dido and Aeneas reflects a poignant revision of the circumstances Virgil describes. As readers of the *Aeneid* knew well, Dido

is not reunited with Aeneas when they meet each other again during his
visit to the underworld:

> Among them, wandering in that great forest,
> and with her wound still fresh: Phoenician Dido.
> And when the Trojan hero recognized her
> dim shape among the shadows . . .
> he wept and said with tender love:
> "Unhappy Dido, then the word I had
> was true? That you were dead? That you pursued
> your final moment with the sword? . . .
> But stay your steps.
> Do not retreat from me. Whom do you flee?
> This is the last time fate will let us speak." (6.593-96; 599-602; 612-14)

But Dido refuses to respond to Aeneas at all:

> She turned away, eyes to the ground, her face
> no more moved by his speech than if she stood
> as stubborn as flint or some Marpessan crag.
> At last she tore herself away; she fled—
> and still his enemy—into the forest
> of shadows, where Sychaeus, once her husband,
> answers her sorrows, gives her love for love. (6. 617-23)

Antony's invocation, then, of the only other classical (and similarly im-
perial) lovers who might rival Cleopatra and himself in fame—the soon
to be Roman Aeneas and his African queen, Dido—involves a hopeful
rewriting of that poem. In his imagining, Dido's sorrows would be undone by her joyful meeting with the lover who provoked her suicide,
rather than assuaged by her former husband, Sychaeus, to whom she
had sworn, and later broken, a vow of fidelity in her widowhood.[32]

Cleopatra, for her part, fully reciprocates Antony's wish for an afterlife together, or rather, she possesses the exact same wish herself; it is
important that they never discuss their hopes for a posthumous life
together but that each of them expresses the same desire independently.

In other words, the promise to meet in the afterlife is not made to convey the depth of love to the other; it is not part of the love test that Cleopatra sets out in her very first utterance: "If it be love indeed, tell me how much" (1.1.14). Instead, the desire that each of them expresses outside the hearing of the other seems to reflect his or her individual, private will. This is a departure from Plutarch's text, in which only Antony hopes for a posthumous reunion. After the report of Cleopatra's death, he berates himself for further delay in dispatching with his own life: "Why dost thou longer delay, Antony? Fortune has taken away thy sole remaining excuse for clinging to life." Then, Plutarch relates, Antony "went into his chamber. Here, as he unfastened his breastplate and laid it aside, he said, 'O Cleopatra, I am not grieved to be bereft of thee, for I shall straightway join thee.'"[33]

Plutarch's Cleopatra makes no comparable declaration—in fact she anticipates something quite to the contrary:

> For though in life nothing could part us from each other, in death we are
> likely to change places; thou, the Roman, lying buried here, while I, the
> hapless woman, lie in Italy, and get only so much of thy country as my
> portion. (325)

Cleopatra's regret that Antony is likely to be buried in Egypt while she will be buried in Italy, and her desire to "embrac[e] the urn which held [Antony's] ashes," reveals her preoccupation with only the mortal remains of her lover, and not with their shared posthumous fate.

Shakespeare, by contrast, abandons all discussion of joint burial on Cleopatra's part, emphasizing only her ambition for an immortal life together. Upon learning of Antony's death, Cleopatra declares the world to be emptied of all meaning:

> Shall I abide
> In this dull world, which in thy absence is
> No better than a sty? O see, my women,
> The crown o' th' earth doth melt. My lord!
> O, withered is the garland of the war.
> The soldier's pole is fall'n. Young boys and girls

Are level now with men. The odds is gone,
And there is nothing left remarkable
Beneath the visiting moon. (4.16.62–70)

In preparation for her own death, she utters first, "I am again for
Cydnus / To meet Mark Antony" (5.2.224–25), reminding us of the location of their first encounter as if Cydnus were itself magically transposed to the afterlife, becoming a private Elysium that reflects their own
personal history. She next initiates what she hopes will be her complete
transformation from matter to spirit:

Give me my robe. Put on my crown. I have
Immortal longings in me. Now no more
The juice of Egypt's grape shall moist this lip.
Yare, yare, good Iras, quick—methinks I hear
Antony call. I see him rouse himself
To praise my noble act. I hear him mock
The luck of Caesar, which the gods give men
To excuse their after wrath. Husband, I come.
Now to that name my courage prove my title.
I am fire and air; my other elements
I give to baser life. (5.2.271–81)

"I have immortal longings in me," "Husband, I come": these are the
sentiments expressed by Bandello's Giulietta and Groto's Hadriana, but
Shakespeare reserves them for his Egyptian queen.

In *Romeo and Juliet*, the statues to be erected in Verona for the two
lovers are understood to represent the only afterlife that the couple will
have together; as we have seen, there is no suggestion that the monument is the earthly manifestation of a love that will continue elsewhere.
In *Antony and Cleopatra*, the monument that Caesar announces he will
erect for Antony and Cleopatra is his attempt to reclaim their posthumous lives as strictly earthly, mortal, and retrospective, but this attempt
is compromised by a different eschatological system to which the lovers
have already laid claim. "Take up her bed," Caesar commands,

And bear her women from the monument.
She shall be buried by her Antony.
No grave upon the earth shall clip in it
A pair so famous. (5.2.346-50)

The ambivalence of Caesar's utterance is embedded in the verb *clip*, which can mean on the one hand to embrace, hug, or grip and, on the other hand, to check or cripple. What Caesar would count as the most one could hope to have—a record of one's earthly fame—feels like a trifle, an irrelevance, to the immortal aspirations of the lovers. As Cleopatra puts it, "'Tis paltry to be Caesar" (5.2.2).

Shakespeare's play does not ultimately deliver a vision of the Elysian fields and what they might bring; there is nothing comparable, for example, to what Virgil gives us in the *Aeneid* or Dante in the *Divina Commedia*. This kind of conjuring up of the afterlife seems to lie far outside either Shakespeare's interests or his ambitions as a playwright. What he does give us, in effect, is a version of the tomb Caesar proposes, but a more generous—and more successful—one. *Antony and Cleopatra* does not bury the lovers "clipped" in embrace. Instead, it perpetuates their memory through the medium of the play itself. In this respect, the poet gives the lovers the identical gift to that bestowed upon Romeo and Juliet: the gift of immortality experienced through generation after generation of audiences and readers. As we shall now see, it was this alternative form of immortality that attracted the most successful Elizabethan sonneteers, including Shakespeare, who imagined that love might remain alive, if not in heaven, then through the poetic artifact itself.

The Afterlife of Renaissance Sonnets

Statues and tombs with age consume and die,
'Tis verse alone has immortality.

—Ovid, *Amores*

In *Antony and Cleopatra*, Shakespeare gives the most famous lovers of antiquity the gift of literary immortality. The play keeps alive what the tomb that Caesar proposed to build can only bury: a complex and vital depiction of who the couple was and what their love was like. Something similar can be said about *Romeo and Juliet*, which far exceeds whatever the golden statues in Verona might do to preserve the passion of the lovers. In his plays, Shakespeare bequeaths this form of immortality upon his characters. But in his sonnets, and the sonnets of his most ambitious contemporaries, the same project becomes personal.

The idea that the poem—and not the heavens—could serve as the locus for posthumous love represents a significant departure from the Petrarchan tradition. Petrarch certainly strove to achieve immortality for his poetry, but this desire was distinct from the eternal life that he anticipated sharing with Laura. Poetic fame was, in effect, an earthly complement to love's ultimate transcendence. "I have always burned with a love of eternity," Petrarch explains to St. Augustine in the *Secretum*, adding: "I use mortal things for what they are worth and do not intend to do violence to the natural order of things."[1] "The greater glory will have to be enjoyed in heaven when we get there," he continues, "and no longer even think of earthly glory. And so I think the proper order is that mortal men should first think about mortal things and that eternal things should follow transitory things, because the most logical order is to proceed from the transitory to the eternal" (137). To this Augustine responds with a curt dismissal: "Silly little man! So you imagine that whatever pleasure there is in heaven and earth will be at your disposal for enjoyment." Petrarch neither challenges this conclusion nor retracts his words. Instead, he maintains that mortal glory is a worthy goal while one is on this earth and that it poses no problem for the enjoyment of eternal pleasures later on.

In the *Rime sparse* the dual ambitions of earthly fame and eternal love are comfortably intertwined. Among many possible examples, poem 333 nicely captures the general pattern. This sonnet begins with the poet's sending his "rime dolenti" (sorrowing rhymes [1]) to Laura's tomb to deliver two different messages: first, that he continues to spread her fame "a ciò che 'l mondo la conosca et ame" (so that the world may know and love her [11]); and second, that he is ready now for her summons: "siami a l'incontro, et quale / ella è nel Cielo, a sé me tiri et chiame" (let her meet me, and let her draw and call me to herself, to be what she is in Heaven [13–14]). The pursuit of Laura's fame in the world does not seem either discordant or trivial in relation to her heavenly state; there is no corrective reminder from Laura's spirit that worldly praise is irrelevant to the elect above. Instead, Petrarch affirms simultaneously that he continues to praise Laura "viva et morta" (9), and that his own passage to the other world, where he expects to join her, is now nearby.

When Renaissance English love poets imagine the possibility of immortal love, by contrast, they do not envision it as a separate achievement from their poetic fame. The only kind of immortality they imagine occurs in and through the poem itself. Hence the immortality conferred by poetry does not complement the shared heavenly life of the lovers, as it does in Petrarch, but substitutes for it. The result of this substitution of poetic immortality for personal immortality was an unprecedented empowerment of the literary work. Far beyond what we find in

Petrarch, where there is always the further prospect of union with the beloved in heaven, the only posthumous future that English love poets imagine resides in the sonnets themselves.

I. Ancient Roots

In their bids for literary immortality, Renaissance English sonneteers were greatly influenced by the examples of classical Roman poetry. Although pagan conceptions of the afterlife had little in common with those of Protestant England, the two cultures shared the fundamental belief that earthly couples would not be happily reunited after death. In this respect the Roman poets provided a strong alternative to Petrarch and his Italian followers, who imagined heaven as the place for love's fulfillment. Latin love elegy in effect supplied English poets with the essential tools for thinking through alternative—and exclusively literary—modes of preservation.

The idea that poems might confer immortality was given its most famous expression in the final poem of Horace's third book of odes.[2] Horace's ode is not a love poem written to one of his many mistresses— it is instead a poem of self-love—but it articulates the central principles of poetic durability that lie behind Elizabethan love sonnets. In a world as deeply preoccupied with monumental commemoration as Augustan Rome, Horace articulated more clearly than any of his contemporaries the claim that poetry could make:

> I have completed a monument more lasting than bronze
> and higher than the [royal] Pyramids of kings,
> which cannot be destroyed by gnawing rain
> nor wild north wind, or by the unnumbered
> procession of the years and flight of time.
> I shall not wholly die. A great part of me
> will avoid Libitina.[3]

"Non omnis moriar" (I shall not wholly die): this is the boldest possible affirmation of poetry's power, surpassing even the monuments of kings as a means of preservation. Monuments might house, for as long as they last, the bodily remains of their inhabitants, but the poem does more than this. It keeps some part of the poet alive.

What is the "great part of me" (multaque pars mei) that will escape the grip of Libitina, the Roman goddess of funerals?[4] Horace makes the radical claim that it is not simply his name or earthly fame, but a physical part of him. Unlike the remainder of the corpse, which will decompose inside his tomb, which will itself decompose (even the pyramids, Horace declares, are subject to devouring rain), this single "part" will be impervious to decay. "I shall continue to grow," Horace continues, "fresh with the praise of posterity, as long as the priest climbs the Capitol with the silent virgin" (usque ego postera / crescam laude recens).[5] The language he uses here is decidedly organic: both the verb *crescere* (to spring forth or grow) and the adjective *recens* (fresh) invoke a living creature. And yet this living creature can only be the poem itself: it is his poem that will stay alive, and in doing so will renew through each act of reading or reciting the voice and thought and person that Horace understands himself to be. The only end that he can imagine to his personal immortality is the end of Roman civilization itself, when the procession of vestal virgins and priests will no longer climb to the temple of Jupiter on the Capitol. In this one respect, Horace's enormous ambition turns out to have been too modest—or his faith in Rome too great—since we are still reviving him, as it were, long after the arrival of the barbarians.

In Horace's ode Elizabethan love poets found a compelling articulation of the idea that poets could produce their own immortality through verse.[6] In the love poetry of Horace's contemporaries (which they read either directly or through its distillation in the Continental poetry of Ronsard and others), they discovered the related idea that immortality could serve as a gift from the poet to his mistress, or would-be mistress—a reward, in effect, for the reciprocity of the poet's love.[7] This is how Ovid puts it at the beginning of his love elegies, the *Amores*:

> Give me yourself as happy matter for my songs—and my songs will come forth worthy of their cause. Through song came fame to Io frightened by her horns, and to her a lover beguiled in guise of the river-bird, and to her

who was carried over the deep on the pretended bull while she grasped with virgin hand his bended horns.[8]

It was not, Ovid claims, through their status as former lovers of Jove that Io, Leda, and Europa earned their fame (although any such encounter should, according to classical tradition, confer immortality upon them).[9] Instead, the lovers—or victims—of Jove earned their fame through the transformation of their stories to song, a task accomplished most fully, of course, in Ovid's own *Metamorphoses*.[10] The fame Ovid offers his mistress will similarly come through song, but it will also reflect a consensual union: unlike Io and Leda and Europa, Ovid's mistress will provide the "happy matter" of his poetry after she willingly gives herself to him. This will bind the couple's names together for eternity: "You and I, too, shall be sung in like manner through all the earth, and my name shall be ever joined with yours" (1.3.25–26).

Propertius makes a similar offer to any woman fortunate enough to receive his praise, declaring his poetic prowess to be the exclusive means for lasting fame:

> Lucky girl, if you are celebrated in my book!
> these poems will be so many monuments to your beauty.
> The wealth of the pyramids shooting toward the stars,
> the abode of Jove Eleus at Olympus, which imitates heaven,
> the wealth and fortune of the Mausolean tomb—
> none is free from the ultimate condition of death.
> Either fire or flood will carry away their honors,
> or they will collapse from the blow of years, defeated by weight.
> [But f]rom genius desired fame will not fade
> with age: in genius deathless glory inheres.[11]

It is striking, and no coincidence, that both Horace and Propertius compare their poems almost exclusively to funerary monuments. In both cases, the poet understands his central artistic rival to be the architect: the maker of grand pyramids and tombs that memorialize, if not preserve, the dead. Poetry exceeds pyramids and tombs, Propertius claims, because these elaborate graves are subject to material decay—they inevitably succumb to the "ultimate condition"—but the poet's "genius," forever renewed through his poems, is immune to the negative effects of nature or time. It cannot be undone by fire or rain or the sheer burden of maintaining physical stature. It alone remains "sine morte" (3.2.26), without death.

In poems like these, English love poets would have glimpsed an alternative model to Petrarch's: a model in which a posthumous future for love was possible through the vehicle of poetry, and not only through heavenly salvation. The difference between the Renaissance English articulation of this idea and the classical one was a difference in both cultural resonance and poetic affect. For the English poets, the idea of poetic immortality was tinged with a poignancy that the Latin poets lacked. In a pagan tradition that did not on the whole regard the afterlife as a place for self-fulfillment and reward, the possibility that lovers would reunite after their deaths played little or no part in the poetic imagination. In the few instances when Latin poets imagined earthly lovers having some form of afterlife together, they did not depict the happy resumption or resolution of erotic ties. Instead, there are descriptions like the one we have already seen from Virgil, in which he describes the fields of mourning ("lugentes campi") where lovers dwell in a state of perpetual sorrow; or this account from Propertius, who gives us an entirely elegiac depiction of Elysium as a place where injured lovers rehearse their stories amidst beautiful trees and flowers and music:

> Beyond the ugly Stream twin mansions are allotted. . . .
> The one bears Clytemnestra's taint, another
> conveys the monstrous wooden mimic-cow of Crete.
> Observe these others swept along in a garlanded hoy,
> where happy airs caress Elysian roses,
> and many strings and Cybebe's rounded bronze
> and turbaned choirs with Lydian plectra sound.
> Andromeda and Hypermestra, guileless wives,
> narrate the tales of their egregious times. . . .
> with tears in death we ratify life's loves.[12]

Although Propertius, speaking here through the voice of his dead lover, Cynthia, distinguishes between two groups of shades—those who were guilty of criminal passions and those who were innocent victims—this is not a Christian afterlife with punishments and rewards, and neither group enjoys any pleasures. Both the guilty and the innocent are positioned along the "foul river" ("turpem amnem") and spend their time in acts of nostalgic recording.

The one notable exception to the Latin poets' lack of positive vision for an afterlife filled with love comes in Tibullus, who describes the myrtle groves of Elysium as a blissful playground, but still not as a place where former lovers meet again:

> It will be Venus herself (she has always found me faithful)
> who will lead me along the way to the Elysian fields
> where song and dancing go on forever, and overhead, curving
> and fluting and falling, song from the delicate throats of birds.
> The fields, untilled, will bear trees of a cinnamon sweetness,
> and roses cover the earth and fill the air with their scent.
> Young men and girls will meet in sport and easy laughter;
> there will be no wars but Love's, waged always on every front.
> And here are those whom death robbed of both life and lover,
> there make a wreath of myrtle laid lightly on the hair.[13]

In this gorgeous scene of singing birds and scented roses and men and women joyfully at play—a seeming ekphrasis of a wall painting from a wealthy Roman's villa—there are no particular reunions or resumed intimacies between earthly lovers. In place of couples, Tibullus describes a communal frolic in which lovers are rewarded for their former pains by a generalized, atmospheric eros.

II. Eternal Sonnets

Although marked by a similar disavowal of posthumous bliss, Renaissance English poetry differs from its classical counterpart in that it is haunted by the prospect of eternal love that has been definitively left behind. In this respect, these poems are perhaps best understood as palimpsests, with Petrarchan traces hovering behind them; they write over, but never completely erase, the banished possibility of erotic transcendence. The rejection of Petrarch's idea of merging what he refers to in *Rime sparse* 327 as "memoria eterna" with the full expectation of posthumous love in heaven brought a new mood to English love poetry, which can best be described as compensatory. In the English sonnet series, poets routinely draw attention in a manner unprecedented in either the classical or the Petrarchan tradition to the physical devastation that death visits upon love; from that position of despair, they offer a form of consolation. This consolation is decidedly secular: English love poets rarely, if ever, invoke the eternal salvation promised to faithful Christians, and equally scarce are mentions of the immortality of the soul. Instead, they offer poetry as the locus not only for the commemoration of love but also—in an extension of the Horatian model—for keeping some form of that love alive.[14]

Readers of English literature have long associated the idea that poetry might combat physical deterioration and death to render the beloved immortal with Shakespeare's *Sonnets*. There is no question that Shakespeare's poems expanded and complicated this idea in ways that had not been done before, but the tropes he adopted were already very familiar to his contemporaries. The conceit of the poem as a means to resist the ravages of time was one of the absolutely central concerns of the sonnet sequences that appeared in the decade or so before Shakespeare's. This conceit is notably absent from the miscellanies of poems that were published in the sixteenth century—collections like *Tottel's Miscellany* that include individual sonnets but not sonnet series—an absence that speaks to a meaningful link between the idea of battling time and the genre of the sonnet cycle, as if the accumulation of little fourteen-line warriors produced a formidable army against death. Moreover, the relatively narrow range of expressive possibilities within the late Elizabethan sequences—the circulation of a shared vocabulary or grammar to describe erotic arrangements—suggests that the sonnet sequence functioned as a rather closed semantic system, committed to a particular kind of project. This project was not exclusively or even primarily about erotic satisfaction in this world. In fact, one of the surprising features of these poems is their relative inattention to the present moment. To a much greater degree than we tend to register, the English sonnet series is preoccupied with the fate of the poet and his beloved after death.

A focus on the posthumous future does not characterize all Elizabethan sonneteers, and interestingly does not seem to apply to the earliest. Both Thomas Watson and Sir Philip Sidney, the authors of the first love sonnet sequences in English (both were penned in the early 1580s), treat their works as less serious achievements than many of their contemporaries do a decade later, and this dismissive attitude toward their poems corresponds to their lack of interest in claiming immortalizing powers. In his prefatory verses to *Hekatompathia*, Watson calls his volume a "toye," and the dedicatory poem written by his friend George Peele, which we looked at briefly in chapter 2, reminds the reader that Watson has done "broader worke then this," naming his Latin translation of Sophocles's *Antigone*.[15] Sidney likewise insists in *Astrophil and Stella* that Stella "think not that I by verse seeke fame," exclaiming that he does not want "Graved in my Epitaph, a Poet's name."[16] However much we might dismiss such claims as coy, it is striking that subsequent sonneteers tend not to follow suit. As the sonnet vogue develops over the course of the following decade, poets represent themselves more and more confidently as working in a genre capable of competing with other forms of preserving memory, beauty, or even—in the Horatian manner—some part of the lovers themselves.

Claims for bestowing immortality upon the beloved pervade the Elizabethan sonnet series, from the least canonical to the most celebrated texts. In Barnabe Barnes's *Parthenophil and Parthenophe* (a series, like Petrarch's, that combines sonnets with other poetic forms), the speaker makes the standard claim for his mistress's immortal fame:

> Do this, and let eternities enroule
> Thy fame and name, let them enroule for ever
> In lasting recordes of still lasting steele:
> Do this, ah this and famous still persever,
> Which in another age thy ghost shall feele.
> Yet (howsoever, thou, with me shall deale)
> Thy bewtie shall persever in my verse.[17]

Having first proposed Parthenophe's immortalization through historical records of "still lasting steele." Parthenophil shifts to the comparably durable vehicle of poetry.

In the anonymous series *Zepheria* (1594), the poet likewise affirms the power of his verse to resist the defacing powers of death:

> No never shall that face so fayre depaynted
> Within the love-limn'd tablet of mine hart,
> Emblemisht be, defaced or unsaynted,
> Till death shall blot it, with his pencill dart:
> Yet then in these limn'd lines enobled more,
> Thou shalt survive richer accomplisht then before.[18]

By picturing death as a rival artist who threatens to "emblemish" and "blot" the beloved's fair face, the poet's own talents become viable means to conquer mortality. Like the resurrected body whose flaws and imperfections are erased, the sonnet renders the beloved even more worthy of praise than when she was alive.

In Samuel Daniel's immensely popular *Delia* (1592), which underwent five printings in the 1590s alone, the poet envisions himself as not only combating death but even competing with God as the bestower of immortal life. In *Delia* 37, the poet suggests that whereas "God and nature" may have bequeathed Delia's earthly gifts, her posthumous life depends upon his own gifts of poetic making:

> When Winter snowes upon thy golden haires,
> And frost of age hath nipt thy flowers neere;
> When dark shal seeme thy day that never cleeres,
> And all lies withred that was held so deere.
> Then take this picture which I heere present thee,
> Limned with a Pensill not all unworthy:
> Heere see the gifts that God and nature lent thee;
> Heare read thy selfe, and what I suffred for thee.
> This may remaine thy lasting monument,
> Which happily posteritie may cherrish;

These colours with thy fading are not spent,
These may remaine when thou and I shall perrish.
If they remaine, then thou shalt live thereby.
They will remaine, and so thou canst not die.[19]

Daniel begins here in the manner of a *carpe diem* poem, warning Delia of the imminent loss of her beauty and the consequent urgency of acting upon love. This theme picks up from the preceding few poems in the sequence: sonnet 37 is the fourth within a "corona" of five linked poems, in which each begins with the final line of the previous poem. As we shall see in chapter 6, the two opening sonnets within this corona have strong *carpe diem* messages. In sonnet 37, however, Daniel distinctly leaves *carpe diem* behind.[20] Far from invoking his mistress's future loss of beauty in order to urge her to take advantage of the present, as he does in the earlier sonnets, here he proposes simply that she take solace in the power of his poetry to compensate for her anticipated loss. The challenge that the poem raises, in other words, is not how Delia might maximize her pleasure while she can but how she might ensure her beauty's preservation, something that only the poet's art can do.

Daniel positions his poem as battling material dissolution—"These may remaine when thou and I shall perrish"—issuing an unambiguous reminder of both his and Delia's inevitable mortality. The verb *to perish* was routinely used in the period in contrast to living an eternal life: in the King James Bible, for example, Jesus explains to the doubting Pharisee Nicodemus: "And as Moses lifted up the serpent in the wildernesse, even so must the Sonne of man be lifted up / That whosoever beleeveth in him, should not perish, but have everlasting life" (John 3:14-15). Within the logic of Daniel's sonnet, the poet's reminder to Delia of her future perishing is treated as a conditional possibility: should she not be preserved in his poetry, this will be her fate. The final couplet moves from an "if" to an assertive "will" as it affirms the power of his "lasting monument": so long as the poem itself "remaines," he contends—a verb repeated four times in the sestet—not only will Delia be spared from oblivion, but she will "not die."

This theme of Delia's eternal preservation through the lines of Daniel's poetry reaches its fullest articulation in sonnet 38, the final poem in the five-sonnet corona, in which Daniel compares his poetic gifts to those of Petrarch:

> Thou canst not die whilst any zeale abound
> In feeling harts, that can conceiue these lynes;
> Though thou a *Laura* hast no *Petrarch* founde,
> In base attyre, yet cleerely Beautie shines.
> And I (though borne in a colder clime,)
> Doe feele mine inward heate as great, (I knowe it,)
> Hee neuer had more faith, although more rime,
> I loue as well, though he could better shew it.
> But I may add one feather to thy fame,
> To helpe her flight throughout the fairest Ile.
> And if my pen could more enlarge thy name,
> Then shouldst thou liue in an immortall stile.
> For though that *Laura* better limned bee,
> Suffise, thou shalt be lou'd as well as shee.

Although Daniel declares Petrarch the greater poet (due in part to his Italian "inward heate"), he maintains that so long as "feeling harts . . . can conceiue these lynes," his poems will keep Delia alive. The power of his love is entirely at the service of preserving his beloved: whatever the merits of his pen, its dedication to Delia allows her to live on "in an immortal stile."

In *Idea* (1593), Michael Drayton frames his bid to immortalize his mistress as a response to the pressing realities of her mortality:

> How many paltry, foolish, painted things,
> That now in coaches trouble ev'ry street,
> Shall be forgotten, whom no poet sings,
> Ere they be well wrap'd in their winding-sheet!
> Where I to thee eternitie shall give,
> When nothing else remayneth of these days,
> And Queenes hereafter shall be glad to live
> Upon the almes of thy superfluous prayse.

Virgins and matrons reading these my rimes,
Shall be so much delighted with thy story,
That they shall grieve, they liv'd not in these times,
To have seene thee, their sexes onely glory:
So shalt thou flye above the vulgar throng
Still to survive in my immortall song.[21]

This sonnet has as its central opposition those who will be "wrap'd in their winding-sheet"—those who, in effect, have corporeal bodies that will die—and those who, by virtue of being praised in poetry, are given the gift of "eternitie." On the one hand, there is no reason to think that the speaker's mistress will be spared the winding sheet, nor is there any mention of a soul that would leave the body behind on its way to higher things. (Here as elsewhere in Elizabethan sonnets, there is very little discussion of the soul.) On the other hand, the "eternity" described is clearly meant as a competing form of transcendence. Drayton's beloved will "flye above the vulgar throng" on the wings, as it were, of his "immortall song." The sonnet takes the place of the Neoplatonic *scala* or the Christian path to salvation.

When Edmund Spenser takes up the trope of poetry as the vehicle to preserve his beloved Elizabeth in the *Amoretti*, he first imagines his poems as having a strictly commemorative purpose, more or less in the manner of the Latin elegists. Spenser's familiarity with this classical precedent had already been established in his earlier work *The Shepheardes Calender*, in which the final gloss to the final eclogue, December, quotes Horace's *Ode* 3.30 and declares that the poet has made a "Calendar, that shall endure as long as time &c. folowing the ensample of Horace and Ovid in the like."[22] In *Amoretti* 69, Spenser compares his poem to the ancient trophy, a monument erected to record military triumphs at the site of victory:

The famous warriors of the anticke world,
  used Trophees to erect in stately wize:
in which they would the records have enrold,
  of theyr great deeds and valorous emprize.
What trophee then shall I most fit devize,

in which I may record the memory
of my loves conquest, peerelesse beauties prise,
adorn'd with honour, love, and chastity?
Even this verse vowd to eternity,
shall be thereof immortall moniment:
and tell her prayse to all posterity,
that may admire such worlds rare wonderment,
The happy purchase of my glorious spoile,
gotten at last with labour and long toyle.

What kind of trophy, Spenser asks, might "record the memory / of my loves conquest"? The answer, not surprisingly, is a monument made not of stone but of words. "Vowd to eternity," the sonnet becomes an "immortal moniment," erected by the poet with "labour and long toyle."

Within this classical conceit, there are limits to what the poem can do. It cannot promise that Elizabeth will in any way escape death or that she will enjoy a heavenly future. It can promise, however, that her beauty, as well as the poet's struggle to possess that beauty, will be remembered. The editors of the Yale Spenser suggest that *Amoretti* 69 should be read as an erroneous (and ironic) assumption that the poet's own labors have had anything to do with winning the lady, whereas Elizabethan readers, they argue, would understand that "God's grace transcends human understanding and human efforts."[23] But to read the poem in this way is to mistake the larger context in which it was written. Questions about Protestant grace do surface in the *Amoretti*, but in this instance Spenser is responding more directly to the challenge raised by so many of his fellow sonneteers: namely, how best to "tell [the beloved's] prayse to all posterity." And the solution he proposes involves the relatively straightforward task of creating an artifact that will preserve her memory.[24]

As the *Amoretti* progresses, Spenser expands the possibilities for granting Elizabeth immortality, leaving the classical machinery for commemoration behind. *Amoretti* 82 begins by declaring the inadequacy of the poet's verse as a means to preserve Elizabeth's "glorious name," but over the course of its fourteen lines this professed inability is transformed into an unabashed celebration of his own poetic prowess:

Joy of my life, full oft for loving you
I blesse my lot, that was so lucky placed:
but then the more your owne mishap I rew,
that are so much by so meane love embased.
For had the equall hevens so much you graced
in this as in the rest, ye mote invent
some hevenly wit, whose verse could have enchased
your glorious name in golden moniment.
But since ye deignd so goodly to relent
to me your thrall, in whom is little worth,
that little that I am, shall all be spent
in setting your immortall prayses forth.
Whose lofty argument uplifting me,
shall lift you up unto an high degree.

As this sonnet imagines it, the lady's purpose in finding a lover is not to enjoy his love and adoration while she is alive but to secure her memorial preservation when she is dead. The purpose, that is, of being loved now is to be remembered well later. This is the ultimate justification for why poets are the best lovers, and Spenser, like Ovid before him, is quick to apprehend it. To be "graced" with love is to have as one's lover a poet "whose verse could have enchased / your glorious name in golden moniment."

The verb *to enchase* is one that Spenser uses on multiple occasions to convey his own practice of ornamentation or praise. In *The Shepheardes Calender*, he describes the engraving carved on a mazer, a wooden drinking bowl, "Wherein is enchased many a fayre sight / Of Beres and Tygres, that maken fiers warre"; and in *The Faerie Queene*, he despairs over the inadequacy of his verse, exclaiming: "My ragged rimes are all too rude and bace / Her heauenly lineaments for to enchace."[25] In *Amoretti* 82 Spenser uses this verb to describe what another poet may have done for Elizabeth had he been her lover, and he does so to emphasize the poverty of his gifts in comparison.

The display of modesty does not extend, however, beyond the *volta*, or turn, at line 9, where Spenser comes back with an even bolder claim for what his own poems will do. And here he subtly draws out the less positive, or certainly less immortalizing, connotations of *enchase*, which can be traced etymologically to the French *enchasser*, to put in a casket or shrine. Spenser will not simply erect a "golden moniment" to house Elizabeth's memory; he will instead devote himself to bestowing "immortall prayses" upon her. The final couplet of the poem is filled with terms of elevation—"lofty," "uplifting," "lift," "high"—which point to a poetic transcendence beyond the monumental achievement of the rival poet. This transcendence, moreover, is not limited to Elizabeth; it redounds as well upon the poet himself. (The doubling effect of praise, which Joel Fineman brilliantly analyzed in Shakespeare's sonnets, underlies nearly all of the poets' claims for the beloved's immortality— they are always at the same time ensuring their own fame—but Spenser is the first to acknowledge it so frankly.)[26]

Spenser's strongest bid for the power of poetry to grant immortality is in *Amoretti* 75, where he pushes further than any of the sonneteers before him the limits of what sonnets might do. This poem begins by rehearsing the difficulty of securing Elizabeth's posthumous fame:

> One day I wrote her name upon the strand,
> but came the waves and washed it a way:
> agayne I wrote it with a second hand,
> but came the tyde, and made my paynes his pray.
> Vayne man, sayd she, that doest in vaine assay
> a mortall thing so to immortalize;
> for I my selve shall lyke to this decay,
> and eek my name bee wyped out lykewize. (1–8)

The charge that his beloved levels against him—of attempting "a mortall thing so to immortalize"—could be an indictment of the genre of the Elizabethan sonnet sequence on the whole, and were this to come at the end of the poem, we might imagine Spenser to be conceding the futility of his poetic project.

But the accusation from Elizabeth is made at the end of the octet, enabling Spenser to take full advantage of the *volta* at line 9, where he begins his retort:

Not so, (quod I) let baser things devize
to dy in dust, but you shall live by fame:
my verse your vertues rare shall eternize,
and in the hevens wryte your glorious name.
Where whenas death shall all the world subdew,
our love shall live, and later life renew. (9–14)

This response takes two different but related forms. First, Spenser makes the familiar claim that his verse will "eternize" Elizabeth's name (although, of course, she is never named in this poem), inscribing her praise "in the hevens."[27] The mention of the heavens is in itself unusual—bids for poetic immortality among Elizabethan love poets tend not to venture into the celestial realm—and this leads to the second, unprecedented response. Not only will Elizabeth be spared the oblivion brought by death (she shall not, he exclaims, "dy in dust," a quiet warning of her material fate should Spenser not continue to celebrate her), but their love itself will be spared the annihilation visited upon other mortal couples: "Where whenas death shall all the world subdew / our love shall live, and later life renew."

The syntax of this final couplet is somewhat ambiguous, but taken in the context of the sestet as a whole, it yields an unequivocal message: the renewal of their love will occur in their shared posthumous future, and not only indirectly or vicariously through the fame of the poem ("where" in line 13 must refer to "the hevens" in line 12, since there has been no competing place mentioned). This reading is reinforced by line 14, which imagines two separate phases of their immortal lives: their love "shall live" now through the power of his verse, *and* it shall live later, when it is renewed in heaven. Or rather, their love, sustained by Spenser's "eterniz[ing]" verse, shall itself be the vehicle of their joint renewal: the eschatology Spenser hints at positions poetry as the agent of their mutual resurrection. Of course, outside of the reference to the "hevens," there is no mention of God, nor any hint of a Christian metaphysics, and in this respect the poem remains firmly secular. But the suggestion that poetry might do what nothing else can—namely, secure a posthumous future for the two lovers—extends the reach of the sonnet, in its final half-line, to a nearly divine power.

III. Uncommon Graves

When Shakespeare began to write his sonnets in the late 1590s, he was embarking on a poetic genre whose preoccupation with immortality was well established. As we have already observed, the Elizabethan sonnet series became increasingly focused on securing a posthumous future for the poet's beloved; this focus often overshadowed the pursuit of reciprocal love in the mortal world. If we consider Shakespeare's poems in this light, his aim to address the challenge posed by the mortality of his "lovely boy" seems much less idiosyncratic than it is often imagined to be. Like so many poets before him, Shakespeare seeks to preserve his beloved for posterity. Thus he did not alter the genre's primary concerns so much as thematize those concerns; he brought to the surface, and rendered visible, what the stakes of the genre had become.

What is unusual about Shakespeare's sonnets is not his concern with the beloved's preservation, but the explicitness with which he stages the transition from advocating immortality through procreation to advocating immortality through poetry. This shift from a biological to an artifactual means of pursuing immortality emerges forcefully in sonnet 18, "Shall I compare thee to a summer's day?," in which Shakespeare affirms the magic of his poetry to conquer the cycles of time and render the short-lived summer "eternal":

> Shall I compare thee to a summer's day?
> Thou art more lovely and more temperate.
> Rough winds do shake the darling buds of May,
> And summer's lease hath all too short a date.
> Sometime too hot the eye of heaven shines,
> And often is his gold complexion dimm'd,
> And every fair from fair sometime declines,
> By chance or nature's changing course untrimm'd;
> But thy eternal summer shall not fade,
> Nor lose possession of that fair thou ow'st,
> Nor shall Death brag thou wand'rest in his shade

When in eternal lines to time thou grow'st.
So long as men can breathe or eyes can see,
So long lives this, and this gives life to thee.

The sonnet becomes not only a portrait of the beloved's beauty but also that which bequeaths to him continual life: death will never possess the young man so long as he "grow[s]" in the poem itself. This suggestion of organic growth through the vehicle of the poem—the poem is breeding and not only recording—obviates the necessity of offspring. Unlike Horace, who imagined that his poetry would survive as long as Roman civilization, Shakespeare's poem is not limited by the duration or reach of the English nation; its only imagined limit is the end of the human race. So long as there are living, breathing men, so long will the poem endure. The poem's endurance becomes, then, the guarantee of the youth's continuous vitality: "So long lives this, and this gives life to thee."

Once Shakespeare has affirmed the power of his verse to keep the beloved alive, the poem becomes superior to all other means of combating mortality. Now clearly echoing the boasts of Horace's Ode 3.30, Shakespeare's Sonnet 55 opens with a contemptuous dismissal of all competing forms of preservation:

Not marble, nor the gilded monuments
Of princes, shall outlive this powerful rhyme,
But you shall shine more bright in these contents
Than unswept stone, besmeared with sluttish time.
When wasteful war shall statues overturn,
And broils root out the work of masonry,
Nor Mars his sword nor war's quick fire shall burn
The living record of your memory.
'Gainst death and all-oblivious enmity
Shall you pace forth; your praise shall still find room
Ev'n in the eyes of all posterity
That wear this world out to the ending doom.
So, till the judgement that yourself arise,
You live in this, and dwell in lovers' eyes.

Marble tombs and gilded statues are vulnerable to "sluttish time" in a manner that the poem is not: the beloved "shines more bright" through the lines of the sonnet than through the shimmer produced by "unswept stone." Such a claim depends entirely, of course, upon the poem's very different relationship to its medium: whereas the tombs and monuments of princes are understood as strictly physical objects, the sonnet is imagined as independent of the individual piece of paper or parchment on which it is printed or written. Of course, unless the poems are committed to memory, they are also ultimately dependent on their medium, but this medium is understood to be renewable in a way that a monument made of even the strongest material is not.

The only limit that Shakespeare acknowledges to the continued renewal of the youth's vitality is the arrival of the apocalypse itself. The final couplet of Sonnet 55 is unusual for its direct invocation of Christian eschatology; as we have seen, English love sonnets tend to evade discussion of judgment or resurrection while declaring their powers to preserve the beloved. But Shakespeare invokes the Last Judgment only to draw an outer limit for the power of his poetry. And the power he claims is prodigious, accumulating force over the course of the sonnet itself. Shakespeare moves from affirming the endurance of the "living record of your memory" and "your praise . . . in the eyes of all posterity" to the much bolder claim that not only testimonials about the beloved but the beloved himself will "live" in the space of the poem. This idea was already hinted at in the idea of his "pac[ing] forth," as if the iambs of the sonnet were granting him a kind of mobility. The poem's final line— syntactically free from any enjambment or dependence, and hence not tainted by the contingency implied in line 13—doubles the *domus* of the immortal youth. He will live both in the poem and in the eyes of future lovers who read the sonnet and thereby reanimate its inhabitant. Like *Romeo and Juliet* or *Antony and Cleopatra*, the sonnet becomes the alternative to the tomb: a work of art that manages to keep its inhabitants alive.

It is important to register that this fantasy, at least as expressed, applies only to the beloved and not to the poet himself. Hence in a poem like Sonnet 71, Shakespeare warns the young man against mourning for him after his death, and describes his anticipated flight "from this vile world with vilest worms to dwell":

O, if I say, you look upon this verse
When I perhaps compounded am with clay,
Do not so much as my poor name rehearse,
But let your love even with my life decay,
Lest the wise world should look into your moan,
And mock you with me after I am gone. (9–14)

The self-negation the poet describes depends upon an understanding of his fate as exclusively material: he will be nothing but his physical remains, eaten by worms and mixed with clay in the earth.

When Shakespeare does imagine some kind of self-preservation after death, that preservation is entirely limited to the active care of the young man. In Sonnet 74, he maintains that worms will consume his flesh but also envisions a separate and more enduring fate for his spirit:

But be contented when that fell arrest
Without all bail shall carry me away.
My life hath in this line some interest,
Which for memorial still with thee shall stay.
When thou reviewest this, thou dost review
The very part was consecrate to thee.
The earth can have but earth, which is his due;
My spirit is thine, the better part of me.
So then thou hast but lost the dregs of life,
The prey of worms, my body being dead,
The coward conquest of a wretch's knife,
Too base of thee to be remembered.
The worth of that is that which it contains,
And that is this, and this with thee remains.

The "spirit" that constitutes the "better part of me" is not identified with the poet's soul; this is not a traditional metaphysical division between flesh and spirit. Instead, the "better part of me" is clearly aligned with his verse. And his verse is not given the gift of eternal life but is limited to the lifespan of the beloved, who will be its only guardian. "My life hath in this line some interest / Which for memorial still with thee shall stay": what will keep the enduring part of the poet alive is entirely bound up with, and dependent on, the will of the beloved.

The contrast between Shakespeare's vision of his own posthumous fate and the fate of the young man comes to the fore in Sonnet 81. Here he abandons even the limited claim to posthumous survival that he describes in Sonnet 74, while giving full expression to the beloved's chance for immortality:

> Or I shall live your epitaph to make,
> Or you survive when I in earth am rotten.
> From hence your memory death cannot take,
> Although in me each part will be forgotten.
> Your name from hence immortal life shall have,
> Though I (once gone) to all the world must die.
> The earth can yield me but a common grave
> When you entombed in men's eyes shall lie. (1–8)

Whereas every part of Shakespeare's self will be forgotten—he will be buried, he says, in a "common grave"—the youth will be "entombed" in the eyes of future readers.

At the *volta* in the sonnet at line 9, Shakespeare leaves behind altogether the prospect of his own dismal fate in order to celebrate the triumph of his poems in relation to the young man's future:

> Your monument shall be my gentle verse,
> Which eyes not yet created shall o'er-read,
> And tongues to be your being shall rehearse
> When all the breathers of this world are dead.
> You still shall live—such virtue hath my pen—
> Where breath most breathes, even in the mouths of men. (9–14)

As in Sonnet 55, the extent of the youth's immortality is ratcheted up as the poem progresses: the claim to keep the beloved's "memory" protected from death shifts to the more prospective notion that his name will have "immortal life" until the poet finally reaches the climactic idea, familiar from the earlier poem, that the youth "shall live" so long as there are breathing men on this earth. ("Still" carries here its now obsolete meaning "forever.") In Sonnet 74, Shakespeare limited his own preservation to the active maintenance of his "line" by the young man. In Sonnet 81, by contrast, the act of keeping the young man alive falls on the survival of all breathers and readers: he will continually be renewed through the eyes that read and the tongues that pronounce the poem. The survival of the poem does not simply depend, in other words, on its perdurance as scripted text. It is not only artifactual but generational.

There are many obvious ironies to Shakespeare's bold claims for the youth's preservation, since of course it is Shakespeare himself who is reborn to each new generation of readers, whereas the youth's identity remains unknown and unsung. And this is more or less true of all of the successful sonnet series: it is Spenser, not Elizabeth, Sidney, not Stella, Daniel, not Delia, who have been celebrated over the centuries, and thereby in some sense kept alive. But what is remembered of these sonnets in general is less the particular identity of poet or beloved than the intensity of feeling expressed. This act of preserving the experience of love finds its fullest expression in John Donne's *Songs and Sonnets*, which were written at the tail end of the sonnet vogue of the 1590s and which extend more fully than any of his predecessors the prospect of immortality from the individual poet or beloved to the couple itself.

IV. Donne's Urns

Donne's focus in the *Songs and Sonnets*—a collection of love poetry that does not, in fact, contain any fourteen-line sonnets but includes an extraordinary range of metrical forms[28]—typically falls on the present moment rather the future of love. In this respect, his poems have more in common with *carpe diem* poetry than with the Elizabethan sonnets that expend terrific energy in attempting to shape the beloved's posthumous fate. But Donne is not nearly so indifferent to the pursuit of immortality as the *carpe diem* poets are, and his interest in that immortality concerns both himself and his beloved as a unit of two. When Donne imagines the power of his poetry in relation to the posthumous future, he imagines it in terms of capturing, and keeping alive, the affective bond shared between lovers. This represents a final stage in the history that this chapter has been tracing. With Donne, the Elizabethan love lyric moves firmly in the direction only glimpsed in the couplet of Spenser's *Amoretti* 75. It offers immortality not only to the beloved but to the couple.

Donne acknowledges both his familiarity with the Petrarchan model and his decision to reject its allures in "The Anniversarie," in which (as we saw briefly in the introduction) he weighs the range of possibilities awaiting him and his mistress or wife after death:

> Two graves must hide thine and my coarse,
> If one might, death were no divorce.
> Alas, as well as other Princes, wee,
> (Who Prince enough in one another bee,)
> Must leave at last in death, these eyes, and eares,
> Oft fed with true oaths, and with sweet salt teares;
> But soules where nothing dwells but love
> (All other thoughts being inmates) then shall prove
> This, or a love increased there above,
> Where bodies to their graves, soules from their graves remove. (11–20)

Here the enticing idea of sharing a grave is deemed impossible, for reasons that are not explained; since married couples were routinely buried in shared graves, this suggests the poem was written either to Ann More before she and Donne married or to an earlier mistress, although the reference to "divorce" and the poem's celebration of an anniversary would suggest the poem was indeed written to his wife. But whatever obstacles Donne imagines to a joint burial, he moves quickly from this regrettable separation of their corpses to the possibility of their souls' meeting in the heavens, where their love may even be "increased."

No sooner has he proposed this reunion of their souls, however, than he pushes it away, fearing that such a reunion will deny them the superior privileges of their earthly bond:

> And then wee shall be thoroughly blest,
> But wee no more, then all the rest;
> Here upon earth, we'are Kings, and none but wee

Can be such Kings, nor of such subjects bee.
Who is so safe as wee? Where none can doe
Treason to us, except one of us two.
True and false feares let us refraine,
Let us love nobly, and live, and adde againe
Yeares and yeares unto yeares, till we attaine
To write threescore: this is the second of our raigne. (21–30)

"Here upon earth, we'are Kings": this is the realm in which Donne wants to have his love, for as many years as it might last. Nothing could be further from Petrarch's vision of Laura's awaiting him in heaven, a long-delayed reward for a life of longing and grief. Donne's vision of heaven, replete with potential subterfuge and treason, cannot compare with the privacy and security and exclusivity of an earthly life together. "Let us love nobly," he urges, and have sixty long years together; since they had just embarked on year two, this was eternity enough.

The strong embrace of this world at the expense of the world to come does not, however, fully capture Donne's attitude toward posthumous love in the *Songs and Sonnets*. He may reject the idea of a paradisiacal reunion, but he nonetheless imagines an afterlife for the couple through, and within, his poems. This vision of the future specifically satisfies his wish in "The Anniversarie" that he and his beloved might have an afterlife that does not confuse them with "all the rest" but instead is unique to them. Donne wrote two poems that answer to this fantasy directly. In "The Relique," the poet grants himself the partial satisfaction of joint burial that he dismisses in "The Anniversarie," imagining the unit formed in his grave by a strand of his mistress's hair wrapped around his bone as a "loving couple":

When my grave is broke up againe
Some second ghest to entertaine,
(For graves have learn'd that woman-head
To be to more then one a Bed)
And he that digs it, spies
A bracelet of bright haire about the bone,
Will he not let'us alone,

And thinke that there a loving couple lies,
Who thought that this device might be some way
To make their soules, at the last busie day,
Meet at this grave, and make a little stay? (1–11)

Donne does not, however, regard the couple made of hair and bone as sharing a meaningful afterlife per se: he does not seem to believe in Browne's account of mingling remains as an attempt to "continue their living Unions."[29] Instead, he understands the purpose of forming this couple merely as a "device" to provoke the reunion of the souls. This re-union, moreover, is not envisioned as more than fleeting. Coming to re-trieve their missing parts to prepare for their last judgment, the souls of the earthly lovers have a short visit, a "little stay," before parting again.

If Donne does not think that the "bracelet of bright haire about the bone" indicates a shared afterlife in the earth or in the heavens, what exactly is he proposing? He is proposing that the combination of these earthly remains, accompanied by the poem itself, will bring the couple posthumous fame:

If this fall in a time, or land,
Where mis-devotion doth command,
Then, he that digges us up, will bring
Us, to the Bishop, and the King,
To make us Reliques; then
Thou shalt be a Mary Magdalen, and I
A something else thereby;
All women shall adore us, and some men;
And since at such time, miracles are sought,
I would have that age by this paper taught
What miracles wee harmelesse lovers wrought. (12–22)

In this tongue-in-cheek anticipation of a time of restored Catholicism, the hair and bone become "reliques." These relics are worshiped not for their owners' religious piety but for the supposed purity of their love. That purity can be conveyed only by the poem ("this paper"), which tells future readers what their love was like:

First, we lov'd well and faithfully,
Yet knew not what wee lov'd, nor why,
Difference of sex no more wee knew,
Then our Guardian Angells doe;
Coming and going, wee
Perchance might kisse, but not between those meales;
Our hands ne'r toucht the seales,
Which nature, injur'd by late law, sets free:
These miracles wee did; but now alas,
All measure, and all language, I should passe,
Should I tell what a miracle shee was. (23–33)

What "this paper" relates on the surface of things is a love that sounds very much like the love that the two souls celebrate in Donne's poem "The Extasie"—before they remember, that is, to reclaim their bodies and end their self-congratulatory "dialogue of one." This is a love that Donne himself, in other words, does not really believe in, a love stripped of corporeal pleasures. The real "miracle" he wants to record is not the chaste love compromised by only a few kisses, but the intensity of his love for his beloved. This is what the poem (rather than the relic of hair and bone) can record, and this is what we experience in Donne's sudden shift in tone from mock piety to seeming frankness and candor in the final lines. "But now alas," he exclaims, as if shaking off all pretense and play: here is what I really want you to know, here is what this poem should—and will—keep alive.

The second poem in the *Songs and Sonnets* that conjures up a posthumous future for Donne and his beloved in poetry rather than in heaven is "The Canonization." This poem begins in the spirit of "The Anniversarie," with Donne fretting over how he and his mistress might be left alone to enjoy their love in the present without disruptions or protestations from the world that surrounds them:

For Godsake hold your tongue, and let me love,
Or chide my palsie, or my gout,
My five gray hairs, or ruin'd fortune flout,
With wealth your state, your minde with Arts improve,

Take you a course, get you a place,
Observe his honour, or his grace,
Or the Kings reall, or his stamped face
Contemplate, what you will, approve,
So you will let me love. (1–9)

This initial concern with the present—with making room for the couple to be left alone to their mutual pleasures—shifts over the course of the poem to a second, and far less immediate, preoccupation: how the poet might best ensure that the love he and his beloved share will somehow survive their deaths. This shift in focus from their experience now to their memory later begins in the third stanza, in which Donne twice describes the couple's miraculous ways of "dying":

Call us what you will, wee are made such by love;
Call her one, mee another flye,
We'are Tapers too, and at our owne cost die,
And wee in us finde the Eagle and the Dove.
The Phoenix riddle hath more wit
By us, we two being one, are it.
So to one neutrall thing both sexes sit,
We dye and rise the same, and prove
Mysterious by this love. (19–27)

The poet assumes the first-person plural "we" (the first two stanzas still operate in the world of "she and I"), and the series of metaphors he unravels—from flies to tapers to birds—moves from one image to the next in search of a simultaneously discrete but shared identity. Hence the first mention of their mutual deaths—as inanimate "tapers" or candles whose burning affects no one but themselves—is improved upon in the second image of death by burning, with the mythical figure of the phoenix. The phoenix, when consumed by fire, is said to be reborn from its own ashes. To this traditional symbol of immortality Donne adds a new layer, envisioning himself and his beloved as this single creature now endowed with both male and female sexual attributes.

"We dye and rise the same, and prove / Mysterious by this love": the sexual suggestiveness of this claim, with its boast of the lovers' ever-renewable climaxes, has tended to distract critical attention from the metaphysical point that Donne makes in these lines about the nature of mortality and rebirth. Judging from the direction in which the poem progresses, this latter point seems to have grabbed the poet's imagination more firmly than the idea of inexhaustible eros. The next stanza moves to a straightforward use of the verb *to die* and the question of what kind of future awaits the lovers after death:

> We can dye by it, if not live by love,
> And if unfit for tombes and hearse
> Our legend bee, it will be fit for verse;
> And if no peece of Chronicle wee prove,
> We'll build in sonnets pretty roomes;
> As well a well wrought urne becomes
> The greatest ashes, as half-acre tombes,
> And by these hymnes, all shall approve
> Us *Canoniz'd* for Love. (28–36)

According to Cleanth Brooks, one of the pioneers of the New Criticism, the "well wrought urne" is the poem as a complex aesthetic object.[30] But it is crucial to recognize that the vehicle and tenor can be reversed. The poem is also the receptacle for the lovers' ashes, the shared grave in which their remains are mingled. The poem, that is, becomes the urn.

Playing on the Italian word *stanza*, Donne's envisions the sonnet as a kind of burial chamber whose "pretty roomes"—both poetic and architectural spaces—will house the "legend" of the lovers. But he describes the sonnet not only as a mechanism for commemoration: he is also imagining a form of immortalization. Like those of the phoenix, the ashes that the poem contains are poised to rise again. In the poem's last stanza, Donne fantasizes about his and his beloved's future admirers who have "canoniz'd" them for the wonders of their love, and he makes clear that their status as saints is not a memorial designation but a description of their active position in the afterlife:

And thus invoke us: You whom reverend love
Made one anothers hermitage;
You, to whom love was peace, that now is rage;
Who did the whole worlds soule contract, and drove
Into the glasses of your eyes
(So made such mirrors, and such spies,
That they did all to you epitomize,)
Countries, Townes, Courts: Beg from above
A patterne of your love! (37–45)

The final couplet turns fully to the new role of the erotic saints: the crowd of worshipers petitions the canonized pair to intercede on their behalf in order to obtain the lovers' "patterne" for love. This "patterne" has transcended the earthly sphere; it has been absorbed, like a Platonic idea, into the world above. Thus the poem containing the lovers' remains becomes the earthly instantiation of the heavenly template. It is not only immortal but also sacred.

Donne's claim here, needless to say, is hyperbolic: the idea that he and his mistress will be appealed to as heavenly saints in the unspecified (and less harmonious) future is of a piece with his claim in "The Relique" that the "bracelet of bright haire about the bone" will be worshiped in a future time of idolatry. In both cases, Donne playfully draws upon Catholic beliefs or practices outlawed by Protestantism in imagining modes of elevation for his love. It is easy to overlook, however, the serious claim that is being made as well: a claim for the power of the poem to convey more successfully than hair or bone or tomb or urn what it was that passed between them. This is what the future admirers are asking for, and this is what Donne's poem can deliver. If we cannot ourselves share an eternal life in the heavens, he suggests, we can at least have enduring poems that capture what it felt like to love and be loved at this particular moment for these particular lovers. Donne's lyric becomes the poetic equivalent of the Etruscan tomb with which this book began: a representation of love that, while we are in its presence, feels palpably alive.

6

Carpe Diem

Let's feast and frolick, sing and play,
And thus lesse last, then live our Day.
                    —Robert Herrick, "A Paranoeticall"

The idea of the poem as the site for posthumous love shifted expectations for a shared afterlife from the heavenly sphere to the literary artifact. But at its core this idea still retained the belief that love could somehow transcend mortality. In the bids for poetic immortality made by Spenser or Shakespeare or Donne, there were still traces of an attachment to the prospect of extending earthly passion to the afterlife, even if this extension took the form of sonnets rather than souls. The next and final phase of the history we have been exploring—the history of how English love poetry evolved through an understanding of human love as mortal—comes with the seventeenth-century *carpe diem* lyric. These are poems that magnify the pleasures of this world at the expense of the next, poems that do not compensate for, but instead capitalize on, the nothingness that awaits lovers in the afterlife in order fully to embrace what this life has to offer.

The *carpe diem* lyric builds on—and reverses—the strain of Elizabethan poetry described in chapter 3, in which death is welcomed as a permanent release from erotic suffering. For *carpe diem* poets death is equally decisive in terminating love, but far from being the desired end, it serves as the looming threat against which they make their case for seizing the day. English *carpe diem* poetry exploits the positive consequences of denying the continuity of love across the grave. Following very much in the path of *Romeo and Juliet*, these poems imagine the intensification of erotic experience by virtue of its temporal limits.

I. Carpe diem

In their search for poetic models that regarded love's restriction to this world as a strength, not a weakness, Renaissance poets turned once again to the ancient Romans. Unlike the topos of poetic immortality, which spanned both the classical and the Petrarchan tradition, the genre of *carpe diem* had no presence in Petrarch's poetry. The message of seizing the day ran counter to the project of sustaining love over long stretches of time, whether in life or in death; Petrarch also generally shied away from the physical intimacy that drives the majority of *carpe diem* poems and did not frame Laura's beauty in terms that were vulnerable to time.[1] Thus the English poet's primary inspiration for *carpe diem* came from a body of pagan poetry that provided the strongest possible alternative—both poetically and emotionally—to the idea of transcendent love.

The phrase *carpe diem* comes from book 1 of Horace's *Odes*, in which Horace cautions Leuconoe, who was probably his lover and possibly also his servant or slave, not to venture to predict when they may meet their ends:

> Don't you ask, Leuconoe—the gods do not wish it to be known—
> what end they have given to me or to you, and don't meddle with
> Babylonian calculations. How much better to accept whatever comes,
> whether Jupiter gives us other winters or whether this is our last
> now wearying the Tyrrhenian Sea on the pumice stones
> opposing it. Be wise, strain the wine and cut back long hope
> into a small space. While we speak, envious time will have
> flown past. Harvest the day and leave as little as possible for tomorrow.[2]

This is a short poem—eight lines in all—and its message is simple. Let us not worry about when death will come, and let us not attempt to alter our fates; that would all be futile. Live each day, rather, as if it were your last, and reserve nothing for tomorrow. *Carpere* is a verb used for harvesting crops, for plucking and gathering from the fields. To do this to the day is to pluck the day bare, to exhaust its resources until there is nothing left behind. For Horace, death is neither to be welcomed nor feared; it lies outside human control and is not worth any expenditure of time. In this ode that gave to Western poetry the resonant command *carpe diem*, Horace advocates for the most modest of pleasures: "Be wise, strain the wine, and cut back long hope / into a small space."

Horace's turn in this poem away from the abstract prospect of death toward the immediate needs of the present is typical of his odes as a whole: their energy falls on luxuriating in the moment at hand and not on anticipating the inevitable end. In *Ode* 1.9, Horace encourages his friend Thaliarchus:

> Thaw out the cold. Pile up the logs
> on the hearth and be more generous, Thaliarchus,
> as you draw the four-year-old Sabine
> from its two-eared cask. . . .
> Don't ask what will happen tomorrow.
> Whatever day Fortune gives you, enter it
> as profit, and don't look down on love
> and dancing while you're still a lad. (5–8, 13–16)

The scene conjured up is a cold winter day, and Horace's message once again is a simple one: use more wood, pour more wine, don't shun love and dancing. What awaits Thaliarchus tomorrow is not something Horace can predict, and hence he wastes little time imagining it. Instead, he focuses on taking what the day gives him as profit or gain:

> Now is the time for the Campus and the squares
> and soft sighs at the time arranged
> as darkness falls.

Now is the time for the lovely laugh from the secret corner
giving away the girl in her hiding-place,
and for the token snatched from her arm
or feebly resisting finger. (18–24)

The pressure of the present, expressed in the anaphora "Now" (Nunc), is meant to propel Thaliarchus from the company of his friend to the company of the girl, from the hearth to the piazza.

Horace's emphasis on the immediate possibilities of the present as a means of pushing away the future characterizes much of classical *carpe diem* poetry, where death plays little role except as a distant boundary that recedes further and further the more fully the "now" is apprehended. Propertius describes his sexual intimacy with Cynthia as a transformation of mortal time into something that feels like immortality:

If she is willing to grant me such nights
With her, it will be a huge year in my life;
And if she'll give many nights, I'll become immortal in them:
In a single night, she makes anybody feel like a god.[3]

The goal is not long, steady love but single nights of such pleasure that they produce the sensation of exiting time altogether.

In Catullus's great *Carmina 5*, "Let us live, my Lesbia, and let us love" (Vivamus mea Lesbia atque amemus)—a poem widely translated and imitated during the Elizabethan period[4]—he describes what a night like the one Propertius desires might feel like, multiplying exponentially the kisses that he and Lesbia will exchange so that they may escape from the world of numbers and time:

Lesbia, live with me
& love me so
we'll laugh at all
the sour-faced strict-
ures of the wise.

This sun once set
will rise again,
when our sun sets
follows night &
an endless sleep.
Kiss me now a
thousand times &
now a hundred
more & then a
hundred & a
thousand more again
till with so many
hundred thousand
kisses you & I
shall both lose count
nor any can
from envy of
so much of kissing
put his finger
on the number
of sweet kisses
you of me &
I of you,
darling, have had.[5]

On the other side of their pleasure there is nothing that the poet cares to imagine: it is only "night & / an endless sleep." "Nox est perpetua una dormienda": this is a more or less Stoical account of what awaits us in the afterlife, and in the hands of someone like Seneca, such a vision would serve as a consoling reminder that there is nothing to fear from our extinction. For Catullus, however, it is no consolation but the strongest of incentives to enjoy the short light that he and Lesbia may share. Death does not hover over the poem as a menace, nor does it actively threaten to pull the lovers from each other. It is simply that which will put an end to their pleasure, pleasure that therefore needs to be enjoyed now.

II. Carpe florem

When Renaissance English poets began to write *carpe diem* lyrics, the models of Horace and Propertius and Catullus remained firmly in their minds. But they also brought to the poems a different understanding of death and its aftermath, one that was informed by the Petrarchan idea of transcendent love that they had left behind. As we have seen, Latin love poets did not generally imagine a shared afterlife for lovers, but they were also not actively rejecting such a tradition. The idea of heavenly reunion simply formed no part of their ontological universe. For English *carpe diem* poets, by contrast, the refusal of the idea of a transcendent erotic reunion not only intensified the preciousness of the present but also cast a dark shadow across it. The result was a body of poems that reflects an intense awareness of both the religious and the literary traditions that it had more or less overturned.

Literary scholars tend to treat Renaissance *carpe diem* poetry as a lighthearted genre of love lyrics indifferent to the pains of tomorrow. This is, in effect, also the message of Sir Walter Ralegh's poem "The Nymph's Reply to the Shepherd," which offers a strong indictment of the realities that *carpe diem* poetry either ignores or turns to its advantage. Ralegh's poem begins by stating a hypothetical condition that would be required for his speaker—the nymph—to return the shepherd's love:

> If all the world and love were young,
> And truth in every shepherd's tongue,
> These pretty pleasures might me move
> To live with thee and be thy love.

Over the course of the next few stanzas, the nymph explains why these conditions could never be met. In order to return the shepherd's love, the nymph suggests, she would require assurances that contradict every feature of the *carpe diem* tradition:

> But could youth last and love still breed,
> Had joys no date nor age no need,

Then these delights my mind might move
To live with thee and be thy love.[6]

The poem to which Ralegh is responding, Christopher Marlowe's "The Passionate Shepherd to His Love," is not a *carpe diem* poem per se; it lacks the awareness of eventual darkness that characterizes this genre. Instead Marlowe's poem is, in effect, a prelapsarian vision of a pastoral world that does not recognize the fragility of either beauty or love. At the end of Marlowe's poem, the shepherd declares:

The shepherd swains shall dance and sing
For thy delight each May morning:
If these delights thy mind may move,
Then live with me and be my love.[7]

The nymph's answer to the shepherd—or Ralegh's answer to Marlowe—is more or less the answer that Leuconoe might have made to Horace: I won't come to you today unless today can be repeated over a long stretch of time; I can't live in a *carpe diem* world because, despite your claims to the contrary, there will be a tomorrow.

English *carpe diem* poetry does not generally occupy the innocent world of Marlowe's shepherd, nor is it in any way frivolous or naive. Whatever surface frivolity there may be typically masks, in fact, a very serious engagement with both theological and philosophical ideas about the consequences of death.[8] For English Renaissance poets, the act of writing *carpe diem* lyrics required a decisive break with Christian metaphysics. There could be no mention of the soul's eventual journey to heaven in poems that urge an immediate seizing of the present; there could be no deferral of joy in poems that imagine this day as the lovers' only chance for bliss. *Carpe diem* poetry always depended upon a physical basis for love, but this physical basis became all the more pronounced when the idea of a spiritual afterlife for lovers was actively rejected.

The most obvious register of a shift in emphasis from classical to English *carpe diem* lies in the heightened attention given by Renaissance poets to the material consequences of aging and death. This is not to say that the theme of fading beauty was altogether absent from Roman poetry. In Ovid's *Ars Amatoria* he warns his female readers:

> There'll come a time when
> You who today lock out your lovers will lie
> Old and cold and alone in bed, your door never broken
> Open at brawling midnight, never at dawn
> Scattered roses bright on your threshold! Too soon—ah horror!—
> Flesh goes slack and wrinkled, the clear
> Complexion is lost, those white streaks you swear date back to
> Your schooldays suddenly spread,
> You're grey-haired.[9]

The solution that Ovid proposes represents the subgenre of the *carpe florem* poem. "Pluck the flower [*carpite florem*]," Ovid tells the young women, "left unplucked / It will wither and fall" (80–81). Of course the flower will wither regardless of whether it is plucked; once plucked, in fact, it will die more quickly, but at least it will give pleasure. The resonance of the flower as a metaphor for virginity makes Ovid's point all the more explicit: the unplucked virgin, like the unplucked flower, cannot be preserved for a better, future purpose. She needs to be enjoyed now.

For English poets, the *carpe florem*—or in its most popular form, *carpe rosam*—poem fit very well within a tradition that preferred on the whole neither to imagine the elevation of love from the material to the spiritual level nor to allow for passage between the earthly and the heavenly sphere.[10] At issue was simply the fleeting moment of the beloved's bloom, which had no possibility of renewal or transformation. Moreover, because these poets did not typically represent the loss of beauty as adequately compensated by a gain in spiritual virtue or wisdom, the onset of age brought nothing to look forward to other than corporeal decay. The threat of aging was the perfect complement to the threat of death: both put an absolute end to erotic bonds.

Although the real flourishing of the *carpe diem* lyric did not occur until the mid-seventeenth century, there were a number of these poems written in the Elizabethan period, most notably of the *carpe florem* or *carpe rosam* variety.[11] On the whole, however, they are missing from the sonnet sequences most celebrated by literary history: Spenser's *Amoretti* and Shakespeare's *Sonnets* lack any sustained examples, and Sidney's *Astrophil and Stella* includes a *carpe diem* motif only within one of its longer poems, the "Fourth Song."[12] This absence is almost certainly not coincidental: the message of seizing the day is fundamentally at odds with the narrative thrust of the sonnet series, which depends upon sustained attention to a single beloved and endurance of the erotic drama as it slowly unfolds. *Carpe diem* is also at odds with the pursuit of poetic immortality that we considered in the last chapter, a pursuit whose energies are directed at creating long-lasting artifacts and not on enjoying immediate pleasures. The *carpe diem* poem is much better suited to the freestanding individual lyric that makes its case independently of any other poems that come before or after it. It is best as a wager of its own.

The one important exception to this general rule is Daniel's *Delia*, which includes several *carpe florem* sonnets that capture what will become one of the most characteristic features of the English *carpe diem* lyric: namely, a tendency to tilt the balance of the poem away from the pleasure of the moment itself toward the impending reversal of the beloved's fortune. (This tendency was, as we have already seen with Ovid, particularly compatible with *carpe florem* lyrics due to the flower's short lifespan and fragile bloom.) In the last chapter we looked at the corona of five sonnets that culminates with Daniel's affirmation that his poems will grant Delia the gift of immortality. As I briefly noted, this embedded corona begins with several *carpe diem* sonnets in which Daniel reminds Delia of her imminent decline:

> Looke *Delia* how wee steeme the half-blowne Rose,
> The image of thy blush, and Sommers honour:
> Whilst in her tender greene she doth inclose,
> That pure sweete beauty Time bestowes upon her.
> No sooner spreades her glory in the ayre,
> But straight her ful-blowne pride is in declining;
> Shee then is scorn'd that late adorn'd the fayre:
> So clowdes thy beauty after fairest shining.
> No Aprill can revive thy withred flowers,
> Whose blooming grace adornes thy glory now:

Swift speedy Time, feathred with flying howers,
Dissolves the beautie of the fairest brow.
O let not then such riches waste in vaine,
But love whilst that thou maist be lov'd againe.[13]

The focus of this poem falls on the single moment of the rose's perfection, when it is no longer closed nor yet fully in bloom—"half blowne," it is on the cusp of revealing the "glory" that will then lead precipitously to its decline—and its message is clearly admonitory.[14] "Looke Delia," Daniel warns, understand that your beauty is like that of the rose, your "blooming grace" only temporary. Not only will Delia's beauty wither and fade, he predicts: it will even "dissolve." *Dissolve* conjures up a more thorough undoing, a disintegration or decomposition associated with Epicurean accounts of what happens to the body after death. According to Lucretius, matter is never annihilated, but is simply broken down into its elemental forms: "nature resolves everything into its constituent particles, she never annihilates anything."[15] For Delia's beauty to dissolve suggests not only the addition of wrinkles to the brow but the unmaking of the brow altogether. This dissolution of beauty is directly linked, as the final couplet makes clear, to the dissolution of love: "O let not then such riches waste in vaine, / But love whilst that thou maist be lov'd againe." To be loved is a temporary condition.

The *carpe florem* message continues in *Delia* 35, which begins, in the corona manner, with the warning that closed *Delia* 34:

But love whilst that thou maist be lov'd againe.
Now whilst thy May hath fill'd thy lap with flowers;
Now whilst thy beauty beares without a staine;
Now use thy Sommer smiles, ere Winter lowers.
And whilst thou spread'st unto the rysing sunne,
The fairest flowre that ever saw the light:
Now ioy thy time before thy sweete be done,
And (*Delia*,) thinke thy morning must have night.
And that thy brightnes sets at length to West:
When thou wilt close up that which now thou showest:
And thinke the same becomes thy fading best,

Which then shall hide it most, and cover lowest.
Men doe not we[igh] the stalke for that it was,
When once they finde her flowre, her glory passe.

The urgency of Daniel's message is conveyed, as in Horace's *Ode* 1.9,
through the anaphora "now." This is repeated three times in the first
quatrain and leads to the first of the poem's commands: "Now ioye thy
time before thy sweete be done."

Delia, it seems, cannot imagine any of this: unlike Horace's Leuconoe, she is not fretting about what the future might bring but seems
altogether indifferent to its dangers. It is for this reason that Daniel exhorts her, twice, to "thinke." However beautiful the morning may be, he
reminds her, it will inevitably fade into night; however bright she might
be now, she will soon, like the glowing sun, be shrouded in darkness. In
place of the personal petition that concluded the previous sonnet—"But
love whilst that thou maist be lov'd againe"—Sonnet 35 ends with an axiomatic warning about what men value. And what men do not value is a
stalk without a bloom—a strange image that conjures up less a withered
flower than a decapitated corpse.

The rather extreme, threatening tone—a foretaste, as it were, of
what Marvell will do some sixty or seventy years later—does not continue past *Delia* 35. In the next poem Daniel begins to relent:

Fresh shalt thou see in mee the wounds thou madest,
Though spent thy flame, in me the heat remaining,
I that have lou'd thee thus before thou fadest,
My faith shall waxe, when thou art in thy waining.
The world shall finde this myracle in mee,
That fire can burne, when all the matter's spent. (*Delia* 36, 5–10)

His love, he concedes, will continue even when his beloved is for all
practical purposes beyond loving—when her "matter," as he coolly puts
it, is "spent." This recuperation of his love for her after her physical decline undermines, of course, the force of the earlier two sonnets in the
corona. It also repositions *Delia* within the more common framework of
the Elizabethan sonnet series, which, as we have seen, is typically more

interested in the long-term project of immortality than in the short-term project of satisfaction.

III. *Herrick's* Hesperides

It is only in the mid-seventeenth century that the *carpe diem* becomes a powerful genre of its own, untempered in its assessment of mortality by the compensations of the Elizabethan sonnet tradition. There is no obvious reason why *carpe diem* became so prominent a genre at this time, but several different explanations come to the fore. First, works of classical materialism and Epicurean philosophy began to circulate more widely in the mid-seventeenth century than in earlier decades, and their idea of the afterlife as a meaningless category for the individual's experience fit well with a *carpe diem* message that there is nothing awaiting us after death.

Second, the instability of the political climate leading up to and during the English Civil War created more incentives for seizing immediate and temporary pleasures; the idea that the world was coming to its end had a sufficiently wide reach, attracting not only millenarian radicals but also more ordinary Protestants on both sides of the political divide. Many responded to this threat by devoting themselves to repentance and prayer, but others translated this anxiety into a kind of seductive energy, urging the pleasures of the day before the day was no more.

Finally, within the framework of literary history, *carpe diem* is the logical consequence of the poetic development that began with Wyatt's rejection of Petrarch's conception of posthumous love. It is a stripping from the afterlife of all forms of pleasure that could compensate for erotic loss, including even the pleasure of poetic immortality or fame. In overturning both Petrarchan ideas of heavenly continuity and English reactions to this Petrarchan paradigm, the *carpe diem* lyric becomes a revolutionary poetic form, considerably raising the stakes of the classical model from which it sprang.

The most prolific practitioner of English *carpe diem* was Robert Herrick, whose celebrated opening lines in "To the Virgins, to make much of Time"—"Gather ye rosebuds while ye may / The time is still a flying"—have become virtually synonymous with the genre itself.[16] But

Herrick's collection of verse *Hesperides* (1648) could almost be considered an anthology of *carpe diem* lyrics, and the breadth of its examples is quite startling.[17] First, *Hesperides* includes a large number of epigrams or very short *carpe diem* poems that are not directed at a lover and that tend to be axiomatic in nature: "Let's live in hast; use pleasures while we may / Co'd life return, 'twod never lose a day"; or "Drink Wine, and live here blithefull, while ye may / The morrows life too late is, Live to day"; or "While Fate permits us, let's be merry; / Passe all we must the fatall Ferry / And this our life too whirles away, / With the Rotations of the Day." Behind each of these poems is a bracingly frank recognition of death's proximity, which he summarizes perhaps best in his poem "Anacreontike":

> Born I was to be old,
> And for to die here:
> After that, in the mould
> Long for to lye here.
> But before that day comes,
> Still I be Bousing;
> For I know, in the Tombs
> There's no Carousing.

Here and elsewhere, Herrick does not push aside the threat of mortality (as Horace, for example, regularly does). Instead, the acknowledgment of the threat is what drives the poet forward, what leads him to his "bousing" (boozing) and "carousing."

The second category of *carpe diem* poems in *Hesperides* are addressed directly to a lover or potential lover, each of whom is given a classical name that ties the poems back to their classical predecessors. "To Electra" begins with a personal plea to his mistress to come out that evening—"Tis Ev'ning, my Sweet, / And dark; let us meet / Long time w'ave here been a toying" (1–3)—and concludes:

> Time flyes away fast;
> Our houres doe waste:
> The while we never remember,

How soone our life, here,
Growes old with the yeere,
That dyes with the next *December*. (13–18)

In "To Sappho," Herrick sets his *carpe diem* message against a vision not only of aging or death but also of lying dormant in the earth:

Let us now take time, and play,
Love, and live here while we may;
Drink rich wine, and make good cheere,
While we have our being here:
For, once dead, and laid' i'th grave,
No return from thence we have.

This is, once again, exactly the kind of message that is characteristic of English *carpe diem* and not of its classical counterpart. The emphasis on the corpse and the impossibility of its revival seems designed specifically to overturn Christian ideas of resurrection, a note that is especially surprising given Herrick's position as a vicar in the English church.

Third, there are a group of lyrics in *Hesperides* that are not strictly *carpe diem* poems but are imbued with a spirit of celebrating the local and particular pleasures of the moment. We might think of them as applied *carpe diem*. These are poems that show us what it might look like, or feel like, to live a life inspired by *carpe diem*; they are performative rather than descriptive. In "The Shooe tying," for example, Herrick describes a rather modest ascent up his mistress's leg:

Anthea bade me tye her shooe;
I did, and kist the Instep too,
And would have kist unto her knee,
Had not her Blush rebuked me.

Or, in a bolder poem, "Upon Julia's breasts," he asks Julia to lay bare her breasts for his kisses:

Display thy breasts, my *Julia*, there let me
Behold that circummortall purity:
Betweene whose glories, there my lips Ile lay,
Ravisht, in that faire *Via Lactea*.

Herrick coined the word *circummortall* in these lines, meaning "more than mortal": here he anticipates the intense pleasure of burying his lips within the "*Via Lactea*," or "Milky Way," of her bosom.[18] There are many more examples of these ebullient poems, and in all of them we glimpse Herrick's wonderful capacity to be absorbed by the immediate erotic occasion.

Finally, there are two long and complex *carpe diem* poems in *Hesperides* that represent major contributions, and even transformations, of the genre. The first of these has been almost entirely overlooked by modern readers, perhaps due in part to its unwieldy title: "A Paranoeticall, or Advisive Verse, to his friend M. John Wicks." "A Paranoeticall" is the second lyric in *Hesperides* addressed to Herrick's friend John Weekes, and it expands on the earlier poem's *carpe diem* themes. In "His age, dedicated to his peculiar friend, M. John Wickes, under the name of Posthumus," Herrick laments their mutual aging—"Ah *Posthumus*! Our yeares hence flye / And leave no sound" (1–2)—and urges his friend to join him in making the most of the present:

A merry mind
Looks forward, scornes what's left behind:
Let's live, my *Wickes*, then, while we may,
And here enjoy our Holiday. (13–16)

Death is handled in a fully classical vein, with the afterlife described alternately as "the doome of cruel *Proserpine*" and "where *Anchus* and rich *Tullus* blend / Their sacred seed" (8; 26–27). (Anchus and Tullus were both ancient Roman kings.) The consolation Herrick offers Weekes is also fully consistent with classical *carpe diem*: "Why then, since life to us is short, / Let's make it full up, by our sport" (31–32).

In "A Paranoeticall, or Advisive Verse," Herrick complicates the strictly classical message, bringing to the poem a more contemporary English preoccupation with death and its material consequences. This poem begins by asking the simple and profound question of what constitutes a life worth living:

> Is this a life to break thy sleep?
> To rise as soon as day doth peep?
> To tire thy patient Oxe or Asse
> By noone, and let thy good dayes passe,
> Not knowing This, that *Jove* decrees
> Some mirth, t'adulce mans miseries? (1-6)

Criticizing his friend for laboring too hard, he advises Weekes to "Let your servant strut thy barnes with sheafs of Wheat":

> Time steals away like to a stream,
> And we glide hence away with them.
> *No sound recalls the houres once fled,*
> *Or Roses, being withered:*
> Nor us (my Friend) when we are lost,
> Like to a Deaw, or melted Frost.
> Then live we mirthfull, while we should,
> And turn the iron Age to Gold.
> Let's feast, and frolick, sing and play,
> And thus lesse last, then live our Day.
> *Whose life with care is overcast,*
> *That man's not said to live, but last:*
> *Nor is't a life, seven yeares to tell,*
> *But for to live that half seven well:*
> And that wee'l do; as men, who know,
> Some few sands spent, we hence must go,
> Both to be blended in the Urn,
> From whence there's never a return. (22-39)

The central distinction Herrick draws is between "lasting" and "living": "Let's feast, and frolick, sing and play, / And thus lesse last, then live our Day." He advocates for shorter, but better, time on earth.

The editor of the Oxford edition of *Hesperides*, L. C. Martin, draws a parallel between "A Paranoeticall" and the central *carpe diem* passage in book 3 of Ovid's *Ars Amatoria*, but the differences are in fact more telling. In the lines preceding those we looked at earlier—in which Ovid warns his female readers that one day they will lie alone, unloved, in their beds—he declares:

> Have fun while you can, in your salad days; the years glide
> Past like a moving stream,
> And the water that's gone can never be recovered,
> The lost hour never returns. (61–64)

There is no subsequent account, however, of the horrors that await us after death. Instead, as we have seen, Ovid goes on to describe only the awkward circumstances that await the older, less attractive woman.

For Herrick, by contrast, the message of *carpe diem* is not set against the chances for love in old age or the fading of beauty. Instead, it is set against the more absolute material fate of the body. First, he describes a process of evaporation similar to what Hamlet describes in his wish that his "too too solid flesh would melt, / Thaw, and resolve itself into a dew" (1.2.129–30): "*No sound recalls the houres once fled, / Or Roses, being withered: / Nor us (my Friend) when we are lost, / Like to a Deaw, or melted Frost.*" Herrick then juxtaposes this vision of matter dissolving to an even more stubbornly materialist vision of their posthumous bodies, a vision of the two friends "both blended in the Urn."

The specific prospect of becoming a heap of ashes mixed in the urn certainly does not conform to church doctrine: cremation was not a sanctified means of burial in the Church of England, nor were urns commonly used in seventeenth-century parishes.[19] (It is also tempting to read the "both," along with the "blended," as a suggestion of a shared urn, but there is little else in the poem to support the idea that Herrick imagines his eventual burial with his friend.) Herrick's insistence, moreover, that the urn is a place "From whence there's never a return" flouts all Christian reassurances of resurrection. Once again, we are reminded of Hamlet's musings on death as the "undiscovered country from whose bourn / No traveller returns" (3.1.81–82).

That "A Paranoeticall" departs from Protestant eschatology is abundantly clear, but this could be said of seventeenth-century *carpe diem* lyrics on the whole. What is unusual about this poem is its almost aggressive overturning of Christian expectations about death, burial, and the afterlife in a manner that is not present, for example, in a poem like "To the Virgins, to make much of Time." In "To the Virgins," Herrick does not refer to the remains of the flesh at all; there is no mention of dew or frost or ashes. The attention to these remains in "A Paranoeticall," and the total lack of any complementary reference to Christian salvation, both intensifies the imperative for pleasure ("Let's feast, and frolick, sing and play") and frames it within a much darker context. The future is not a *nox perpetua* but a place of decomposed matter.

The second remarkable *carpe diem* poem in *Hesperides* is the well-known lyric "Corinna's *going a Maying*." In this poem, Herrick's acknowledgment of what will come on the other side of the present day—whether heralded by the arrival of tomorrow, or old age, or death—is deferred until the very last stanza, while the pleasures of the moment are dilated, as it were, over the course of the prior fifty-six lines. The immediate task of rousing Corinna from her bed and bringing her to the May Day festivities is so all-consuming, and so full of pastoral charm, that we might easily imagine ourselves in a very different kind of poem, a more innocent version—or in fact, an inversion—of a poem like Donne's "Elegy XIX: To His Mistress Going to Bed," which spends all of its poetic energy trying to get his mistress into bed rather than out of it.

The opening stanzas of "Corinna's *going a Maying*" suggest a combination of holiday mirth and seduction that carries few hints of the *carpe diem* message that awaits us:

Get up, get up for shame, the Blooming Morne
Upon her wings presents the god unshorne.
   See how *Aurora* throwes her faire
   Fresh-quilted colours through the aire:
   Get up, sweet-Slug-a-bed, and see
   The Dew-bespangling Herbe and Tree.
Each Flower has wept, and bow'd toward the East,
Above an houre since; yet you not drest,

Nay! not so much as out of bed?
When all the Birds have Mattens seyd,
    And sung their thankful Hymnes: 'tis sin,
Nay, profanation to keep in,
When as a thousand Virgins on this day,
Spring, sooner then the Lark, to fetch in May.

Rise; and put on your Foliage, and be seene
To come forth, like the Spring-time, fresh and greene;
    And sweet as *Flora*. Take no care
    For Jewels for your Gowne, or Haire:
    Feare not; the leaves will strew
    Gemms in abundance upon you:
Besides, the childhood of the Day has kept,
Against you come, some *Orient Pearls* unwept:
    Come, and receive them while the light
    Hangs on the Dew-locks of the night:
    And *Titan* on the Eastern hill
    Retires himselfe, or else stands still
Till you come forth. Wash, dresse, be briefe in praying:
Few Beads are best, when once we goe a Maying. (1–28)

Leah Marcus has persuasively shown the extent to which Herrick inter-
weaves in these stanzas aspects of pagan and Anglican rituals; even
those gestures that seem most heathen, she argues, have liturgical resonances that reveal symmetries between pagan and Christian modes of
May Day celebration.[20]

What is jarring about the poem, however, is less its mingling of
paganism and church practice than its abrupt darkening of mood in the
final stanza, a shift in tone that has little precedent in either classical or
early modern *carpe diem*. From its intense focus on the rhythms of the
present day with its festivities and rites and sexual liberties, the poem
suddenly widens its lens to the life cycle itself:

Come, let us goe, while we are in our prime;
And take the harmlesse follie of the time.

> We shall grow old apace, and die
> Before we know our liberty.
> Our life is short; and our dayes run
> As fast away as do's the Sunne:
> And as a vapour, or a drop of raine
> Once lost, can ne'r be found againe:
> So when or you or I are made
> A fable, song, or fleeting shade;
> All love, all liking, all delight
> Lies drown'd with us in endlesse night.
> Then while time serves, and we are but decaying;
> Come, my *Corinna*, come, let's goe a Maying. (57–70)

The nature of the urgency moves from the threat of missing this one particular occasion of May Day to the threat of missing all of life's opportunities for pleasure; the familiar *carpe diem* conceits at the opening of the stanza—"we shall grow old"; "our life is short"—shifts to much less conventional ideas of their posthumous fate. Herrick first compares human life to "a vapour, or a drop of raine," echoing the two earlier mentions of "dew" in the poem ("the Dew-bespangling Herbe and Tree" and "the dew-locks of the night"), but the outcome is not that he and Corinna will evaporate into the air. Instead, he imagines their becoming "A fable, song, or fleeting shade" (66). This is a strange combination of possibilities, intertwining the idea of their gaining immortality through poetry ("A fable, song") with the idea of their wandering as classical ghosts ("fleeting shade[s]") in the Elysian fields. Whichever fate it is, however, Herrick is clear that it will be devoid of all pleasure: "All love, all liking, all delight / Lies drown'd with us in endlesse night" (67–68).

In the final couplet the poem darkens even further: the ethereal and immaterial image of Herrick and Corinna as songs or shades is now compromised by a new emphasis on their physical bodies and the process of deterioration that is already well under way. To describe them as "but decaying" is to draw attention to their organic qualities, to treat them above all as matter and not also as spirit. This is the context in which Herrick reiterates his petition to "go a-Maying," a refrain that becomes eerily dissonant once it is paired with so different a message from the earlier stanzas. To "go a-Maying" hardly seems an adequate response, that is, to the existential threat that engulfs them—it feels extravagantly modest—and it is this juxtaposition that finally gives the poem its power. At the end of "Corinna's *going a Maying*," Herrick quietly exposes the huge disparity between the bleak posthumous reality—the comfortless vision of decay and eternal darkness—and the responses that are available: drink good wine, share many kisses, celebrate May Day. However great these pleasures may be in the moment (and the poem's opening stanzas make them sound nearly irresistible), they fall dramatically in scale before the prospect of the *nox perpetua*. This extreme adjustment in perspective had been missing from the *carpe diem* tradition up to this point, and its consequences were not insignificant. In "Corinna's *going a Maying*," *carpe diem* becomes ironic.

IV. Marvell's "Coy Mistress"

There is no Renaissance poem more ironic about the possibilities for posthumous love, and more skeptical about the consolations even of *carpe diem*, than Andrew Marvell's "To his Coy Mistress."[21] More than any other single lyric, "To his Coy Mistress" engages the full range of mortal poetics that I have sought to define in this book: a denial of love's transcendence; a concern with death and its physical consequences; a consideration of poetry's compensatory gift of immortality; an interest in seizing the pleasures of the moment; a recognition, or even embrace, of the temporal limits of love. We cannot know whether Marvell personally stood behind the positions advocated in the poem, and biographers and literary critics have hotly debated the question of the poet's identification with his speaker.[22] What matters for our purposes, however, is not whether Marvell identified with his speaker but the fact that through this speaker he gives voice to the most radical exposition of mortal love imaginable. His poem is the limit case, in effect, of what it means to reject posthumous love.

"To his Coy Mistress" begins with a counterfactual utterance that both embodies the central message of *carpe diem* and turns the Petrarchan condition of eternal love on its head: "Had we but world enough and time," Marvell declares, "This coyness, lady, were no crime." And yet, he protests, their situation is urgent. Mocking the implied leisure of Petrarchan conventions of praise, he imagines a slowing down of time that would enable their love to evolve:

> We would sit down, and think which way
> To walk, and pass our long love's day.
> Thou by the Indian Ganges' side
> Shouldst rubies find; I by the tide
> Of Humber would complain. I would
> Love you ten years before the Flood,
> And you should, if you please, refuse
> Till the conversion of the Jews.
> My vegetable love should grow
> Vaster than empires, and more slow;
> An hundred years should go to praise
> Thine eyes, and on thy forehead gaze;
> Two hundred to adore each breast,
> But thirty thousand to the rest:
> An age at least to every part,
> And the last age should show your heart.
> For Lady you deserve this state;
> Nor would I love at lower rate. (1–20)

These lines are often compared to Catullus's *Carmina* 5, "Let us live, my Lesbia, and let us love"; in that poem, as we saw earlier, Catullus envisions deceiving both jealous observers and time itself by multiplying exponentially the kisses that he and Lesbia exchange.[23] Marvell, however, dismisses the efficacy of dilation as a means to ward off death. He deems incompatible, that is, what Catullus regards as intertwined: on the one hand the urging of *carpe diem*, and on the other hand the prolonging of love. Of course, the delay that Catullus describes is itself a form of erotic satisfaction (kisses upon kisses), whereas Marvell hypothesizes only about the courtly prelude to any such thing. But the contrast between the two poems brings out the rigor of Marvell's. There is no time for any of the minor pleasures (kissing, praising, adoring) in the circumstances he describes.

The pressure that propels all *carpe diem* lyrics—the exigency of time—makes itself centrally felt in Marvell's second stanza, where time emerges at the heels of the lovers:

> But at my back I always hear
> Time's winged chariot hurrying near;
> And yonder all before us lie
> Deserts of vast eternity. (21–24)

No longer the domain of the distant gods who lurk in the inscrutable background of Horace's words to Leuconoe—"Don't you ask, Leuconoe—the gods do not wish it to be known— / What end they have given to me or to you"—time is ready to overtake these lovers at any moment. The urgency of what pursues them is set off against the blankness of what awaits, and this transformation of time ("eternity") into space ("Deserts") conjures up a seemingly godless expanse emptied of any comforts.[24] In comparison, even Catullus's "nox est perpetua una dormienda" has a certain cozy charm.

The posthumous landscape soon shifts, however, from the infinite space of the desert to the narrow confinement of the grave:

> Thy beauty shall no more be found,
> Nor, in thy marble vault, shall sound
> My echoing-song; then worms shall try
> That long-preserved virginity,
> And your quaint honor turn to dust,
> And into ashes all my lust.
> The grave's a fine and private place,
> But none, I think, do there embrace. (25–32)

We might recall Romeo's astonishment at Juliet's beauty when he finds her lifeless in the Capulet tomb: "Ah, dear Juliet, / Why art thou yet so fair?" This image of Juliet as a type of Persephone retaining her earthly beauty as Death's "paramour" turned out to be mistaken, of course: Juliet is not yet dead, and her corpse is destined to the same fate as the rest, a fact that Romeo himself acknowledges some lines later, when he refers to the "worms that are thy chambermaids" (5.3.109). Marvell invokes the same prospect of vermiculation within his mistress's "marble vault," but here the description is in the service of the attempted seduction. Better me, he proposes, than the worms.

Behind this seemingly simple choice lies a complete dismissal of the idea that his mistress's virginity carries any metaphysical worth whatsoever. It will not be preserved for a spiritual marriage with Christ, nor will it garner her rewards in heaven.[25] Like her "quaint honor," virginity is reduced to a strictly material possession (the common Renaissance pun on the word *quaint*, a medieval term for female genitalia, evokes this all the more).[26] Marvell also dispenses with any of the familiar seduction strategies deployed by earlier English poets, who urge the beloved's parting with his or her virginity in order to perpetuate beauty in the form of children; in these instances, sexual activity is treated as a necessary means to an end rather than openly acknowledged as the goal itself. This utilitarian position is the governing premise of the first group of sonnets in Shakespeare's sequence; it also surfaces in his *Venus and Adonis*, when Venus tries to lure Adonis to her bed by explaining that "By law of nature thou art bound to breed / That thine may live when thou thyself art dead / And so in spite of death thou dost survive / In that thy likeness still is left alive" (171-74). Likewise in Milton's *Comus*, the enchanter Comus exhorts the Lady to surrender her virginity in order not to hoard her beauty:

> List, lady, be not coy, and be not cozened
> With that same vaunted name Virginity;
> Beauty is Nature's coin, must not be hoarded,
> But must be current, and the good thereof
> Consists in mutual and partaken bliss,
> Unsavory in th'enjoyment of itself.
> If you let slip time, like a neglected rose
> It withers on the stalk with languished head. (737-44)

Sexual pleasure is acknowledged as the "good" that comes from beauty's use—the pleasure of "mutual and partaken bliss"—but Comus still deploys an economic argument for why such pleasure should be pursued.

In "To his Coy Mistress," Marvell does not justify his mistress's losing her virginity in terms of perpetuating her beauty or fulfilling her obligations to nature; he simply advocates for allowing him to have her. By replacing the traditional threat of the mistress's fading like a "neglected rose" with the much harsher vision of the decomposing corpse consumed by worms, Marvell exposes the *carpe rosam* conceit for the gentle metaphor that, of course, it always was. He also does not spare his own eventual return to base matter: his desire, he announces, will itself be reduced to corporeal remains ("into ashes all my lust"). There is nothing transcendent about either her virtue or his passion, both of which will lie dead in the tomb.

There is also nothing transcendent, he declares, about his poetry. Marvell's denial of his "echoing song" is a particularly aggressive note to strike, since the marble tomb, unlike the "deserts of vast eternity," would be as good an echo chamber as any. By refusing the comfort of his poetry within the tomb, Marvell negates the idea that was held so dear by many of his English counterparts (even Herrick, who is hardly sentimental, played with the idea of becoming a "fable" or "song"). For Marvell, there will be no "echoing song" in his coy mistress's tomb because poems, it would seem, are more like bodies after all. Very much against the spirit of Shakespeare's Sonnet 55, in which, as we saw, the poet affirms that his beloved will "pace forth" through the poem for "all posterity," Marvell declares that poems do not continue to echo once their originating voice is gone. Even the adjective *echoing* carries with it the lack of autonomous sound he imagines his poem to possess. It is only a trace.

There is another reason that the tomb will be bereft of Marvell's poetry. Marvell has no intention to lie alongside his mistress when he, too, is dead. It is not that he hopes to find a more suitable companion but rather that he has no interest in posthumous companionship whatsoever. Unlike generations of English men and women who desired burial with their spouses, Marvell describes the grave as entirely solitary: "The grave's a fine and private place / But none, I think, do there embrace." In this quiet but forceful demurral, intensified by the understated irony of "I think," Marvell issues a second blow to the compensatory pleasures that might accrue from within the bounds of mortal love.

Not only does poetry seem unable to offer immortality to lovers, but the tomb itself is no longer a site for posthumous intimacy. We might recall for the last time the words of Marvell's slightly older contemporary Sir Thomas Browne, who described the longing that even the lovers' physical remains felt to be together: "they affectionately compounded their bones, passionately endeavouring to continue their living Unions."[27] In the world of Marvell's poem, however, there is no satisfaction to be had from a reunion in the earth.

It is not altogether surprising that Marvell would take such a decisive position against posthumous intimacy. Elsewhere in his poetry, he describes paradise as a place of absolute solitude. In the midst of his soul's ecstatic flight from the body in "The Garden," he exclaims:

> Such was that happy garden-state,
> While man there walked without a mate:
> After a place so pure, and sweet,
> What other help could yet be meet?
> But 'twas beyond a mortal's share
> To wander solitary there:
> Two Paradises 'twere in one
> To live in Paradise alone. (57–64)

In the immediate context of "The Garden," the pleasure Marvell imagines of being in paradise has to do with the pleasure he experiences in liberation from the flesh. As in his "Dialogue between the Soul and the Body," he reveals his general dissatisfaction with human dualism, however necessary such an arrangement may be, and relishes the thought of "casting the body's vest aside" (51) in order to become pure soul. But the specific analogy Marvell draws—to Adam walking alone in Eden—points to a different kind of solitariness, the solitariness that Adam in fact protested when he beseeched God for a mate. In rewriting this episode from Genesis, Marvell assigns to Adam a pleasure that Adam is never described as experiencing, but that suggests Marvell's idea of the ultimate paradisiacal condition. "Two Paradises 'twere in one / To live in Paradise alone": Calvin's idea of our dispensing with our earthly loved ones in order to have only the company of God takes a hard, secularizing turn.

"To his Coy Mistress" is simultaneously the logical culmination and the deepest critique of the love poetry written in English over the course of the preceding century; it strips all expectation of posthumous love, it rejects the immortality of poetic verse, it denies even the possibility of sharing a single tomb.[28] In its last stanza, it also both epitomizes and strains to the very limits the central conceit of *carpe diem*:

> Now therefore, while the youthful hue
> Sits on thy skin like morning dew,
> And while thy willing soul transpires
> At every pore with instant fires,
> Let us sport us while we may;
> And now, like amorous birds of prey,
> Rather at once our time devour
> Than languish in his slow-chapped power.
> Let us roll all our strength, and all
> Our sweetness, up into one ball:
> And tear our pleasures with rough strife,
> Through the iron gates of life.[29]
> Thus, though we cannot make our sun
> Stand still, yet we will make him run. (33–46)

The invitation to beat time at its own game—to consume "at once" what time can do only slowly—is a direct overturning of the usual submission to time within the genre. And this is what Marvell's poem teaches us: it forces us to see that what may at first glance seem to be a challenge is in fact a form of yielding. Traditional *carpe diem* poetry, Marvell reveals, does not triumph over time so much as work within its confines. We might once again recall Horace's advice to Leuconoe not to attempt to negotiate with the fates, or we might look to Daniel's concession at the end of his lyric "A Pastorall": "Let's love: this life of ours / Can make no truce with time that all devours."[30]

In the final stanza of "To his Coy Mistress" Marvell offered a new response to the problems that had plagued English love poets since they fundamentally rejected the idea that love would continue past the grave. The solution Marvell proposed was not to operate within the boundaries of this world but to exit from this world violently: to combine the act of lovemaking with the act of death-taking in a sublime instance of *Liebestod*. The lovers may later lie in separate tombs, isolated for all eternity; at the moment described in this poem, however, they are a single unit, one that has rightly been likened to a cannonball.[31] As in *Romeo and Juliet*, to die together seems to represent the apex or *telos* of their love, but in Marvell's poem, unlike Shakespeare's play, death is entirely coincident with the sexual union itself.[32] This is the most, Marvell concludes, that earthly love may achieve: a fully consuming union whose sheer intensity rips through this world to the abyss of death with neither regrets nor expectations for anything more. The heavens have been left behind.

Limit Cases
Henry King and John Milton

From Wyatt's rejection of Petrarch's *in morte* sonnets in the early 1500s through the *carpe diem* lyrics of Herrick and Marvell written more than a hundred years later, this book has traced the poetic evolution of the idea that human love is mortal. There are two well-known poems from the end of this period that seem to defy this general trend, poems in which a posthumous reunion between lovers is either anticipated or momentarily experienced. Although they represent very different genres—the first is technically an "exequy," or form of elegy; the other is a sonnet—Henry King's "An Exequy To his Matchlesse never to be forgotten Freind" and John Milton's "Methought I saw my late espousèd saint" share as their central concern a desire for renewed intimacy with the poet's deceased spouse.

At the same time that both of these poems express the desire for posthumous reunion, however, they both also register the difficulty of conceiving of such a reunion as transcendent or eternal. King's "Exequy" dwells on the idea of a posthumous marriage between corpses, not heavenly souls; Milton's sonnet privileges the tempting allure of the immediate, fleeting moment rather than the solace of what lies further ahead. In both instances, the prospect of a heavenly meeting is entertained in a manner that seems uncharacteristic for English poets, but this prospect is buried within the middle of the poem and subsequently overwhelmed by stronger and more corporeal impulses. The urgency of each lyric lies not in its distant vision of heavenly satisfaction but in its expression of desire for more immediate gratification. In these important respects, King's "Exequy" and Milton's "Methought I saw my late espousèd saint" do not ultimately thwart our expectations for how English love poetry understands posthumous love. On the contrary: in the very act of imagining a reunion with the deceased spouse, both King and Milton unwittingly confirm some of the fundamental features of the tradition they had inherited. These two examples test, and corroborate, the degree to which the conception of love in Renaissance England was ultimately bound to this world.

I. King's Second Marriage

King's "Exequy" is not technically a love poem—it was not included among the love lyrics that are grouped together at the beginning of the 1657 edition of King's poetry (*Poems, Elegies, Paradoxes, and Sonnets*) but sits instead among his epitaphs and elegies—and hence it does not necessarily belong to the body of verse that has been the focus of this book. I include it here because it exemplifies how deeply the established conventions surrounding posthumous love shaped even a poem that sought to do something entirely different—how, in spite of himself, King managed to recapitulate many of the anxieties surrounding the idea of a heavenly afterlife for earthly lovers. King's commitment as a Protestant minister to the idea of the resurrection of the body and his hope for the reunion of the blessed in heaven sit awkwardly alongside his more materialist and earth-bound preoccupations typical of English love poets. In its emphasis on the body over the soul, and on the time in the grave over eternity in heaven, "An Exequy" interestingly aligns with those English lyrics that eschewed any extended imagining of a transcendent afterlife. However much King desires a permanent reunion with his deceased wife, he seems most comfortable imagining such a reunion within the confines of the earth below.

Anne Berkeley King died in 1624 at the age of twenty-four and was buried in St. Paul's inside the tomb of her father-in-law, John King, the former bishop of London. According to Henry King's friend Thomas

Goffe, the bishop welcomed his daughter-in-law as a cohabitant in his tomb.[1] Since she died three years after Bishop King and had not been ill when he died, it strains the imagination to believe this burial arrangement had been discussed, let alone shared with friends. But it is worth keeping in mind the complexities of this family ménage given King's preoccupation in "An Exequy" with the plot of earth where Anne is laid. In King's will, drawn up in 1653 (sixteen years before his death), he laments that due to the political unrest surrounding him, he is unlikely to be buried either in "Sainte Paules Church, where some deare relacions of myne, a father, formerly a Bishopp of London, a mother, and a Wife lye interred," or in Chichester Cathedral, where he had served as bishop for less than a year before the siege of that city in 1643. But he also declares his ultimate indifference as to his place of burial: "I am not solicitous where my corruptible parte must turne to dust," he writes, "whether in myne owne native or any forraigne country."[2] Despite this later profession, at the time of "An Exequy"'s composition (sometime within a few years of Anne's death) King's wish to lie beside her trumps all other desires.[3]

Judging from its title—the term *exequy* signifies a funeral rite, more commonly used in the plural, *exequies*—readers of "An Exequy To his Matchlesse never to be forgotten Freind" might expect to encounter the poetic equivalent of a funeral sermon or eulogy written for his deceased spouse. But King's poem is not an elegiac poem of praise—over the course of its 120 lines, we learn very little about Anne—nor is it an attempt to commemorate the life he and Anne shared together. To return once again to Panofsky's crucial distinction, "An Exequy" is prospective rather than retrospective in orientation; King focuses not on how Anne might best be remembered but how he might best imagine the next phase of their marital union. The work of the poem, in short, is not to bury the dead but to identify the most comforting account of what might lie ahead.

"An Exequy" begins by announcing its focus on Anne's mortal remains:

Accept, thou Shrine of my Dead Saint!
Instead of Dirges this Complaint;

And, for sweet flowers to crowne thy Hearse,
Receive a strew of weeping verse
From thy griev'd Friend.[4]

This address to the shrine—the container or casket containing the corpse—and the subsequent mention of the "hearse" can in one sense be read as metonymic substitutions for Anne's body, but they are also symptomatic of King's distance from her body and his inability, at this point in the poem, to approach her directly.[5] Over the course of the poem, King propels himself from outside Anne's shrine to within its very walls—from standing above to lying, if only imaginatively, below. It is crucial in this respect that he begins by addressing not Anne but the material structure that keeps him from her. The success of the poem depends upon its ability to produce the equivalent of Romeo's "wrenching iron": the tool that pries the tomb open, allowing the grieving husband to join his wife inside.

Critics of King's poem have emphasized the unusual range and sophistication of his apostrophic mode: the poem addresses, in turn, the shrine, the beloved, the "Earth," and, in its most ambiguous moment, the tomb, or fellow mourners, or the grieving poet himself: "Close the ground, and 'bout his shade / Black Curtaines draw, My bride is lay'd" (79–80).[6] These readings of the poem tend to focus so heavily on King's formal mechanisms, however, that they overlook the poem's metaphysics. For our purposes, the questions raised by this string of apostrophes concern the nature of King's relationship to the dead. What kind of continuity does he seek between himself and his deceased wife? And where does he imagine that the posthumous intimacy he desires might actually transpire?

To answer these questions, we need first to consider a second impressive set of shifts in the poem. In addition to its range in apostrophic address, the poem includes several different, and competing, temporalities: it moves from the present (the burial or funeral) to the distant future (the prospect of resurrection and reunion in heaven) to the more immediate future (the time following the poet's own death). It is this final period—the period following King's death—that dominates the poet's imagination, and the burden of the poem is to transform Anne's belonging only to the earth to her belonging, once again, to him. This effort first becomes apparent in King's attempt to remove the obstacle of the earth that stands between them, which he describes, in a conceit worthy of Donne, as a "strange eclipse":

> And 'twixt mee and my Soule's deare wish
> The Earth now interposed is,
> Which such a straunge Ecclipse doth make
> As ne're was read in Almanake. (35–38)

The relationship between the grieving husband and the ground that contains Anne lies at the very heart of this poem, as King attempts to negotiate the period between now—when his wife lies apart from him—and later, when he will be able to join her in the earth.

This negotiation formally begins at line 61, with the poet's apostrophe to the earth—"Meane time, thou hast Hir Earth"—and continues for nearly sixty lines, through the end of the poem. It is worth pausing over the phrase "Meane time," which delineates the temporal sphere the poet wants to manage. This line functions, in effect, as the *volta* in the poem, pulling him definitively away from the celestial realm of transcendent love that he has just invoked in the intervening lines, back toward the present. Between the image of the "straunge Ecclipse" and this return to the earth, there has been an unusual interlude in which King reaches a kind of theological rapture, envisioning the resurrection at the Last Day when their bodies will be rejoined with their souls:

> . . . Never shall I
> Be so much blest, as to descry
> A glimpse of Thee, till that Day come
> Which shall the Earth to cinders doome,
> And a fierce Feaver must calcine
> The Body of this World, like Thine,
> My Little World! That fitt of Fire
> Once off, our Bodyes shall aspire

To our Soules' blisse: Then wee shall rise,
And view our selves with cleerer eyes
In that calme Region, where no Night
Can hide us from each other's sight. (49-60)

If "An Exequy" were a strictly devotional poem, it would rightly end
here: the movement from the corpses in the ground to the souls in eternal bliss reproduces a trajectory of ascension and salvation that neatly
corresponds to the fate of the blessed in Protestant literature. In King's
own sermon preached for Lent at Whitehall two years after Anne's
death, he declares: "The proper Motion of my soule is to ascend. . . .
Our Meditations must rather glance, than fix upon the businesse of the
World. And therefore the Soule (in Boetius), sensible of her owne Elevation, confesses shee hath wings to lift her farre above the contemptible
earth."[7] Despite this more public declaration that the "proper Motion" of
our meditation should be toward the heavens, however, the motion of his
private thoughts runs in the opposite direction. Immediately following
the invocation of the "calme Region" of the heavens above, "An Exequy"
leaves that region behind, investing all of its concern in the earth. This is
not to say that King dismisses or negates his vision of the souls' mutual
bliss. Instead, it is to say that his attention in the poem shifts elsewhere,
that the exigencies of the present interval are either more pressing or
more poetically manageable than the depiction of what might await him
in heaven. As he contemplates how to reconcile himself to the loss of his
wife and how best to conjure up a posthumous life together, he chooses
to focus on the possibilities afforded by the world he inhabits already.

After a lengthy admonition to the earth in which King warns of the
dangers of allowing Anne's flesh to decompose—"See that thou make thy
reck'ning straight / And yeeld Hir back againe by weight / For thou must
Auditt on thy trust / Each Grane and Atome of this Dust" (73-76)—he
turns to address her directly:

Sleep on (my Love!) in thy cold bed
Never to be disquieted.
My last Good-night! Thou wilt not wake

Till I Thy Fate shall overtake:
Till age, or grief, or sicknes must
Marry my Body to that Dust
It so much loves; and fill the roome
My heart keepes empty in Thy tomb.
Stay for mee there: I will not faile
To meet Thee in that hollow Vale. (81–90)

These lines are startling for their entirely unorthodox idea that Anne's corpse will reawaken not only when it is called on the Last Day to rejoin her soul but also much sooner, when it is joined in the tomb by her husband. She is to sleep, King instructs, until the time of his own death, when they will be married anew. This second marriage will be contracted between bodies of two different sorts: Anne will already be reduced to dust, while he, newly dead, will retain his bodily integrity. But what matters is simply the fact that they will meet again—whatever this meeting may mean or whatever form it may take—long before any heavenly encounter. It is this encounter, in the earth, or "hollow Vale," which preoccupies the poet and becomes the sole focus of his attention.

We might pause here to recall a comparable moment in Petrarch simply to measure how far from the Petrarchan account of transcendent love "An Exequy" really is.[8] In *Rime sparse* 302, Petrarch speaks to the heavenly Laura, who reassures him that following his death he will meet her in heaven:

Per man mi prese et disse: "In questa spera
sarai ancor meco, se 'l desir non erra;
i' so' colei che ti die' tanta guerra
et compie' mia giornata inanzi sera.
Mio ben non cape in intelletto umano;
te solo aspetto, et quel che tanto amasti
et là giuso è rimaso, il mio bel velo." (5–11)

(She took me by the hand and said: "In this sphere you will be with me, if my desire is not deceived. I am she who gave you so much war and completed my day before evening. My blessedness no human intellect can comprehend. I only wait for you and for that which you loved so much and which remained down there, my lovely veil.")

Petrarch never imagines the reunion following his death to be exclusively between their bodies, nor does he envision a long delay between his death and his meeting Laura in heaven. Even if Laura eagerly awaits the return of her body (here figured as her "lovely veil"), the resurrected body is not required for the heavenly union of their souls. The idea that the reunion of lovers will occur only after the resurrection of the body finds no place in the *Rime sparse*.

In "An Exequy," by contrast, the heavenly reunion between King and Anne depends upon the prior reunion of both their bodies and souls; he anticipates that the occasion of their seeing each other "with cleerer eyes / In that calme region" will occur when "our Bodyes shall aspire / to our Soules' blisse" (58-59, 56-57). Because there is no expectation of a prior meeting of the souls alone, the poem at this point leaves the heavenly realm behind. For King's concern is overwhelmingly with the bodies—the bodies that receive no attention once stripped of their souls in the Petrarchan imaginary—and "An Exequy" assumes real urgency as it looks forward to their imminent encounter in the earth:

> And think not much of my delay;
> I am already on the way,
> And follow Thee with all the speed
> Desire can make, or Sorrowes breed.
> Each Minute is a short Degree
> And e're Howre a stepp towards Thee.
> At Night when I betake to rest,
> Next Morne I rise nearer my West
> Of Life, almost by eight Howres' sayle,
> Then when Sleep breath'd his drowsy gale. (91-100)

Within the narrative of the poem, this hastening toward death produces a kind of magical efficacy. In the final lines, the poet enacts his march toward death, describing his heart as a drum leading him forward, and he shifts his gaze from the distant future to the immediate present:

> But hark! My Pulse, like a soft Drum,
> Beates my Approach, Tells Thee I come;
> And, slowe howe're my Marches bee,
> I shall at last sitt downe by Thee.
> The thought of this bids mee goe on,
> And wait my dissolution
> With Hope and Comfort. Deare! (forgive
> The crime) I am content to live
> Divided, with but half a Heart,
> Till wee shall Meet and Never part. (111–20)

The idea of "sitt[ing] downe by Thee" fortifies King against the horror of the body's "dissolution," a process that King's fellow churchman Donne describes in a 1620 sermon as our return to "that excrementall jelly that thy body is made of at first, and that jelly which the body dissolves to at last."[9] It is not the prospect of his soul leaving the body behind, but instead of his body joining with Anne's, that gives him "Hope and Comfort." The triumphant reunion anticipated at the end of this poem written by a Protestant minister for his beloved wife is a reunion not between immortal souls but between mortal—and deceased—bodies. To the extent that posthumous love is envisioned as an alluring possibility, that love remains bound to the mortal world.

II. Milton's Dream

Milton's "Methought I saw my late espousèd saint" shares with King's "Exequy" the simple premise of a grieving husband longing to see his deceased wife. There has been much scholarly debate in the past fifty or so years over whether Milton wrote the sonnet after the death of his first wife, Mary Powell (with whom he had a famously difficult relationship), or that of his second wife, Katherine Woodcock, to whom he was married for a little over a year before her death, and about whom the sonnet was, until the mid-twentieth century, assumed to have been written. Recent critics and biographers have largely returned to the idea that the poem describes an encounter with Katherine, although the issue remains unsettled.[10] For reasons that will become clear, my own reading strengthens this case, and in what follows I will refer to Katherine as the poem's subject. But whether Milton describes Katherine or Mary has little bearing on my interest in the sonnet as evidence of the difficulty English poets faced in imagining posthumous love. Milton's sonnet presents, in effect, the ghostly specter of the Petrarchan arrangement in the *in morte* sequence: in place of the heavenly and radiant Laura speaking to Petrarch and affirming their future reunion, Milton's wife is pale and silent, offering neither consolation nor reassurance. As is the case in King's "Exequy," "Methought I saw my late espousèd saint" briefly glimpses, only to move past, the prospect of a heavenly encounter. Milton may invoke with some confidence the idea of seeing Katherine "in heaven without constraint," but this occurs in the middle of the sonnet and is soon supplanted by a more pressing and immediate desire that cannot be satisfied. The power of Milton's poem lies in its depiction not of future bliss, but of present loss.

Katherine Woodcock Milton died on February 3, 1658, some fifteen months after her marriage and less than four months after giving birth to a daughter, who died six weeks after Katherine. Milton was already blind at the time of his second marriage and hence would never have seen Katherine's face. These biographical facts—the recent birth of a child and Milton's blindness—figure significantly in the sonnet's description of his wife's appearance to him in his dream:

Methought I saw my late espousèd saint
Brought to me like Alcestis from the grave,
Whom Jove's great son to her glad husband gave,
Rescued from death by force, though pale and faint.
Mine, as whom washed from spot of child-bed taint
Purification in the old Law did save,
And such as yet once more I trust to have
Full sight of her in heaven without restraint,

Came vested all in white, pure as her mind.
Her face was veiled, yet to my fancied sight
Love, sweetness, goodness, in her person shined
So clear as in no face with more delight.
But O as to embrace me she inclined,
I waked, she fled, and day brought back my night.

The opening quatrain of the sonnet employs two different similes, each of which resonates with Milton's own circumstances. The first draws on the story of Alcestis, who sacrifices herself to die in place of her husband, Admetus, king of Thessaly, who had been sentenced to death for failing to make adequate sacrifices to the goddess Artemis. In the best-known version of the story, Euripides's *Alcestis*, Alcestis is ultimately rescued from the underworld by Heracles, who returns her, alive, to her husband. The second simile refers to a woman purified after childbirth according to the rites described in Leviticus: "And she shall then continue in the blood of her purifying three and thirty days; she shall touch no hallowed thing, nor come into the sanctuary, until the days of her purifying be fulfilled. But if she bear a maid child, then she shall be unclean two weeks, as in her separation: and she shall continue in the blood of her purifying threescore and six days" (12:4–5).

Each of these images raises a set of questions that scholars have considered at length. Why does Milton put himself in the position of Admetus, who allowed his wife to die for him and is subsequently ridden by terrible guilt? Why does he invoke Old Testament rituals of purification that he, as a left-leaning Protestant, would not have practiced? Does the fact that Mary Powell, Milton's first wife, died three days after giving birth suggest that the sonnet is in fact about her, since Katherine died after the postpartum period of supposed uncleanness had passed?[11]

It is a third simile, however, that I want to focus on here, in the lines immediately following the pagan and biblical references: "And such as yet once more I trust to have / Full sight of her in heaven without restraint." To call this a simile depends upon our reading "And such as" to mean "like"—in other words, Katherine came to him not only like Alcestis, and not only like one purified from "child-bed taint," but also like one whom he will see in full heavenly glory once he arrives in heaven. I emphasize the status of these two lines as a simile because it has implications for what Milton actually wants to claim. For he does not say in these lines that he sees Katherine's heavenly self per se (this is, in effect, what Petrarch claims repeatedly in the *Rime sparse*). Instead, he declares that he sees something that resembles what he (as someone, again, who never saw her on earth) imagines her heavenly self will be. He is not, in other words, glimpsing her "without restraint" so much as experiencing what that might feel like when he does. This helps to explain why she is still veiled, as we learn in line 10, and it leads to a description of the veiled yet radiant vision: "Her face was veiled, yet to my fancied sight / Love, sweetness, goodness in her person shined / So clear as in no face with more delight" (10–12).

In tracing Milton's multiple sources or inspirations for this poem, scholars have noted similarities between his conception of Katherine's appearance to him and one of the *in morte* sonnets that the sixteenth-century Italian poet Berardino Rota wrote about his wife, Portia:[12]

In lieto e pien di riverenza aspetto
Con vesta di color bianco e vermiglio
Di doppia luce serenato il ciglio
Mi viene in sonno il mio dolce diletto
Io me l'inchino, e con cortese affetto
Seco ragiono e seco mi consiglio,
Com'abbia a governarmi in quest'esiglio;
E piango intanto, e la risposta aspetto.
Ella m'ascolta e fisa, e dice cose
Veramente celesti, ed io l'apprendo,
E serbo ancor nella memoria ascose.
Mi lascia alfine, e parte, e va spargendo
Per l'aria nel partir viole e rose:
Io gli porgo la man, poi mi riprendo.

(With aspect mild and full of awe she appeared, wearing robes of white and vermillion; in double light she came to me in my sleep, my heart's beloved. Bowing toward the fair vision, with courteous affection, I asked her to advise me, how I might best comport myself through this time of exile; I wept, and awaited her response. Intent she heard me, and the words she spoke were truly heavenly—such they were that still I keep them as treasure hidden away in my breast. At length she left me, scattering violets and roses through the air as she goes: I offer to her my hand, and then I take it back.)[13]

Whatever surface similarities exist between the two sonnets, however, their differences are more telling. First, in Rota's sonnet the beloved is not merely a vision but an interlocutor; the former spouses engage in actual dialogue. In his wife's response to his question about how to conduct himself in his grief, she gives him pearls of heavenly wisdom—"cose veramente celesti"—and he accepts this wisdom as precious, storing it in his heart. When she leaves him "alfine" (at last)—suggesting that more than a fleeting moment has passed—the departure is smooth and serene: she scatters flowers in the air as she ascends, and he, witnessing this graceful flight, takes back the hand he had belatedly offered.

In Milton's sonnet there is no conversation between the poet and his wife, nor does either of them attempt to speak; the poem does not center on dialogue but on the vision itself. More important, Milton's sonnet does not end with his wife's ascension but with her abrupt departure: "But O, as to embrace me she inclined / I waked, she fled, and day brought back my night" (13-14). Whereas Rota's sleep is never broken, Milton's is shattered. And what shatters his dream is an attempt at physical intimacy, an attempt that seems to be initiated by the ghostly figure herself.[14] This reverses the usual order of things in the poetic tradition, as in book 2 of the *Aeneid*, in which Aeneas attempts to embrace the shade of his wife, Creusa:

> When she was done with words—I weeping and
> wanting to say so many things—she left
> and vanished in transparent air. Three times
> I tried to throw my arms around her neck;
> three times the Shade I grasped in vain escaped
> my hands—like fleet winds, most like a winged dream.[15]

Whether Milton or Katherine initiates the embrace, the effect is the same: the prospect of touch cannot be contained within either the dream or, it would seem, the sonnet, and the poem ends with a line as choppy as its first line is smooth. (Compare the fluidity of the iambs in "Methought I saw my late espousèd saint" with the jolting pace of "I waked, she fled, and day brought back my night.")

The end of Milton's sonnet may be jarringly different in its poetic rhythms from the opening, but in an important sense its haunting power depends upon returning to where the poem began, with the myth of Alcestis and the fantasy of a physical reunion between the dead and the living spouse. In this respect, it does not progress forward so much as loop backward, forming a closed circle of longing. To say, as one critic has, that Milton "undermines the hollow and fanciful promises of the [Alcestis] myth and gives us instead a strenuously Protestant and Neoplatonic vision of mourning, faith, and hoped for restoration," or, in the words of another critic, that Milton shows that "Alcestis was a physical reality, but pale and faint, the poet's wife a dream, but radiantly present; the pagan agent, Heracles, could not give eternal life, but Christ the redeemer did," is gravely to mistake the trajectory of these fourteen lines.[16] The restoration that is finally dangled before the poet is one of physical intimacy in this world between the living and the dead; it is more Heathcliff and Catherine than Petrarch and Laura. Milton builds, that is, toward an erotic encounter that does not look to the heavens but remains firmly on the ground.[17]

At the end of his sonnet, Milton does not reject the Alcestis myth; he returns to its very terms only to be left empty-handed. What slips from the poet's grasp is exactly what Admetus joyfully receives: the presence of his beloved, now and not later, here and not there. From the perspective of Protestant theology or Neoplatonic philosophy, the rewards of Ademtus may be paltry and short-lived. From the perspective of the grieving husband wanting to receive his dead wife's embrace, the rewards of Admetus are entirely enviable.

The implicit presence of Admetus at the end of Milton's sonnet as a husband who does not lose his wife permanently, but manages to bring her (or have her brought) back from the dead, points us to a second pagan myth, one whose emotional textures are perhaps even closer to Milton's own: the myth of Orpheus and Eurydice. In this story, the poet-husband's attempt to retrieve his dead wife tragically fails when he breaks the sole condition of his journey: never to look back at her until they have reached the earth above. Given the status of vision at the center of this myth—the one unforgivable act was to see Eurydice before the appointed time—the resonances with Milton's poem are compelling. It is very surprising, in fact, that the myth has not received serious attention as one of Milton's central sources; its complete absence from the Milton *Variorum*, published in the 1970s, and its only passing mention in more recent criticism suggest that the extensive discussion of the Alcestis myth has stood in the way of scholarly engagement with this second story.[18]

There are multiple versions of the Orpheus story that Milton is likely to have known, and it seems possible that he had several of them in mind when writing this sonnet. In Ovid's description in the *Metamorphoses* of Orpheus's fatal turning to see Eurydice and her tragic slipping away, we glimpse another source for the failed embrace at the end of Milton's sonnet:

> . . . longing so to see her, [Orpheus] turned to gaze
> back at his wife. At once she slipped away—
> and down. His arms stretched out convulsively
> to clasp and to be clasped in turn, but there
> was nothing but the unresisting air.[19]

As with Virgil's account of Aeneas and Creusa in the *Aeneid*, Ovid describes the horrible frustration of the desire to "clasp and be clasped" (*prendique et prendere certans*) with an ethereal shade, the futility of attempting to touch with body what has become only spirit.

But the version of the Orpheus myth that puts the forbidden act of seeing most fully at its narrative center, and that employs metaphors of vision and blindness eerily close to Milton's own, belongs to Virgil's *Georgics*. In book 4 of that poem, after Orpheus fatally succumbs to the temptation to see his wife and thereby ensures her second death, Eurydice bemoans her fate:

"What madness beyond measure? Once more a cruel fate
Drags me away, and my swimming eyes are drowned in darkness.
Good-bye. I am borne away. A limitless night is about me
And over the strengthless hands I stretch to you, yours no longer."
Thus she spoke, and at once from his sight like a wisp of smoke
Thinned into air, was gone.[20]

The scene that Virgil conjures up twice frames the loss of love as a loss of vision. First, Eurydice describes her experience of dying again as losing her "swimming eyes" (*natantia lumina*) to darkness (literally *somnus*, or sleep); and second, Orpheus describes Eurydice's vanishing from his eyes (*ex oculis*) like a vapor into the air.

If Milton had this passage from the *Georgics* in mind when composing his sonnet—and we are certain he had the *Georgics* in mind when he wrote *Paradise Lost*—he did something quite remarkable with it.[21] Far from simply assuming the role of the grieving husband, as he does with Admetus, Milton occupies both the role of Orpheus and that of Eurydice: he is at once husband and wife. On the one hand he is Orpheus, left behind by a dead wife who is momentarily returned to him, only to have her disappear once again from his sight. On the other hand he is Eurydice, abruptly pulled away from a moment of near happiness, and then plunged back into an all-consuming night (*feror ingenti circumdate nocte*), which she experiences specifically through her eyes. More than any other possible source or inspiration, Virgil's lines seem to possess the complex swirl of emotions that makes the ending of Milton's poem so moving: the immensely pleasurable but unsustainable act of seeing the dead spouse; the temptation, and failure, of renewed intimacy; the horrible re-severing of the bond; the cruel return from the tantalizing promise of day into darkness. The punishment allotted to Orpheus for the sheer act of looking prematurely intensifies the tragic nature of Milton's sonnet, as if the blind poet were being punished for seeing what he is not yet meant to see. (The presence of Katherine's veil now takes on more poignancy: Milton is protecting himself, in effect, from fully seeing what might be forbidden to him; he is hedging his bets.)

"Methought I saw my late espousèd saint" is the closest that Renaissance English poetry comes to inhabiting the Orpheus myth, a myth that has at its core the fantasy shared by so many husbands and wives and lovers: that death need not be final, that one's husband or wife or lover might be returned to this world again. The Orpheus myth has at its core as well a fantasy shared by many poets: that through the incantatory power of their words they might bring the dead back to life. This is what Horace gently accuses Virgil of wishing after the death of their mutual friend Quintilius in book 1 of the *Odes*. "What if," Horace chides, "you were to tune a sweeter lyre than Thracian Orpheus / And trees came to listen? Would blood come back / Into the empty shade which Mercury has once herded?"[22] This is also, in the deepest sense, what Shakespeare and Spenser and Daniel and Donne hope to do through their poems: to keep the blood running through the veins of the beloved in whatever way they can.

But finally, the story of Orpheus is not only a story of restoring the dead, nor is it only a story of extraordinary lyric power. It is also the archetypal story of absolute limits, of a boundary that cannot be crossed no matter how passionate the love or talented the lover. Renaissance English love poets understood this boundary in all of its complexity, and mined its depths for all of its riches.

"An Arundel Tomb"

In the graceful medieval cathedral of Chichester stands the monument for Richard Fitzalan II, the earl of Arundel, and his wife, Eleanor of Lancaster, erected in the late fourteenth century. Unlike the semi-upright and intertwined posture of the Etruscan *Sarcophagus of the Bride and Bridegroom* sculpted some two thousand years earlier with which this book began, the Arundel couple lie stiffly on their backs, their bodies parallel to each other. And unlike the obvious eros of the Cerveteri spouses, who exude a kind of sexual confidence, the earl and countess seem primly chaste, with only their hands clasped together.

It was the unexpectedness of this affectionate gesture—unexpected because of the blank severity of the couple's repose—that attracted the notice of the twentieth-century poet Philip Larkin during a visit to the cathedral. In his celebrated poem "An Arundel Tomb" (1956), he describes the sensation he felt when he saw the clasped hands as "a sharp tender shock":

Side by side, their faces blurred,
The earl and countess lie in stone,
Their proper habits vaguely shown
As jointed armour, stiffened pleat,
And that faint hint of the absurd—

The little dogs under their feet.
Such plainness of the pre-baroque
Hardly involves the eye, until
It meets his left-hand gauntlet, still
Clasped empty in the other; and
One sees, with a sharp tender shock,
His hand withdrawn, holding her hand.[1]

The tomb looked just like any other, Larkin thought—indistinct faces, unrevealing garments, an altogether unremarkable "plainness"—until he noticed the couple's hands. It was the seeming dissonance of the touch in relation to everything else about them that drew him into his musings.

The Arundel tomb is one of many medieval English monuments with a full-length effigy of a couple across its top, and by itself it would not warrant our attention. But Larkin's reflections on this tomb capture many of the poignancies and ironies raised both by the spousal tombs reviewed in the introduction and the scores of poems considered in subsequent chapters addressing the fate of love after death. "An Arundel Tomb" asks us to ponder, in a way we are now prepared to do, the relationship between the artifact that endures and the love that is long past. How much of that love is actually preserved? Was the love experienced at the time in a manner at all consonant with its posthumous representation? What, in short, does the passage of time do to the survival of love?

Larkin begins his inquiry by questioning whether the earl and the countess ever imagined they would remain like this, lying side by side, as the world changed irrevocably into a place they would no longer recognize. "They would not think," he declares, "to lie so long":

Such faithfulness in effigy
Was just a detail friends would see:
A sculptor's sweet commissioned grace
Thrown off in helping to prolong
The Latin names around the base.
They would not guess how early in

Their supine stationary voyage
The air would change to soundless damage,
Turn the old tenantry away;
How soon succeeding eyes begin
To look, not read. Rigidly they
Persisted, linked, through lengths and breadths
Of time. Snow fell, undated. Light
Each summer thronged the grass. A bright
Litter of birdcalls strewed the same
Bone-littered ground. And up the paths
The endless altered people came,
Washing at their identity. (13–31)

After contemplating the stubborn persistence of the tomb over the centuries that have passed—centuries filled with winter and summers, with streams of visitors who pass by without even reading the names on the base of the tomb, with the fading of the stone and the blurring of their faces—Larkin asks what it means for the couple to be reduced to a single "attitude" that they may not even have chosen:[2]

Now, helpless in the hollow of
An unarmorial age, a trough
Of smoke in slow suspended skeins
Above their scrap of history,
Only an attitude remains:
Time has transfigured them into
Untruth. (32–38)

Larkin asks us to consider the other side, as it were, of artistic immortality: what it feels like to be Petrarch's Laura or Spenser's Elizabeth or Shakespeare's young man, who played no role in choosing how they would be, to borrow Spenser's term, "eternized." "Time has transfigured them into / Untruth": it has made the couple's eternal posture what was perhaps never felt or intended to be.

Years after writing the poem, in a further twist of irony, Larkin learned that the couple's hands—the source of his "sharp tender shock"—were not necessarily part of the tomb's original design. Sketches of the monument from a collection of eighteenth- and early nineteenth-century drawings show the earl missing one arm and the countess with no arms at all; the current arms were added to the tomb during repairs in the mid-nineteenth century. We will never know exactly how the hands were originally conceived.[3] Larkin was disturbed by this discovery, and in an interview in 1981 he disparaged the poem both for the particular error he made with the hands and for its uncharacteristic sentimentality. It's "a rather romantic poem," he quipped. "I don't like it much, partly because of this. . . . Everything went wrong with that poem: I got the hands wrong—it's a right hand gauntlet really—and anyway the hands were a nineteenth century addition, not pre-Baroque at all."[4]

For a poet as sour and cynical as Larkin, the fact that he had been so moved by a Victorian (and not even medieval) gesture of sentiment was clearly too much to bear. But the discovery of the hands as a decision on the part of a nineteenth-century restorer to imagine not only what may have been for the earl and countess but also what could still be ultimately only strengthens the poem's conclusion:

> The stone fidelity
> They hardly meant has come to be
> Their final blazon, and to prove
> Our almost-instinct almost true:
> What will survive of us is love. (38–42)

Why does it matter, we might ask Larkin, whether the clasped hands were sculpted right after the earl's and countess's deaths or added several hundred years later? In neither case does he imagine that the couple's "stone fidelity" reflected their own choice; in neither case does he think they intended this as "their final blazon." Regardless of when the hands were made to touch one another, the earl and countess are the victims—and the beneficiaries—of art. And it is this art that not only survives them but also changes them, making them something new. The tomb has transformed them into a loving couple that they may or may not ever have been.

"What will survive of us is love": this is one of Larkin's most famous lines of verse, and read on its own, it sounds like a simple affirmation of love's immortal powers. Within the context of the poem, however, "what will survive of us is love" testifies not only to the power of love lived, but also to the power of love made. It is a testament, that is, to the ability of sculptors and artists and poets to create—whether from experience or *ex nihilo*—works that move us, surprise us, survive.

NOTES

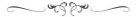

Introduction

1. There is a nearly identical tomb, also from Cerveteri and dated to the sixth century BCE, in the Louvre Museum in Paris, known as *The Sarcophagus of the Spouses*.

2. On Etruscan burial, see J. M. C. Toynbee, *Death and Burial in the Roman World* (Baltimore: Johns Hopkins University Press, 1973).

3. The medieval poem *Sir Orfeo* (ca. 1300), the longest version of the Orpheus myth written in English, has a happy ending: King Orfeo's wife, Dame Heurodis, is seized by the king of the land of Fairye, a kind of medieval otherworld, but is ultimately rescued, and she and Orfeo resume their rule in Britain.

4. As I discuss in chapter 2, this division was not in fact Petrarch's own; see pp. 52–53 below.

5. John Milton, *Paradise Lost*, in *The Complete Poetical Works of John Milton*, ed. Douglas Bush (Boston: Houghton Mifflin, 1965), bk. 8, 591–92; bk. 9, 890, 906–7.

6. Ibid., bk. 11, "The Argument."

7. John Stow, *Survay of London* (London, 1598) A3v. Other antiquarians, such as John Weever, describe their projects more polemically as interventions against the iconoclasm that has swept the nation. See the "Author to the Reader" in *Ancient Funerall Monuments within the united Monarchie of Great Britaine, Ireland, and the Ilands adjacent with the dissolved Monasteries therein contained . . . As also the Death and burial of certaine of the Bloud, Roiall, the Nobilitie and Gentrie of these Kingdomes entombed in forraine Nations . . .* (London, 1631).

8. Erwin Panofsky, *Tomb Sculpture: Four Lectures on Its Changing Aspects from Ancient Egypt to Bernini*, ed. H. W. Janson (New York: H. N. Abrams, 1964).

9. See John Garstang, *The Burial Customs of Ancient Egypt, as Illustrated by Tombs of*

the Middle Kingdom (London, 1907), and Wolfram Grajetzki, *Burial Customs in Ancient Egypt: Life in Death for Rich and Poor* (London, 2003).

10. To a greater degree than Panofsky acknowledges, Roman tombs also include prospective features: sarcophagi figuring Elysian banquets and celebrations are relatively common, for example, as are images of gods or cosmic figures connected with one's posthumous life. Consider, for example, the twin mausoleums in the Vatican cemetery with a vivid wall painting of Lucifer and Hesperus, whose depiction was associated with the idea of rebirth after death; or the regular appearance of souls carried to safety in the next world on the backs of dolphins. For further discussion of this, see Jocelyn Toynbee and John Ward Perkins, *The Shrine of St. Peter and the Vatican Excavations* (London: Longmans, Green, 1956), 79.

11. See Toynbee, *Death and Burial in the Roman World*, esp. chap. 2, "Roman Beliefs about the Afterlife," 33–42.

12. See for example, Nigel Llewellyn's *Funeral Monuments in Post-Reformation England* (Cambridge: Cambridge University Press, 2000), which emphasizes the role of *memoria*. Two important exceptions to this general trend in early modern historiography are Peter Marshall, *Beliefs and the Dead in Reformation England* (Oxford: Oxford University Press, 2002), esp. chap. 5; and Peter Sherlock, *Monuments and Memory in Early Modern England* (Aldershot, UK: Ashgate, 2008).

13. John Weever, *Ancient Funerall Monuments within the united Monarchie of Great Britaine, Ireland, and the Ilands adjacent with the dissolved Monasteries therein contained . . .* (London, 1631), 649–50. No date is given for this epitaph.

14. For further evidence of this conclusion, see Sherlock, *Monuments and Memory in Early Modern England*, 110–12.

15. Stow, *Survay of London*, 515–16. Unless otherwise noted, all epitaphs are from Stow. I am grateful to T. Corey Brennan for help with this translation.

16. Thomas Ravenshaw, *Antiente Epitaphes* (London: Joseph Masters, 1888), 40.

17. All references to Donne's poetry are from *The Poems of John Donne*, ed. Herbert J. C. Grierson (London: Oxford University Press, 1933); here "The Relique," lines 10–11.

18. F. A. Greenhill, *Incised Effigial Slabs: A Study of Engraved Stone Memorials in Latin Christendom, c. 1100 to c. 1700*, 2 vols. (London: Faber and Faber, 1976), 1:342.

19. According to Barbara J. Harris, aristocratic widows regularly paid for or directed the construction of their husbands' and their own tombs, and also chose with which husband they wanted to be buried. Among women with multiple husbands, many seem to have chosen the husband with whom they had their first son or child, or the husband of the highest rank. (Barbara J. Harris, "The Fabric of Piety: Aristocratic Women and Care of the Dead, 1450–1550" *Journal of British Studies* 48 [April 2009]: 308–35.)

20. For a good example of a tomb for a wife with multiple husbands, see Stow's description of the monument for Barbara Champion, whose effigy is placed between those of her two husbands, Henry Heardson (d. 1555) and Sir Richard Champion (d. 1568), on a single tomb (Stow, *Survay of London*, 139).

21. H. R. Mosse, *The Monumental Effigies of Sussex (1250 to 1650)* (Lewes, UK: Farncombe, 1928).

22. This epitaph is not dated.

23. For more on the relationship between prayer and poetry, see Ramie Targoff, *Common Prayer: The Language of Public Devotion* (Chicago: University of Chicago Press, 2001), esp. chap. 3, "Prayer and Poetry: Rhyme in the English Church," 57–84.

24. E. W. Badger, *The Monumental Brasses of Warwickshire* (Birmingham: Cornish Brothers, 1895), 24.

25. Marcus Tullius Cicero, *Tusculan Disputations*, trans. J. E. King (Cambridge, MA: Harvard University Press, 1950), 1.36, pp. 86–87.

26. Cicero, *Tusculan Disputations* 1.43, pp. 122–25.

27. Sir Thomas Browne, *Hydriotaphia, Urne-Buriall, or A Discourse of the Sepulchrall Urnes lately found in Norfolk*, in *Religio Medici and Urne-Buriall*, ed. Stephen Greenblatt and Ramie Targoff (New York: New York Review of Books Classics, 2012), 116.

28. Browne, *Religio Medici*, in *Religio Medici and Urne-Buriall*, 10.

29. The original Latin and an English translation are printed in *John Donne's Marriage Letters in the Folger Shakespeare Library*, ed. M. Thomas Hester, Robert Parker Sorlien, and Dennis Flynn (Washington, DC: Folger Shakespeare Library, 2005) 62. I have made some small changes to this translation.

30. See the matrimony service in *The Book of Common Prayer*, ed. Brian Cummings (Oxford: Oxford University Press, 2011), 436.

31. "Appendix D.II: Donne's Will," in R. C. Bald, *John Donne, a Life* (New York: Oxford University Press, 1970), 563.

32. See Ramie Targoff, *John Donne, Body and Soul* (Chicago: University of Chicago Press, 2008).

33. My translation.

34. According to Vivien Brodsky, very few widows in late sixteenth-century London married after the age of fifty. See Brodsky, "Widows in Late Elizabethan London: Remarriage, Economic Opportunity and Family Orientations," in *The World We Have Gained: Histories of Population and Social Structure*, ed. Lloyd Bonfield, Richard M. Smith, and Keith Wrightson (Oxford: Basil Blackwell, 1986), 130–31.

35. Alan Bray, *The Friend* (Chicago: University of Chicago Press, 2003), 88.

36. Ibid., 94. Charlton T. Lewis and Charles Short, *A Latin Dictionary* (Oxford: Oxford University Press, 1993), s.b. "conjunx."

37. Bray, *Friend*, 142. The translation is Bray's.

38. Homer, *Iliad*, trans. A. T. Murray (Cambridge, MA: Harvard University Press, 1999), 23.75–92.

39. One famous example is the magnificent tomb that the poet Fulke Greville designed, but never built, for his burial with his dear friend Sir Philip Sidney. As Greville relates in a 1615 letter to John Coke, he intended to erect a double tomb with two beds made of stone, one above the other; this was the identical form used in many of the spousal tombs that graced early modern churches. (See Bray, *Friend*, 42–59.)

Chapter 1

1. *The Bible: Authorized King James Version* (Oxford: Oxford University Press, 1997). All quotations from the Bible, unless otherwise noted, are from this edition.

2. See William Maskell, *Monumenta Ritualia Ecclesia Anglicanae*, 3 vols. (Farnborough, Hants, UK: Gregg, 1970), 1:46.

3. *The Book of Common Prayer: The Texts of 1549, 1559, and 1662*, ed. Brian Cummings (Oxford: Oxford University Press, 2011), 66.

4. William Gouge, *Of Domesticall Duties* (London, 1622), 226.

5. Lawrence Stone, *The Family, Sex, and Marriage in England: 1500–1800* (New York: Harper and Row, 1977). See p. 56 for his discussion of remarriage statistics throughout the ages, as well as the accompanying chart on p. 45.

6. Bernhard Jussen, *Der Name der Witwe, Erkundungen zur Semantik der mittelalterlichen Bußkultur* (Göttingen: Veröffentlichungen des Max-Planck-Instituts für Geschichte, 2000), 158.

7. See Jack Goody, *The Development of Marriage and Family in Europe* (Cambridge: Cambridge University Press, 1983), 41–42, 188–89.

8. Juan Luis Vives, *The Instruction of a Christen Woman*, ed. Virginia Walcott Beachamp, Elizabeth H. Hageman, and Margaret Mikesell (Urbana: Universioty of Illinois Press).

9. Ibid., 165, spelling modernized.

10. Gouge, *Domesticall Duties*, 187.

11. John Calvin, *Corpus Reformatorum* 33.227 (*Opera Quae Supersunt Omnia*). The Latin text reads: "In paradiso esse, et cum Deo vivere, non est alterum alteri loqui, et alteram ab altero audiri: sed tantum Deo frui, sentire bonam eius voluntatem, in eo acquiescere." The English translation is from Coleen McDannell and Bernhard Lang, *Heaven: A History* (New Haven, CT: Yale University Press, 2001), 155.

12. Letter dated April 7, 1549; cited in William Bouwsma, *John Calvin: A Sixteenth-Century Portrait* (New York: Oxford University Press, 1988).

13. Cited by Aquinas in *Catena Aurea*, Gospel of Matthew commentary (London: Baronius, 2009).

14. Calvin, *Corpus Reformatorum* 73.675 (*Opera Exegetica et Homiletica*); the English translation is adapted from McDannell and Lang, *Heaven*.

15. Calvin, *Commentary on a Harmony of the Evangelists: Matthew, Mark and Luke*, trans. William Pringle (Grand Rapids, MI: Eerdmans, 1949), 158–60.

16. Edward Vaughan, *A Divine Discoverie of Death* (London, 1612), cited in Peter Marshall, *Beliefs and the Dead in Reformation England* (Oxford: Oxford University Press, 2002), 217.

17. Alexander Hume, *Treatise of Felicitie of Life to Come* (Edinburgh, 1594), 34–35.

18. John Bunyan, *The Pilgrim's Progress*, ed. James Blanton Wharey, rev. ed. Roger Sharrock (Oxford: Oxford University Press, 1960), 10.

19. Gouge, *Domesticall Duties*, 239.

20. William Whately, *A Bride-Bush, or a Direction for Married Persons, plainely describing the duties common to both, and peculiar to each of them* (London, 1623), 36.

21. *The Sermons of John Donne*, ed. George R. Potter and Evelyn M. Simpson, 10 vols. (Berkeley: University of California Press, 1953–62), 3:249.

22. Philip Stubbes, *A Christal glasse for Christian women* (London, 1592), C2v.

23. Thomas Gataker, *Marriage Duties Briefly Couched Togither* (London, 1620), 48.

24. Robert Bolton, *Boltons Last and Learned Worke of the Foure last Things, Death, Iudgement, Hell, and Heaven* (London, 1632), 49–50.

25. Augustine, sermon 80.7, trans. in *The Early Church Fathers and Other Works* (Edinburgh: Eerdmans, 1867). Letter 92 in *The Works of Saint Augustine: A Translation for the 21st Century*, trans. Roland Teske, ed. John E. Rotelle (Hyde Park, NY: New City, 2001), 371.

26. Bolton, *Boltons Last and Learned Worke*, 145.

27. John Donne, *Letters to Severall Persons of Honour* (London, 1651), 7. Lady Kingsmill's maiden name was Bridget White, and Donne had a lengthy correspondence with her before her marriage.

28. See chapter 2 of Ramie Targoff, *John Donne, Body and Soul* (Chicago: University of Chicago Press, 2008), for a discussion of the relationship between these two pairings.

29. *Sermons of John Donne*, 8:95, 99.

30. Ibid., 3:244–49.

31. See Stone, *Family, Sex, and Marriage in England*, chap. 8, "The Companionate Marriage," 325–404.

32. On the rabbinical tradition of commentary on Genesis 2:18—"it is not good for man to be alone"—see, for example, Jacob Neusner, *Genesis Rabbah: The Judaic Commentary to the Book of Genesis; A New American Translation* (Providence, RI: Brown University Press, 1985), 179–80.

33. Aquinas, *Summa contra Gentiles: Book 3, Providence Part 2*, trans Vernon J. Bourke (Notre Dame, IN: University of Notre Dame Press, 1975), 148 (3.123.6). For the link to Aristotle, see Edmund Leites, *The Puritan Conscience and Modern Sexuality* (New Haven, CT: Yale University Press, 1986), 79.

34. Gataker, *Marriage Duties Briefly Couched Togither*, 43.

35. Whately, *Bride-Bush*, 38, 42.

36. John Milton, *Doctrine and Discipline of Divorce*, in *The Student's Milton*, ed. Frank Allen Patterson (New York: F. S. Crofts, 1936), 580, 578.

Chapter 2

1. See Gordon Braden on the French troubadours and Occitan poets who preceded Dante. *Petrarchan Love and the Continental Renaissance* (New Haven, CT: Yale University Press, 1999).

2. *La Vita Nuova*, ed. and trans. Stanley Appelbaum (Mineola, NY: Dover, 2006), chap. 24, "Tanto gentile," 1.7–8; chap. 19, "Donna ch'avete intelletto d'amore," 1.37–39.

3. All quotations from Petrarch's *Rime sparse*, and all English translations, unless otherwise noted, are from *Petrarch's Lyric Poems: The Rime Sparse and Other Lyrics*, trans. and ed. Robert M. Durling (Cambridge, MA: Harvard University Press, 1976); Poem 72.2–3; Poem 133.12; Poem 159.1–4.

4. For Petrarch's knowledge of Plato, see Christopher S. Celenza, "The Revival of Platonic Philosophy," chap. 5 in *The Cambridge Companion to Renaissance Philosophy* (Cambridge: Cambridge University Press, 2007); and Sears Jayne, *Plato in Renaissance England* (Dordrecht, Netherlands: Kluwer Academic, 1995).

5. Cited in John Charles Nelson, *Renaissance Theory of Love: The Context of Giordano Bruno's "Eroici furori"* (New York: Columbia University Press, 1958), 73.

6. See William Kennedy, *Authorizing Petrarch* (Ithaca, NY: Cornell University Press, 1994).

7. See, for example, *Incominciano li sonetti cõ cãzoni dello egregio poeta misser Frãcesco Petrarcha cõ la interp̃tatione: Dello eximio & excellente poeta. mis. Fran. philepho allo inuictissimo Philippo Maria duca di Millano* (Venice: Bartholomaeus de Zanis, 1497).

8. See, for example, Nicholas of Lyra, *Postilla super Epistolas et Euangelia quadragesimalia* (Venice: Johannes Hamman, 1494).

9. For a discussion of this culture and how it began to fade in the mid-sixteenth century, see Donald L. Guss, "Petrarchism and the End of the Renaissance," in *Francis Petrarch, Six Centuries Later: A Symposium* (Durham: University of North Carolina Press, 1975).

10. This commentary was written by the medical doctor Dino del Garbo in the early 1300s. See Nelson, *Renaissance Theory of Love*, 36–39.

11. Ibid., 137. Another of Varchi's lectures was devoted to *Rime sparse* 132, "S'amor non è," the sonnet that Chaucer translated in *Troilus and Criseyde*. See also Benedetto Varchi, "Lezioni sul Petrarca," in *Opere* (Trieste, 1859), 2.444.

12. *The Complete Works of Thomas Watson*, ed. Dana F. Sutton, 2 vols. (Lewiston, NY: Edwin Mellen, 1997), 1:153.

13. See Sears Jayne, *John Colet and Marsilio Ficino* (Oxford: Oxford University Press, 1963), and "Ficino and the Platonism of the English Renaissance," *Comparative Literature* 4 (1952): 214–38.

14. See Jayne, *Plato in Renaissance England*.

15. See Sarah Hutton, "Introduction to the Renaissance and Seventeenth Century," in *Platonism and the English Imagination*, ed. Anna Baldwin and Sarah Hutton (Cambridge: Cambridge University Press, 2005), 67–75. On Protestants' attempt to divorce Plato from the Neoplatonists and reclaim him for themselves, see E. N. Tigerstedt, *The Decline and Fall of the Neoplatonic Interpretation of Plato: An Outline and Some Observations* (Helsinki: Societas Scientiarum Fennica, 1974).

16. Jill Kraye, "Moral Philosophy," in *The Cambridge History of Renaissance Philosophy* (Cambridge: Cambridge University Press, 1988), 356.

17. See Jayne, *Plato in Renaissance England*, and John Smith Harrison, *Platonism in English Poetry of the Sixteenth and Seventeenth Centuries* (Westport, CT: Greenwood, 1903, rept. 1980). Harrison argues that "the application of the tenets of Platonic theory to the writing of love lyrics in the Petrarchan manner, however, was never anything more than a courtly way of making love through exaggerated conceit and fine writing. . . . The love of the idea of beauty . . . in its absolute nature is nowhere present in the mass of love lyrics written between 1590 and 1600" (137–38).

18. Jayne, *Plato in Renaissance England*, 135.

19. For Petrarch's reputation in northern Europe, see Nicholas Mann, "Petrarch and Humanism: The Paradox of Posterity," in *Francesco Petrarca: Citizen of the World*, ed. Aldo S. Bernardo (Albany: SUNY Press, 1980).

20. A letter survives, for example, from Edmund Bonner, the Catholic bishop of London (1540–49, 1553–59) to Thomas Cromwell, in which he reminds him that "[a]s you wished to make me a good Italian some time since, by promising to lend me the 'Triumphs of Petrarch,' I beg you to send it by Mr. Augustine's servant" (from J. S. Brewer, ed., *Letters and Papers, Foreign and Domestic, of the Reign of Henry VIII* (Vaduz, Liechtenstein: Kraus Reprint, 1965), 4:2850). Thomas More is also likely to have used the poem as the partial model for his wall hangings depicting nine pageants, six of which depict the same triumphs as Petrarch's. See Robert Coogan, "Petrarch's *Trionfi* and the English Renaissance," *Studies in Philology* 67 (1970): 306–27.

21. See Coogan, "Petrarch's *Trionfi*," for details of Lord Morley's translation. For the tapestries, see Thomas P. Campbell, *Henry VIII and the Art of Majesty* (New Haven, CT: Yale University Press, 2007), 149–53.

22. See David Wallace, *Chaucerian Polity: Absolutist Lineages and Associational Forms in England and Italy* (Palo Alto, CA: Stanford University Press, 1997), 262–63.

23. On the lack of circulation of Petrarch's *Rime sparse*, see Mann, "Petrarch and Humanism." Henry Bohn published the first full English translation in 1859 as part of his Illustrated Libraries series.

24. See, for example, E. K. Chambers, *Sir Thomas Wyatt and Some Collected Studies* (London, 1933), 129, and A. K. Foxwell, *The Poems of Sir Thomas Wiat* (London: University of London Press, 1913), 2:48, both cited in Patricia Thomson, "Wyatt and the Petrarchan Commentators," *Review of English Studies* n.s. 10, no. 39 (August 1959): 225–33. Thomas Greene also comments on Wyatt's avoidance of "descriptions of nature and of women." See *The Light in Troy: Imitation and Discovery in Renaissance Poetry* (New Haven, CT: Yale University Press, 1982), 247. The only notable exception is Patricia Thomson, who draws attention to these differences only in passing (*Sir Thomas Wyatt and His Background* [Stanford, CA: Stanford University Press, 1964], 179–80).

25. Eric Ives provides a thorough review of the evidence in his biography of Anne Boleyn and concludes that there is simply no convincing case to be made. The poems remain unreliable for biographical data, and the secondhand testimonials all suggest an infatuation but not necessarily an affair (Eric Ives, *The Life and Death of Anne Boleyn* [Malden, MA: Blackwell, 2004], 73–80). Retha Warnicke reaches a similar conclusion; she claims that "any attempt to establish a close relationship between Wyatt and Anne must rely on a speculative reading of the evidence," and argues that it is nearly impossible that the two were lovers in the summer of 1527, as is often claimed, given Henry's very strong pursuit of Anne during precisely these months. Retha M. Warnicke, *The Rise and Fall of Anne Boleyn: Family Politics at the Court of Henry VIII* (Cambridge: Cambridge University Press, 1989), 64–66.

26. Kenneth Muir, *Life and Letters of Sir Thomas Wyatt* (Liverpool: Liverpool University Press, 1963), 41.

27. Wyatt wrote this poem, a translation of *Canzoniere* 37, from his ambassadorial post in Spain, where he lived from 1537 and 1539, more than a decade after he wrote the

other Petrarchan translations. Petrarch's poem ends with an expression of desire to be with his mistress, in either an embodied or disembodied form: "io sarò là tosto ch'io possa / o spirto ignudo od uom di carne et d'ossa" (I shall be there as soon as I can, / either a disembodied spirit or a man of flesh and bone). Wyatt does not drop this reference to the possibility of his soul visiting his beloved—his poem reads: "Then tell her that I come she shall me shortly se / Yff that for whayte the body fayle, this sowle shall to her fle" (poem 98, lines 99–100).

28. See Wyatt's poem "Stond who so list upon the Slipper toppe."

29. See Gordon Braden, "Wyatt and Petrarch: Italian Fashion at the Court of Henry VIII," *Annali d'Italianistica*, 2004.

30. Thomson, "Wyatt and the Petrarchan Commentators," 225–33. On Wyatt's travels in Italy, see Kenneth Muir, *Life and Letters of Sir Thomas Wyatt* (Liverpool: Liverpool University Press, 1963).

31. On the usefulness in reading the poems as divided between *in vita* and *in morte*, and for more details on the history of publication based on codice Vat. Lat. 3195, see Gerhard Regn, "La decade della bipartizione (RVF 261–70)," in *Il canzoniere: Lettura micro e macrotestuale*, ed. Michelangelo Picone (Ravenna, Italy: Longo Editore, 2007); and Christoph Niederer, "La bipartizione 'in vita / in morte,'" in *Petrarca e i suoi lettori*, ed. Vittorio Caratozzolo and George Guentert (Ravenna, Italy: Longo Editore, 2007).

32. Niederer, "La bipartizione 'in vita / in morte,'" 22.

33. I use *elegiac* here as a reference not to the classical genre of elegy but to a poetics of mourning. For further definition of this form, see Peter M. Sacks, *The English Elegy: Studies in the Genre from Spenser to Yeats* (Baltimore: Johns Hopkins University Press, 1985).

34. See Nancy J. Vickers, "Diana Described: Scattered Woman and Scattered Rhyme," *Critical Inquiry* 8, no. 2 (Winter 1981): 265–79.

35. See *Rime sparse* 287, where Petrarch describes the love poets Guittone d'Arezzo, Cino da Pistoia, Dante, and Franceschino degli Albizzi, all resting in the third sphere.

36. This is an interpretation that modern and Renaissance commentators share. Durling glosses "my lovely veil" as "my body," and Alessandro Vellutello glosses "il mio bel velo" as "il bel corpo di lei" (*Il Petrarca, con l'espositione di M. Alessandro Vellutello* [Venice, 1568]).

37. Petrarca, *Il Canzoniere e I Trionfi* (Milano: F. Valladri, 1924), 499; Petrarch, *The Triumphs of Petrarch*, trans. Ernest Hatch Wilkins (Chicago: University of Chicago Press, 1962), *The Triumph of Death*, chap. 2, lines 88–92.

38. Richard Strier makes the case for certain Petrarchan sonnets as *carpe diem* lyrics in *The Unrepentant Renaissance* (Chicago: University of Chicago Press, 2011), 59–75.

39. Virgil, *The Aeneid of Virgil*, trans. Allen Mandelbaum (Berkeley: University of California Press, 1981), 6.451. I am indebted to Durling for this observation (*Petrarch's Lyric Poems*, 58).

40. *Aeneid of Virgil*, 6. 582–84.

41. There are occasions in the *Rime sparse* in which Petrarch openly embraces the

idea that he could die from unrequited love. See, for example, number 126, in which he conjures up the scene of his death:

S'egli è pur mio destino
e'l cielo in ciò s'adopra,
ch'Amor quest'occhi lagrimando chiuda,
qualche grazia il meschino
corpo fra voi ricopra,
e torni l'alma al priorio albergo ignuda;
la morte fia men cruda
se questa spene porto
a quel dubbioso passo,
ché lo spirito lasso
non poria mai in più riposato porto
né in più tranquilla fossa
fuggir la carne travagliata et l'ossa. (14–26)

(If it is indeed my destiny and Heaven exerts itself that Love close these eyes while they are still weeping, let some grace bury my poor body among you and let my soul return naked to this its own dwelling; death will be less harsh if I bear this hope to the fearful pass, for my weary spirit could never in a more restful port or a more tranquil grave flee my laboring flesh and my bones.)

42. The poetic tradition dates back at least to Ovid's *Remedia amoris*, in which Ovid solicits Cupid's help in curing lovesickness by reminding him of the many deaths he has already caused. *The Art of Love and Other Poems*, trans. J. H. Mozley (Cambridge, MA: Harvard University Press, 1929), 178–79 (11.13–22).

43. William Shakespeare, *As You Like It*, in *The Norton Shakespeare*, ed. Stephen Greenblatt (New York: W. W. Norton, 1997), 4.1.81–83, 91–92. All references to Shakespeare are from this edition.

44. The Latin inscription on the monument reads:

Frigida Francisci tegit hic lapis ossa Petrarcae.
Suscipe, Virgo parens, animam: sate Virgine, parce,
Fessaque jam terris, coeli requiescat in arce.

(This stone protects the lifeless bones of Francesco Petrarca. Receive, O Virgin mother, [his] soul: and you begotten of the Virgin, forgive [it]. Now wearied of the earth, may it rest in high heaven.) Trans. Benjamin Woodring, PhD candidate, Department of English, Harvard University.

45. Wyatt wrote twenty-six poems that are imitations or translations of Petrarch, but two are versions of the same poem.

46. Lines 3–5. All references to Wyatt's poems are to *Collected Poems of Sir Thomas Wyatt*, ed. Kenneth Muir and Patricia Thomson (Liverpool: Liverpool University Press, 1969).

47. The Sherborne burial register simply reads: "Mensis Octobris Illo sepultus est/

Thomas Wyatt, Miles Regis Consilarius, vir venerabilis" (In the month of October in that place was buried Thomas Wyatt, Soldier, Counselor to the King and man of honour). Trans. Benjamin Woodring.

48. Jacques Ferrand, *A Treatise on Lovesickness*, trans. and ed. Donald A Beecher and Masssimo Ciavolella (Syracuse, NY: Syracuse University Press, 1990), 280.

49. Lines 25–26 of "Sweetest love: I doe not goe," in *Poems of John Donne.*

50. I am indebted to Gordon Braden's article "Wyatt and Petrarch" for drawing this Bonifacio poem to my attention.

51. When compared to the Italian original, Wyatt's poem stands out for its emphasis on the recovery of self in the last line. In Bonifacio's madrigal, the poem ends: "si non posso esser vostro, sarro mio" (if I cannot be yours, I will be my own). Wyatt drops the conditional "if" clause from the poem's conclusion and ends with a straightforward affirmation of his would-be, and wished-for, autonomy.

52. In *Tottel's Miscellany*, where Wyatt's sonnets first appeared, one of the only poems that follow the Petrarchan model and address the death of the beloved, "Sythe singyng gladdeth oft the hartes," does not imagine an afterlife for the lovers. After the beloved's death, the speaker merely declares the end of his bliss, and his song: "But cease, for I will syng no more: / Since that my harms hath no redresse: / But as a wretche for everymore / My life will waste with wretchednesse." He also does not imagine his love in heaven—he only laments that "now lieth it [his blisse] under ground." I am indebted to one of my anonymous readers for the University of Chicago Press for drawing this poem to my attention (*Tottel's Miscellany (1557–1587)*, 1966).

53. Pietro Bembo, *Rime*, ed. Andrea Donnini (Rome: Salerno, 2008).

54. Carol Kidwell, *Pietro Bembo: Lover, Linguist, Cardinal* (Montreal: McGill-Queen's University Press, 2004).

55. Berardino Rota, *Rime*, ed. Luca Milite (Milan: Fondazione Pietro Bembo. 2000).

56. See *Rime* 145 and 146.

57. Vittoria Colonna, *Rime*, ed. Alan Bullock (Roma-Bari: Gius. Laterza & Figli, 1982); trans. Ellen Moody, online source: http://www.jimandellen.org/ellen/emschol .htm.

58. Trans. Laura Anna Stortoni (*Women Poets of the Italian Renaissance: Courtly Ladies and Courtesans*, ed. Laura Anna Stortoni [New York: Italica, 1997]).

59. Ronsard's influence is especially strong in the sonnets of Thomas Lodge, Giles Fletcher, Thomas Watson, and Samuel Daniel. See Anne Lake Prescott, *French Poets and the English Renaissance* (New Haven, CT: Yale University Press, 1978).

60. Translation mine.

61. Translation mine. For Ronsard's relationship to Propertius and the other Latin elegists, see Robert E. Hallowell, *Ronsard and the Conventional Roman Elegy* (Urbana: University of Illinois Press, 1954).

62. The *scala*, a scale or ladder to the divine, is an image frequently used by medieval mystical writers such as Walter Hilton and John Climacus, and its use does not depend on direct knowledge of Plato. Knowledge of this metaphor, and others, may well have come through Neoplatonic authors such as Dionysus the Areopagite. I am

indebted to James Hankins, Department of History, Harvard University, for references on this subject.

63. Francesco Petrarch, *Petrarch's "Secretum,"* with introduction, notes, and critical anthology by Davy A. Carozza and H. James Shey, series 17, Classical Languages and Literature 7 (New York: Peter Lang, 1989), 110.

64. The full commentary reads: "E che amore rispose, Non egli haversela ritolta, Ma chi a volse per se, Intendendeno d'Iddio, che prima non a lui solo, ma veramente a tuto l'mondo date l'havea" (*Il Petrarca, con l'espositione di M. Alessandro Vellutello* [Venice, 1568], 128r).

65. Braden, "Wyatt and Petrarch."

66. For the meaning of *price*, I am indebted to private correspondence with Walter Melion, Department of Art History, Emory University.

67. Muir and Thomson make this connection in their commentary on poem 8 in *Collected Poems of Sir Thomas Wyatt*, 277.

68. This is one of the interpretations that Wyatt's early nineteenth-century editor, G. F. Nott, proposes: that Wyatt "designedly departed from the original and meant to intimate that 'a richer rival had taken his mistress from him'" (*The Works of Henry Howard Earl of Surrey and Sir Thomas Wyatt the Elder*, ed. Fred Nott [1816, 2:553]. H. Howarth argues that *price* is "power and majesty. It is Wyatt's half-concealment of a perilous matter: it is a cipher for King Henry, who took Anne Boleyn" ("Wyatt, Spenser, and the Canzone," *Italica* 41 [1964]: 80–81). Both glosses are cited in *Collected Poems of Sir Thomas Wyatt*, 276.

69. J. W. Lever, *The Elizabethan Love Sonnet* (London: Methuen, 1956), 9.

70. Cited in ibid., 10.

71. Although she does not explain what aspect of Englishness (weather, race, etc.) produced this, Thomson similarly presents Wyatt's rejection of Petrarchan transcendence as entirely typical of medieval English poetry. Hence she observes: "Wyatt is therefore no more interested than his English predecessors in the love that survives the death of a beloved mistress, purifies the lover's soul through suffering and separation, and anticipates a reunion of souls in Heaven" (*Sir Thomas Wyatt and His Background*, 179).

72. Geoffrey Chaucer, "Complaint unto Pity," in *The Riverside Chaucer*, 3rd ed., gen. ed. Larry D. Benson (Oxford: Oxford University Press, 1987), 11:113–19.

73. On drawing the boundaries between the living and the dead, see Stephen Greenblatt, *Hamlet in Purgatory* (Princeton, NJ: Princeton University Press, 2001), 244–45. For Tyndale's denouncements of purgatory, see William Tyndale, *An Answer to Sir Thomas More's Dialogue* (Cambridge: Parker Society, 1850), 120–33, 142–43. For Martin Luther's discussion of this, see Luther, *Christian Songs Latin and German for Use at Funerals*, in *Works of Martin Luther* (Philadelphia: Castle, 1932), 6:288.

Chapter 3

1. Walter Benjamin, *The Origin of German Tragic Drama*, trans. John Osborne (London: Verso, 1998), 58. I am grateful to my student Martin Moraw, PhD candidate at Brandeis University, for drawing this passage to my attention.

2. John Donne, "The Extasie," in *The Poems of John Donne*, ed. Herbert J. C. Grierson (London: Oxford University Press, 1933), line 64.

3. Anon, *The Teares of Fancie, or Love Disdained* (London, 1593), sonnet 43. The *Teares of Fancie* was long attributed to the poet Thomas Watson but is no longer believed to be his work. Franklin Dickey claims that *Teares of Fancie* has been proven to be a "Collier forgery" from the nineteenth century (Thomas Watson, *Amyntas* [1585] and Abraham Fraunce's *The Lamentations of Amyntas* [1589], ed. Franklin M. Dickey [Chicago: University of Chicago Press, 1967]). This position is corroborated in *The Complete Works of Thomas Watson*, ed. Dana F. Sutton, 2 vols. (Lewiston, NY: Edwin Mellen, 1997), 2:380.

4. Robert Burton, *The Anatomy of Melancholy*, ed. Thomas C. Faulkner, Nicholas K, Kiessling, and Rhonda L. Blair, 6 vols. (Oxford: Clarendon, 1994), 3:199.

5. Thomas Lodge, *Phillis: honoured vvith pastorall sonnets, elegies, and amorous delights: VVhere-vnto is annexed, the tragicall complaynt of Elstred* (London, 1593), poem 23.

6. Lucretius, *On the Nature of the Universe*, trans. R. E. Latham (New York: Penguin, 1994).

7. Robert N. Watson, *The Rest Is Silence: Death as Annihilation in the English Renaissance* (Berkeley: University of California Press, 1994) 28.

8. Psychopannyism was largely associated with the radical Protestant sect of Anabaptists, although both Tyndale and Luther also seem to have believed in it. Calvin attacked such beliefs in his 1542 treatise *Psychopannychia*. On the related idea of mortalism—that the soul died with the body—see Norman T. Burns, *Christian Mortalism from Tyndale to Milton* (Cambridge, MA: Harvard University Press, 1972).

9. Bartholomew Griffin, *Fidessa, more chaste then kinde* (London, 1596), sonnet 51.

10. Barnabe Barnes, *Parthenophil and Parthenophe Sonnettes, madrigals, elegies and odes* (London, 1593), sonnet 80.

11. See p. 33 in chapter 1.

12. The series itself ends with a surprising consummation of their love, after Parthenophe appears to Parthenophil naked on a goat, an arrangement Parthenophil manages to effect through the use of black magic.

13. This poem is among a series of poems printed in the 1594 edition of *Diana* only, and not in the first edition, printed in 1592. For a full account of the textual history and its problems, see Joan Grundy, ed., *The Poems of Henry Constable* (Liverpool: Liverpool University Press, 1960), 84–100.

14. *The Riverside Chaucer* notes that the "eighth sphere" likely refers either to the sphere of the moon or to the sphere of the fixed stars. Geoffrey Chaucer, *The Riverside Chaucer*, ed. Larry Benson (Oxford: Oxford University Press, 1987). For a defense of the latter, see Gerald Morgan, "The Ending of *Troilus and Criseyde*," *Modern Language Review* 77, no. 2 (April 1982): 257–71. On the multiple endings of *Troilus and Criseyde*, see, among others, Rosemarie P. McGerr, *Chaucer's Open Books: Resistance to Closure in Medieval Discourse* (Gainesville: University Press of Florida, 1998).

15. McGerr argues that Chaucer shows, at the end of his tale, that Christian "*charite* is the only true form of love" (*Chaucer's Open Books*, 116).

16. In Sidney Lee, *Elizabethan Sonnets*, 2 vols. (New York: E. P. Dutton, 1904).

Chapter 4

1. For a very useful anthology of the different versions that circulated on the Continent in the sixteenth century, see Masuccio Salernitano et al., *Romeo and Juliet before Shakespeare: Four Early Stories of Star-Crossed Love*, trans. and ed. Nicole Prunster (Toronto: Centre for Reformation and Renaissance Studies, 2000). For the texts of the English versions of the story that preceded Shakespeare's play, see Geoffrey Bullough, *Narrative and Dramatic Sources of Shakespeare*, 8 vols. (London: Routledge and Kegan Paul, 1957–), vol. 1, lines 1674-80.

2. See Jill L. Levenson, "Romeo and Juliet before Shakespeare," *Studies in Philology* 81, no. 3 (Summer 1984): 325-47.

3. Giovanni Boccaccio, *The Decameron: A New Translation*, ed. Peter Bondanella and Mark Musa, (New York: W. W. Norton, 1977). In *Decameron* 3.8, Boccaccio tells the story of Ferondo, who is taken for dead after swallowing a powder; he is later removed from the tomb by the abbot who in the interim has taken advantage of Ferondo's wife. In *Decameron* 10.4, the gentlewoman, Catalina, is likewise taken for dead and laid in her tomb, only to be discovered living by one who loves her, and who, despite his love, returns her and her child to her husband.

4. Luigi da Porto, *Novellieri del Cinquecento*, ed. Marziano Guglielminetti, vol. 1 (Milano: Ricciardi, 1972); English version from Masuccio et al., *Romeo and Juliet before Shakespeare*, 32.

5. Bandello, *The Novels of Matteo Bandello, Bishop of Agen, now first done into English prose and verse by John Payne* (London: Villon Society, 1890), 3:156.

6. Translation from Payne, slightly altered.

7. Stanley Chojnacki, *Women and Men in Renaissance Venice: Twelve Essays on Patrician Society* (Baltimore: Johns Hopkins University Press, 2000), 153.

8. Vincenzo Forcella, *Iscrizioni delle Chiese e d'Altri Edificii di Roma, Raccolte e pubblicate da Vincenzo Forcella*, 14 vols. (Roma: Tipografia delle Scienze Matematiche e Fisiche, 1869).

9. Forcella, *Iscrizioni delle Chiese e d'Altri Edificii di Roma*, 1.157; 5.47, 53. The only notable exceptions are German and Swiss burials in Rome.

10. Luigi Groto, *La Hadriana Tragedia Nova* (Venezia, 1609), act 2, scene 3, p. 72. Translation mine.

11. Among others, see William Carroll, "'We were born to die': *Romeo and Juliet*," *Comparative Drama* 15, no. 1 (Spring 1981): 54-71; Jonathan Dollimore, *Death, Desire and Loss in Western Culture* (New York: Routledge, 1998); Julia Kristeva, *Tales of Love*, trans. Leon S. Roudiez (New York: Columbia University Press, 1987).

12. William Shakespeare, *Romeo and Juliet*, prol. 6, 9.

13. Kristeva, *Tales of Love*, 233.

14. Carroll makes a strong case for the prevalence of the journey metaphors in the play, always heading toward death as their ending. I share with him, and many other readers, the sense that Romeo and Juliet's love "already contains its own beginning and end," although I disagree, as the following pages will make clear, with the sense of their end as "endless" (65).

15. *Hamlet*, 5.2.302–3.

16. Edmund Spenser, *The Faerie Queene*, in *Edmund Spenser's Poetry*, ed. Hugh Maclean and Anne Lake Prescott (New York: W. W. Norton, 1992), 1.9.40.352–58.

17. Edward Snow, "Language and Sexual Difference in *Romeo and Juliet.*," in *Shakespeare's "Rough Magic": Renaissance Essays in Honor of C. L. Barber*, ed. Peter Erickson and Coppélia Kahn (Newark: University of Delaware Press, 1985), 176, 190. Along with most modern editors, Snow argues here against the text of Q4, which reads "when he shall die" rather than "when I shall die," an emendation that nineteenth-century editors often elected in order to avoid what they otherwise perceived to be too extreme a narcissism on Juliet's part. Most modern editions agree with Snow (and with the Q2, Q3, and the Folio), printing the subject of the line as "I," and there is strong textual evidence to do so.

18. Kristeva, *Tales of Love*, 214.

19. *Hamlet* 4.3.20–21.

20. Although these ideas had little presence in Elizabethan love poetry, there were certainly strains of Neoplatonic philosophy in Elizabethan verse more broadly: Spenser's two "heavenly" hymns ("An Hymne of Heavenly Love" and "An Hymne of Heavenly Beautie") are strong examples. See Edmund Spenser, *The Yale Edition of the Shorter Poems of Edmund Spenser*, ed. William Oram, Einar Bjorvand, and Ronald Bond (New Haven, CT: Yale University Press, 1989).

21. The Variorum, for example, has "throws them down" (*Romeo and Juliet*, New Variorum Edition 1 [Philadelphia: J. B. Lippincott, 1874], 168); the Norton Shakespeare has "putting down the cords." The Quartos and Folio do not include a stage direction here.

22. Although marriage was legally binding once vows had been exchanged, the idea that sexual union validated or confirmed marriage was widespread. For a history of the church's liturgy for marriage, see David Herlihy, *Medieval Households* (Cambridge: Cambridge University Press, 1985).

23. In the Folio, "cord" is in the singular—"come Cord, come nurse."

24. See Iiro Kajanto, *Classical and Christian Studies in the Latin Epitaphs of Medieval and Renaissance Rome* (Helsinki: Suomalainen Tiedeakatemia, 1980). This Latin formula was often abbreviated in epitaphs as o.t.b.q., or more elaborately, O.T.B.Q.T.T.L.S. = o(ssa) t(ibi) b(ene) q(uiescant) t(erra) t(ibi) 1(evis) s(it). The mention of the body's undisrupted rest in the grave was typical for both pagan and early Christian epitaphs. Although it became less common in the medieval period, when the focus moved to the rest or peace of the soul, we need only consider Shakespeare's own epitaph—"GOOD FREND FOR JESUS SAKE FORBEARE TO DIGG THE DUST ENCLOASED HEARE. BLEST BE YE MAN YT SPARES THES STONES AND CURST BE HE YT MOVES MY BONES"—to realize how deeply this fear persisted in the early modern period.

25. On the role of prophecy, and reversal, in Romeo's dream, see Norman Holland's psychoanalytic reading "Romeo's Dream and the Paradox of Literary Realism," *Literature and Psychology* 13, no. 4 (Fall 1963). See also Marjorie Garber, *Dream in Shakespeare: From Metaphor to Metamorphosis* (New Haven, CT: Yale University Press, 1974), 44–47.

26. In Bandello's *novella*, Romeo instructs his servant Pietro to "make shift to find

me such tools as behove to open the tomb where my wife is buried and props to prop
it." Boaistuau similarly specifies that Romeo purchased not only the poison but also
the "tools needed to open Juliet's vault" (115). This detail is omitted from Brooke's translation.

27. The formula *cuius anima requiescat in pace* is cited repeatedly in Weever, *Ancient
Funerall Monuments* (London, 1631).

28. Cited in the New Variorum Edition, 222.

29. The first Quarto (Q1) for *Romeo and Juliet* has "rest" rather than "rust." See New
Variorum Edition, 288, for a summary of early opinions about the two different readings. The central question is whether Shakespeare wanted to emphasize the material
decay of the dagger—its "rusting" in her breast—or simply the replacement of one
sheath for another as the dagger's resting place. For a discussion of the dagger itself,
see Katherine Duncan-Jones, "O Happy Dagger: The Autonomy of Shakespeare's Juliet,"
Notes and Queries 45, no. 3 (1998): 314–16.

30. The partial exception to this is Bandello, who relates that the prince was "willing that they should abide ensepulchred in that same tomb"; he then adds, however,
that an epitaph is placed "upon the two lovers' sepulcher," which suggests that some
sort of private tomb is erected inside the Capulet monument (167–68).

31. Virgil, *The Aeneid of Virgil*, trans. Allen Mandelbaum (Berkeley: University of
California Press, 1981), 6.583–86).

32. See Virgil, *Aeneid* 6.15–19, 24–26. Dido's sister Anna tells Dido that the "ashes or
buried shades" (cinerem aut Manis . . . sepultos) will not care whether she remains
faithful (4.31–34).

33. Plutarch, *Life of Antony*, ed. C. B. R. Pelling (Cambridge: Cambridge University
Press, 1988), 311.

Chapter 5

1. Francesco Petrarch, *Petrarch's "Secretum,"* with introduction, notes, and critical
anthology by Davy A. Carozza and H. James Shey, series 17, Classical Languages and
Literature 7 (New York: Peter Lang, 1989), 135.

2. The idea of writing as delivering a more durable form of fame dates back to the
ancient Egyptians. On a papyrus from ca. 1300 BCE we find this passage: "If there were
made for [them] doors and buildings, they are crumbled. Their mortuary service is
[gone]; their tombstones are covered with dirt; and their graves are forgotten. [But]
their names are [still] pronounced because of their books which they made, since they
were good and the memory of him who made them [lasts] to the limits of eternity."
Cited in James B. Pritchard, ed., *Ancient Near Eastern Texts Relating to the Old Testament*,
2nd ed. (Princeton, NJ: Princeton University Press, 1955), 431–32. The particular text is
from Papyrus Chester Beatty IV (now British Museum 10684), verso ii5–iii 11.

3. *Horace Odes III, Dulce Periculum*, trans. and ed. David West (Oxford: Oxford University Press, 2002), 259.

4. For Libitina as "goddess of death," see *Horace: Odes and Epodes*, ed. and trans.
Niall Rudd (Cambridge, MA: Harvard University Press, 2004). On her role as goddess
of funerals, see *Horace Odes III, Dulce Periculum*, trans. and ed. West, 262.

5. I have departed from West's translation for these lines because the translation is not entirely accurate: he translates "ego postera crescam laude recens" as "my fame will grow ever fresh," thereby substituting "fame" for *ego*. The English for these lines alone is from *Horace, Odes and Epodes*, ed. and trans. Rudd, 3.30.7–9.

6. For a concise account of Horace's transmission to Renaissance poets, see Glenn W. Most, "Horace," in *The Classical Tradition*, ed. Anthony Grafton, Glenn W. Most, and Salvatore Settis (Cambridge, MA: Belknap / Harvard University Press, 2010), 454–57.

7. On Renaissance English poets' access to Latin love poetry, see James A. S. McPeek, *Catullus in Strange and Distant Britain* (Cambridge, MA: Harvard University Press, 1939), and Jacob Blevins, *Catullan Consciousness and the Early Modern Lyric in England: From Wyatt to Donne* (Burlington, VT: Ashgate, 2004).

8. Ovid, *Heroides and Amores* 1.3, 19–24, trans. Grant Showerman (London: William Heinemann, 1914). I am using a prose translation for Ovid's *Amores* because the verse translations available are too free and lose the precise meaning of the lines.

9. On the granting of immortality or immortal fame to lovers of the gods, see Ovid, *Amores: Text, Prolegomena, and Commentary*, trans. and ed. J. C. McKeown, 4 vols. (Liverpool: Francis Cairns Ltd. 1988–), 2.73, n1.3.21–23.

10. See also Ovid's threnody to Tibullus in book 3 of the *Amores*, where he declares, "'Tis song alone escapes the greedy pyre. . . . So Nemesis, so Delia, will long be known to fame" (3.9.28–30).

11. Sextus Propertius, *The Complete Elegies of Sextus Propertius*, trans. Vincent Katz (Princeton, NJ: Princeton University Press), 3.2–17–26.

12. Propertius, *The Poems*, trans. W. G. Shepherd (Harmondsworth, UK: Penguin, 1985), 4.55, 57–64, 70.

13. Tibullus, *The Poems of Tibullus*, trans. Constance Carrier (Bloomington: Indiana University Press, 1969), 1.3.57–66.

14. Aaron Kunin has described this as a state of "quasi-human" preservation. Kunin is interested in the ethics of such a practice, which he regards on the whole as a non-consensual use of the subject—"Either you do not preserve the object of value, or you preserve it in a form that will not allow you to experience it fully, or you preserve it in a form that is toxic to whatever quality you value and that originally made you want to preserve it." (Aaron Kunin, "Shakespeare's Preservation Fantasy," *PMLA* 124, no. 1 [2009]: 100).

15. Thomas Watson, *The Complete Works of Thomas Watson*, ed. Dana F. Sutton, 2 vols. (Lewiston, NY: Edwin Mellen, 1997), 1:153.

16. Philip Sidney, *The Poems of Sir Philip Sidney*, ed. William A. Ringler (Oxford: Clarendon, 1962), sonnet 90, lines 1, 8.

17. Barnabe Barnes, *Parthenophil and Parthenophe Sonnettes, madrigals, elegies and odes* (London, 1593), elegy 15, lines 12–18.

18. Anon., *Zepheria* (London, 1594), canzon 14, lines 9–14.

19. Samuel Daniel, *Delia and Rosamond augmented Cleopatra*, 2nd ed. (London, 1594), sonnet 37, lines 1–14.

20. *Delia*, sonnet 36, "When men shall finde thy flower, thy glory passe," begins the transition from *carpe diem* to the theme of immortality celebrated in *Delia* 37.

21. Michael Drayton, *Poems of Michael Drayton*, ed. John Buxton, 2 vols. (London: Routledge and Kegan Paul, 1953), vol. 1, sonnet 5 (6), lines 1–14. This particular sonnet was first printed in the 1619 edition of the poems.

22. *The Yale Edition of the Shorter Poems of Edmund Spenser*, ed. William Oram, Einar Bjorvand, and Ronald Bond (New Haven, CT: Yale University Press, 1989), 212. This gloss is to "Colins Embleme," which is missing from the poem, perhaps, the editors speculate, intentionally. See the note on 209.

23. Ibid., Sonnet 69, note to line 7, p. 642.

24. At the end of his "Epithalamion," the wedding poem written for Elizabeth and appended to the *Amoretti* in its first publication, Spenser declares, "Be unto her a goodly ornament / and for a short time an endless monument." Whether this "short time" is limited to the occasion of the wedding celebrations or to the duration of their marriage, it is clear that the wedding poem—an occasional poem that narrates the festivities of the day itself—is differentiated from his sonnets in terms of its longevity. The "endless monument" of the "Epithalamion" is endless only to a point.

25. "August," 27–28. See also Spenser's use of *enchase* in *Faerie Queene* 2.9, and *Prosopoia, Or Mother Hubberds Tale*, in *Complaints* 1.624.

26. Joel Fineman, *Shakesperae's Perjur'd Eye* (Berkeley: University of California Press, 1986).

27. Kunin makes much of this, although his point is less persuasive when we consider the sonnet within the sonnet series as a whole, a series that is not shy about naming the beloved (Kunin, "Shakespeare's Preservation Fantasy").

28. In the *OED* the secondary definition of *sonnet* is "a short poem or piece of verse; in early use esp. one of a lyrical and amatory character."

29. See Sir Thomas Browne, *Urne-Buriall*, in *Religio Medici and Hydriotaphia, or Urne-Buriall*, ed. Stephen Greenblatt and Ramie Targoff (New York: New York Review of Books Classics, 2012), 116. For the earlier discussion of this passage, see p. 21 above.

30. Cleanth Brooks, *The Well Wrought Urn* (New York: Harcourt, 1947).

Chapter 6

1. Richard Strier has argued that *Rime sparse* 248 is a *carpe diem* poem that invites those who would like to see "all that Nature and Heaven can do among us" to come gaze upon Laura before death comes. But this does not pertain to the relationship between Petrarch and Laura, nor does it relate to any intimate relationship that needs to be taken advantage of now. The *carpe diem* message, to the extent that it pertains, is merely a reminder to all mortals of their mortality, exemplified by Laura: "this beautiful mortal thing passes and does not endure." Strier, *The Unrepentant Renaissance* (Chicago: University of Chicago Press, 2011), 71–75.

2. Book 1, ode 11. For the suggestion of her status as slave or servant, see Horace, *Odes I: Carpe Diem*, trans. and ed. David West (Oxford: Clarendon, 1995), 51–52. All quotations from book 1 of the *Odes* are, unless otherwise noted, from this edition. Other

commentators claim that Leuconoe is a fictitious name; see R. G. M. Nisbet and Margaret Hubbard, *A Commentary on Horace: Odes Book I* (Oxford: Clarendon, 1970), 136–38.

3. Propertius, *The Complete Elegies of Sextus Propertius* 2.15.37–40.

4. Among others, Ben Jonson, Christopher Marlowe, and Thomas Campion wrote versions of this poem, and Sir Walter Raleigh included a translation of its central lines in his *Historie of the World*: "The Sunne may set and rise / But we contrariwise / Sleepe after our short light / One everlasting night." According to Blevins, Catullus's popularity grew rapidly in mid-sixteenth-century England after the publication of two well-known commentaries, by Achilles Statius (1558) and Joseph Scaliger (1577). Catullus was also taught in both the Eton and Westminster curricula during Henry VIII's and Elizabeth I's reigns. (Blevins, *Catullan Consciousness and the Early Modern Lyric in England* [Aldershot, Hampshire, UK: Ashgate, 2004]).

5. Catullus, *The Poems of Catullus*, trans. Peter Whigham (Harmondsworth, UK: Penguin Classics, 1966).

6. *The Norton Anthology of English Literature*, gen ed. Stephen Greenblatt, 8th ed. (New York: W. W. Norton, 2005), 1:918, 11.1–4, 21–24.

7. Ibid., 1022, 11. 21–24.

8. For a strong refutation of the *carpe diem* as a trivial genre, see Wendy Beth Hyman, "Skeptical Seductions: Carpe Diem, Materialism, and Doubt in English Renaissance Literature," unpublished dissertation, Harvard University, 2005. See also her article "Seizing Flowers in Spenser's Bower and Garden," *English Literary Renaissance*, 2007, 193–214.

9. Ovid, *The Art of Love*, in *Ovid: The Erotic Poems*, trans. Peter Green (Harmondsworth, UK: Penguin Classics, 1982), 3.70–77.

10. In this respect, the Elizabethan poets were also dependent on the poetry of Ronsard. See, among others, Robert E. Hallowell, *Ronsard and the Conventional Roman Elegy* (Urbana: University of Illinois Press, 1954); Malcolm Quainton, *Ronsard's Ordered Chaos: Visions of Flux and Stability in the Poetry of Pierre de Ronsard* (Manchester: Manchester University Press, 1980); and Cathy Yandell, *"Carpe Diem* Revisited: Ronsard's Temporal Ploys." *Sixteenth Century Journal* 28, no. 4 (1997).

11. In addition to Daniel's sonnets discussed below, see also Sonnet 26 of William Smith's *Chloris* (London, 1596):

> Though you be faire and beautifull withall
> And I am blacke for which you me despise,
> Know that your beauty subiect is to fall
> Though you esteeme it at so high a prise.
> And time may come when that whereof you boast,
> (Which is your youths chief wealth and ornament)
> Shall withered be by winters raging froast,
> When beauties pride and flowring yeeres are spent (1–8)

12. See the "Fourth Song," which includes the lines "That you heard was but a mouse / Dumb sleep holdeth all the house; / Yet asleep, methinks they say / Young folks, take time while you may." I am grateful to one of my anonymous readers for the press for reminding me of these lines.

13. Samuel Daniel, *Delia and Rosamond augmented Cleopatra*, 2nd ed. (London, 1594), sonnet 34, lines 1–14.

14. For a discussion of the "halfe-blowne" quality of the rose, see Elizabeth Harris Sagaser, "Sporting the While: Carpe Diem and the Cruel Fair in Samuel Daniel's *Delia and the Complaint of Rosamond*," *Exemplaria* 10, no. 1 (Spring 1998): 145–70.

15. Lucretius, *On the Nature of Things*, trans. Martin Ferguson Smith (London: Sphere Books), 1.215–16.

16. All quotations of Herrick's poetry are from *The Poems of Robert Herrick*, ed. L. C. Martin (London: Oxford University Press, 1965).

17. There are also a few rare anti–*carpe diem* moments in *Hesperides*, such as this short lyric, "Love me little, love me long":

You say, to me-wards your affection's strong;
Pray love me little, so you love me long.
Slowly goes farre: The meane is best: Desire
Grown violent, do's either die, or tire.

18. *OED*, s.v. "circummortal."

19. Herrick was vicar of Dean Prior in Devon.

20. Leah S. Marcus, *The Politics of Mirth: Jonson, Herrick, Milton, Marvell, and the Defense of Old Holiday Pastimes* (Chicago: University of Chicago Press, 1986), 158–65.

21. Nigel Smith dates the poem to the late 1640s–early 1650s; see Andrew Marvell, *The Poems of Andrew Marvell*, ed. Nigel Smith (New York: Pearson Longman, 2007), 75. All quotations of Marvell's poetry are from Smith's edition.

22. See ibid., 78.

23. On the comparison with Catullus, see Stanley Stewart, "Marvell and the *Ars Moriendi*," in *Seventeenth-Century Imagery: Essays on Uses of Figurative Language from Donne to Farquhar*, ed. Earl Miner (Berkeley: University of California Press, 1971), 136. Charles Kay Smith points out that Marvell is parodying Cowley's "My Diet," which includes the lines "An hundred years on one kind word I'll feast / A thousand more will added bee / If you an Inclination have for mee" (Charles Kay Smith, "French Philosophy and English politics in interregnum poetry," in *The Stuart Court and Europe: Essays in Politics and Political Culture*, ed. R. Malcolm Smuts [Cambridge: Cambridge University Press, 1989] 204).

24. As Nigel Smith points out, "vast eternity" is not Marvell's coinage: Herrick used it earlier in his poem "Eternitie," and Cowley, twice, in "My Diet" and "Sitting and Drinking in the Chair made out of the reliques of Sir Francis Drake's Ship" (*Poems of Andrew Marvell*, note to line 24, p. 82).

25. See Hyman, "Skeptical Seductions," for a thorough discussion of the role of virginity in the English *carpe diem* tradition.

26. See Smith, *Poetry of Andrew Marvell*, note to line 29, p. 83.

27. Sir Thomas Browne, *Hydriotaphia, Urne-Buriall, or A Discourse of the Sepulchrall Urnes lately found in Norfolk*, in *Religio Medici and Urne-Buriall*, ed. Stephen Greenblatt and Ramie Targoff (New York: New York Review of Books Classics, 2012), 116.

28. I share this opinion with Jules Brody, who makes a similar argument at the end

of his article "The Resurrection of the Body: A New Reading of Marvell's 'To His Coy Mistress,'" *English Literary History* 56 (1989): 68.

29. There has been much critical discussion of Marvell's idea of tearing through the "iron gates of life," a metaphor which reverses or adjusts both the traditional "gates of death" described in Psalm 9 ("thou hast lifted me up from the gates of death") and the "gates of everlasting life" invoked in the Easter Day collect from the Book of Common Prayer: "Almighty God, which through thy only begotten Son Jesus Christ hast overcome death, and opened unto us the gate of everlasting life . . ." As Nigel Smith has persuasively suggested, Marvell's image seems less dependent on these biblical or liturgical sources than on Lucretius's description of old age in book 1 of *De rerum natura*. Here the Latin poet explains his fear that age may "open the gates of life" before he finishes his exposition of the truths of matter and void to his friend Memmius (a more literal translation is that age will "loosen in us the barriers of life"). In *The Poetry of Andrew Marvell*, note to line 44, p. 184.

30. Daniel, *The Complete Works of Samuel Daniel*, ed. Rev. Alexander B. Grosart, 5 vols. (London: Hazel, Watson, and Viney, 1885), 1:262, lines 91–92.

31. See Ann E. Berthoff, *The Resolved Soul: A Study of Marvell's Major Poems* (Princeton, NJ: Princeton Univ. Press, 1970) 223–24.

32. Stewart also sees the poem as suggesting suicide, although he reads this as a result of sex: "Ironically, by overcoming this fear the lovers hurry their own end—commit suicide (for every act of love one relinquishes a day of life)—but in so doing they exercise a newfound power over Time" (Stewart, "Marvell and the *Ars Moriendi*," 146).

Conclusion

1. See Henry King, *Poems of Henry King*, ed. Margaret Crum (Oxford: Clarendon, 1965), 8. Crum refers to Bodl. MS. Rawl. D. 398, fols. 172–73.

2. From Henry King, *Poems and Psalms*, ed. Rev. J. Hannah (Oxford: F. Macpherson, 1843), "Appendix C.II: Exact Copy of Bishop Henry's Will." The will is dated July 14, 1653.

3. On date of poem: Mary Hobbs, in *The Sermons of Henry King (1592–1669) Bishop of Chichester*, ed. Hobbs (Madison, NJ: Fairleigh Dickinson, 1992), speculates that it was written in 1626 or 1627 and notes its similarities with his Lenten sermons from these years. Crum does not specify in her edition of the poems when the poem was written.

4. King, *Poems of Henry King*, 1:1–5. All notes to "An Exequy" are from this edition.

5. For a discussion of the relationship between the speaker and the metonymic "shrine of my dead saint," see Paul Alpers, "Apostrophe and the Rhetoric of Renaissance Lyric," *Representations* 122, no. 1 (2013): 1–22.

6. As Charles Altieri has noted, the "dynamics of address" are part of the poet's efforts to establish "workable means of establishing connection with his wife." In Charles Altieri, *The Particulars of Rapture: An Aesthetics of the Affects* (Ithaca, NY: Cornell University Press, 2003) 97.

7. King, *Sermons of Henry King*, ed. Hobbs, 129.

8. See pp. 54–55 in chapter 2, above, for further discussion of this poem.

9. John Donne, *The Sermons of John Donne*, ed. George R. Potter and Evelyn M. Simpson, 10 vols. (Berkeley: University of California Press, 1953-62), 3:105. King wrote an elegy to Donne titled "To the Memorie of my ever desired Friend Dr. Donne."

10. This is the conclusion reached by E. A. J. Honigmann in *Milton's Sonnets* (New York: St. Martin's, 1966), 190-94, and by A. S. P. Woodhouse and Douglas Bush, the editors of vol. 2 of *A Variorum Commentary on the Poems of John Milton*, gen. ed. Merritt Y. Hughes (New York: Columbia University Press, 1970-), 486-501. Milton's biographer Barbara Lewalski also maintains that the poem was very likely about Katherine (*The Life of John Milton* [Oxford: Blackwell, 2000], 340).

11. See Lewalski, *Life of John Milton*, who argues that Milton would not have understood his wife's cleansing as a bodily process but instead emphasized her spiritual purity and goodness. She quotes Revelation 19:8: "And to her [the Lamb's bride] was granted that she should be arrayed in fine linen, clean and white: for the fine linen is the righteousness of saints" (655).

12. This comparison was first made by Henry Hallam, *Introduction to the Literature of Europe in the Fifteenth, Sixteenth, and Seventeenth Centuries*, vol. 2 (Paris: Baudry's European Library, 1893), cited in John S. Smart, *The Sonnets of Milton* (Glasgow: Maclehose, Jackson, 1921). For a discussion of Rota, see p. 69 in chapter 2, above.

13. My translation, adapted from the verse translation in John Milton, *Laura, or An Anthology of Sonnets (on the Petrarchan Model) and Elegiac Quatuorzains*, vol 4, trans. Capel Lofft (Ludgate, UK: B. and R. Crosby, 1813), poem 591.

14. Louis Schwartz points out that the odd order of things—"I waked, she fled"—suggests that the poet's waking may still be part of the dream: "It suggests that the vision has not simply been ended by his waking, but that, still within the dream, she reacts to the speaker's waking and *flees from him*" (Schwartz, *Milton and Maternal Mortality* [Cambridge: Cambridge University Press, 2009], 177; italics original).

15. Virgil, *The Aeneid of Virgil*, trans. Allen Mandelbaum (Berkeley: University of California Press, 1981), 2.790-94; see Thomas B. Stroup, "Aeneas's Vision of Creusa and Milton's Twenty-Third Sonnet," *Philological Quarterly* 39, no. 2 (January 1960): 125-26.

16. Schwartz, *Milton and Maternal Mortality*, 172.

17. For a subtle critique of the Neoplatonic interpretation of this poem, see Patrick Cheney, "Alcestis and the 'Passion for Immortality': Milton's Sonnet XXIII and Plato's *Symposium*," *Milton Studies* 18 (1983): 63-76.

18. See *Variorum* 2:486-501. For critics who cite the myth in their discussions of Sonnet XXIII but do not discuss its rich resonances or the classical texts that Milton may have used, see Jonathan Goldberg, *Voice Terminal Echo* (New York: Methuen, 1986), 148-49; or Elizabeth D. Harvey, *Ventriloquized Voices: Feminist Theory and English Renaissance Texts* (London: Routledge, 1995), 100. On the other side of the scholarly spectrum, critics who work specifically on Orpheus's presence in Milton's work but fail to make mention of Sonnet XXIII, see, for example, Patricia Vicari, "The Triumph of Art, the Triumph of Death: Orpheus in Spenser and Milton," in *Orpheus: The Metamorphoses of a Myth*, ed. John Warden (Toronto: University of Toronto Press, 1982), 207-30.

19. Ovid, *Metamorphoses*, trans. Allen Mandelbaum (New York: Harcourt Brace, 1993) bk. 10, p. 327 (lines 56-59 of the Latin poem).

20. Virgil, *The Eclogues; The Georgics*, trans. C. Day Lewis (Oxford: Oxford University Press, 1983), 4.495–500.

21. On Milton's use of the *Georgics* in *Paradise Lost*, see, among others, Juan Christian Pellicer, "*Georgics* II in *Paradise Lost*," *Translation and Literature* 14 (2005): 129–47; and Douglas Bush, "Ironic and Ambiguous Allusion in *Paradise Lost*," *Journal of English and Germanic Philology* 60 (1961): 631–40.

22. Horace, *Odes I: Carpe Diem*, trans. and ed. David West (Oxford: Clarendon, 1995), Ode 24, lines 13–15.

Epilogue

1. Philip Larkin, *The Complete Poems*, ed. Archie Burnett (New York: Farrar, Straus and Giroux, 2012), lines 1–12.

2. There is in fact no inscription on the monument's base; there is only a card placed beside the monument (ibid., 437).

3. The sketch is in Add MS 29925, fol. 26, in the British Library. Cited in H. A. Tummers, "Church Monuments," *Chichester Cathedral: An Historical Survey*, ed. Mary Hobbs (Chichester: Phillimore, 1994), 211.

4. Cited in James L. Orwin, "'An Arundel Tomb'—An Interpretation," *About Larkin* 17 (April 2004): 1.

INDEX